PEOPLE PRACTICS

17 PRACTICAL TACTICS FOR BUSINESS & NONPROFIT SUCCESS

Edited by
Deborah A. Jackson

PEOPLE PRACTICES: 17 PRACTICAL TACTICS
FOR BUSINESS & NONPROFIT SUCCESS

ISBN 978-1-7342605-0-2
Library of Congress Control Number:2019919440

Printed in the United States of America by Ingram Content Group.

Published by Áccent on Words Press
18543 Devonshire Street #327
Northridge, California 91324
accentonwords.com

First Printing

Faces image on cover by Gerd Altmann on Pixabay.
Cover design and copy by Deborah A. Jackson.

Published in the United States, Canada, Europe
the United Kingdom, Australia, and New Zealand.

Address all queries
Áccent on Words Press
18543 Devonshire Street #327
Northridge, California 91324

PEOPLE PRACTICS

17 PRACTICAL TACTICS FOR BUSINESS & NONPROFIT SUCCESS

There is a tide in the affairs of men, which taken at the flood, leads on to fortune.
Omitted, all the voyage of their life is bound in shallows and in miseries.
On such a full sea are we now afloat.
And we must take the current when it serves, or lose our ventures.
— William Shakespeare in *Julius Caesar*

DEDICATION

To our teachers and mentors.
Thank you.

practic *adjective*

prac·tic | \ ˈpraktik\

1: PRACTICAL

(*Source: merriam-webster.com*)

practics *newly coined noun*

prac·tics | \ ˈpraktiks\

1: PRACTICAL TACTICS

(*Source: the authors*)

ACKNOWLEDGMENTS

We would first like to express our gratitude to our professor, Dr. Arnie Dahlke, who required each of us to write a book chapter for our Organizational Behavior course at Phillips Graduate University (recently renamed the Phillips Education Center for Campbellsville University), from which we each earned a Doctorate in Psychology with an emphasis in Organizational Management and Consulting. Those chapters are the basis of this book.

Next, we acknowledge our other professors at Phillips, who imparted wisdom and acted as our mentors as well as our teachers: Dr. Tora Brown, Del Black, Rodney Bolton, Dr. Deborah Buttitta, Dr. Robert Clark, Dr. Nancy Duresky (our program chair), Stacey Gordon, Dr. Yolanda Gorman, Dr. Jim Lott, Pedro Manrique, Dr. Leon Tonkonogy, and Dr. Kevin Walsh. Thank you all.

We would also like to acknowledge the organizations for which we have worked as owners, leaders, employees, or outside business consultants. We have learned much from our experiences with the people in those businesses and nonprofits.

Finally, we want to thank our families—who contributed to this project in ways we cannot count.

The Authors

CONTRIBUTING AUTHORS

Bennett Annan, PsyD, EdD, MBA, MS, MA, LMFT
Margaret Easter, PsyD
Melanie Gharapetian, PsyD
Greg Hilsenrath, PsyD
Raffi Islikaplan, PsyD
Deborah A. Jackson, PsyD
Sherman Lee Mitchell, II, PsyD, MAIOP, MPA
Jamie Menendez-Adamski, PsyD, MA
Ramila Naziri, PsyD
Alice Nkore, PsyD, MBA
Brandy Reid, PsyD, LMFT
Shari Scott, PsyD, MA
Kristyl J. L. Smith, PsyD

CONTENTS

PREFACE

What are "practics"? It's a new term coined by the editor as a combination of the words "practical" and "tactics."

What are "people practics"? Simply put, they are practical tactics to be used for effectively working with people in your business or nonprofit.

What is a business or nonprofit? A collection of *people* with a goal in mind. That's why *People Practics* focuses primarily on the **people** side of organizations, providing seventeen categories of "practical tactics" for managing the workers in your business or nonprofit as well as for understanding and managing your organization overall. These are proven techniques that can make your business thrive.

People Practics covers everything from employee motivation to teamwork to conflict resolution to best practices in leadership to improving organizational culture to strategic planning and process improvement to organizational research and data collection to marketing, and more.

These practical tips come from thirteen members of a graduate cohort who were often required to work as a team as we earned doctorates in organizational psychology. Our aim is to pass on useful knowledge about how to make organizations work better. But this information doesn't only come from what we learned in grad school. It's also based on what we know from our years of experience as business and nonprofit leaders, entrepreneurs, and consultants.

Yet, because you'll see them mentioned in various chapters, you may want to know why we bother with theoretical models. It's because they've been tested, and the research can be replicated so that we know what works and what doesn't in the real world.

In other words, this work is scholarly only in the sense that it has been well researched, and its assertions are backed up by psychological theory, business theory, and empirical research. We all have doctorates, after all, and research is our life's blood.

But the content here is primarily based on business *experience*, business sense, and *common sense*, and it's meant to be readable to the average businessperson, business owner, and business or nonprofit leader.

It's intended to be user-friendly—the kind of business book that you pick up looking for great advice for how to make your business or nonprofit more effective, easier to run, and, ultimately, successful. It's a plus that these ideas are fully backed by really great research.

NOTE: For those who are particular about style, we have used a hybrid of Chicago (*The Chicago Manual of Style*) and APA (*Publication Manual of the American Psychological Association*). Chicago applies to most of the text and formatting. We have used APA only for full references in the notes at the end of each chapter, as most of us used it when we initially wrote our chapters and because this is a text based primarily on ideas from the field of organizational psychology.

Finally, we hope you'll read this book cover to cover, because we believe all of the information to be relevant to achieving success in today's volatile business environment. At the same time, each chapter is designed to be understood independently, so you also have the option to read only the topics most relevant to your current needs.

The Authors

FOREWORD

Several years ago, I had the pleasure of teaching a class in Organizational Behavior at Phillips Graduate University in Southern California. All of the contributors to this book were the students in that class.

At the beginning of the class, I told them that I believe you learn best by teaching. So, instead of me simply lecturing every class session, I would have them teach me what they were learning from the text and any assigned articles using PowerPoint presentations and exercises to demonstrate the subject being covered.

In the end, I required each of them to write a chapter in a book about organizational behavior. This book is the result of that assignment.

Based on my more than thirty-five years of experience assisting both public and private organizations as an industrial/organizational (I/O) psychologist, I asked them to write their chapters as if they were writing a popular psychology book, rather than an academic publication, because I knew that's what most busy clients would prefer. I urged them to make it interesting and easy to read and to include captivating graphics, given that we all are becoming more visual in this new technological world.

The result is this excellent book! They did a great job of providing organizations with helpful tips to bring out the best from their people!

The most valuable resource of any organization is the individual employee, whether an efficient waiter in a restaurant, a highly trained nurse, a talented salesperson, or the conscientious porter who brings you your car in an auto repair facility. The most successful organizations develop a supportive culture that involves every individual employee at every level in the organization.

Think about your experiences dining in a restaurant, going to a doctor's office, purchasing something in a department store, getting your car fixed. What stands out the most as you recall your experiences?

My guess is that it's the people with whom you dealt. The friendly, superb waiter who anticipated your every need. The patient, empathetic nurse who treated you with caring and understanding. The retail clerk who took the time to personally help you find exactly what you wanted. The service technician who carefully explained the problem needing repair on your car and got it done with quality workmanship and no delay.

My guess is that you return to those kinds of places with that kind of culture for further services and purchases.

This book is full of easy-to-grasp practical tactics for building and maintaining that culture. Whether it's leadership or management, a focus on organizational culture, long-range planning, or improving processes in an organization, the authors of this book present clear and practical tactics that focus on the caring development of people, a long-term strategy that builds a solid performance-based component of organizational success.

No matter what kind of organization you are currently working in, large or small, public or private, profit or nonprofit, I believe that you will find the practical tactics offered in this book to be very helpful to you in developing a supportive culture!

Enjoy!

Arnie Dahlke

Arnie Dahlke, PhD
Program Director, Industrial and Organizational Psychology Program
Touro University Worldwide
arnie@arniedahlke.com

Leadership is a choice, not a position.
— Stephen Covey, Businessperson, Author

Leadership is unlocking people's potential to become better.
— Bill Bradley, U.S. Senator, NBA Guard

True leadership stems from individuality that is honestly and sometimes imperfectly expressed . . . Leaders should strive for authenticity over perfection.
— Sheryl Sandberg, Facebook COO

A life is not important except in the impact it has on other lives.
— Jackie Robinson, Businessperson, MLB Second Baseman

The world is before you, and you need not take it or leave it as it was when you came in.
— James Baldwin, Author, Activist

PART ONE

PEOPLE PRACTICS
IN
LEADERSHIP

ONE

PRACTICAL TACTICS FOR LEADING AND MANAGING PEOPLE

by Bennett Annan, PsyD, EdD, MBA, MS, MA, LMFT

An organization cannot get very far toward accomplishing its goals without its employees. It is certainly true that the people who work within an organization are the most important puzzle pieces in it.

Knowing *how* to motivate your workers to perform the best they can to help your organization reach its objectives is a significant part of leading and managing them. Knowing *when* to motivate them is even more significant. There is a delicate balance between knowing *how* to motivate employees and knowing *when* to intervene to keep them motivated or *when* to let them "fly on their own."[1]

For starters, it is critical to know the difference between *leaders* and *managers*.

Leadership vs. Management

Leading and managing people requires making sure they have the resources they need to perform as individual employees, while at the same time being present to support them in their work tasks.[2]

Yet leading and managing people are actually two different skills, each with its own responsibilities and challenges.

It is critical to provide an operational definition of these terms in order to clarify them and avoid possible variations in interpretation.

Management educator and business consultant Peter Drucker noted that, "The only definition of a leader is someone who has followers."[3] According to his definition, because managers have followers, they are leaders.

Management consultants/educators Warren Bennis and Burton Nanus stated it another way: "Managers work toward the organization's goals, using its resources in an effective and efficient manner."[4] According to their definition, since leaders work toward the organization's goals, leaders are also managers.

It is of utmost importance to understand that the two roles, though different in some ways, are similar in others. When one assumes a leadership role, one must also take on the role of manager and vice versa.

The difference is that while managing people requires helping people to adhere to rules, regulations, and principles to achieve organizational goals and objectives, *leading* them requires intervention, innovation, and vision when situations change, as can be expected in our VUCA (Volatile, Uncertain, Complex, Ambiguous) world of business.

It is therefore important to know which leadership styles will help leaders and managers perform their roles most effectively and efficiently.

The Basics of Leadership Styles

One study describes three basic forms of leadership:

1. authoritarian (also called autocratic),
2. participatory (also called democratic), and
3. delegative (also called laissez-faire).[5]

A leader commands at least one of these behaviors, but never all of them simultaneously.

This model supports the concept that in the long-term, the democratic form of leadership is the most productive, because subordinates are able to participate in the decision-making process. Despite its extensive use across a variety of settings—including work, school, and family—employing only one of these styles can make a leader inflexible. That's because leaders are constantly challenged to use all forms of the basic traditional leadership styles (authoritarian, participatory, delegative) when appropriate.

This more adaptable approach, often called *situational leadership*, demands that leaders be autocratic sometimes, democratic at other times, and sometimes laissez-faire, depending on the situation.

It is well-known that situational leadership has stood the test of time in the marketplace and is frequently used for training leaders, including in more than four hundred of the Fortune 500 companies.[6] The most effective leaders generally incorporate all three styles as they lead, using one more predominately than the others. Ineffective leaders often use one style exclusively (typically autocratic).

The **Authoritarian** leadership style creates clear and concise expectations about what needs to be accomplished, when it needs to be accomplished, and how it needs to be accomplished. Authoritarian leadership concentrates on the *leader's* decisions and commands. Use this style if you want to make decisions independently with little input from followers.[7]

Participatory leadership is recognized as the most effective of the three styles. Democratic leaders provide direct feedback to followers while participating in group activities. This leadership style encourages input and participation from followers in the decision-making process. Use this style if you want the final say over decisions. Research has shown that followers are more motivated and creative—as a result of feeling more engaged—when leaders use this style.[8]

The **Delegative** style is useful if you want your followers to make decisions, while you as leader ultimately remain responsible. This style is considered the least effective of the three, as followers generally lack guidance and direction. The delegative style often leads to followers blaming one another for mistakes and refusing to accept responsibility.[9]

Various philosophies of leadership have emerged from these three basic forms of leadership, but the major theories that have dominated much of our thinking in the past century are:

a) *Trait theories*, which emphasize identifying the qualities of great persons.
b) *Behavioral theories*, where the focus is exclusively on what leaders do and how they act, with two general kinds of behaviors (task behaviors and relationship behaviors).
c) *Contingency theories*, in which optimal actions are contingent upon the situation.
d) *Dyadic theories*, an approach to leadership that attempts to explain why leaders vary their behavior with different followers.
e) *Transformational leadership*, which focuses on influencing and transforming followers.[10]

Leadership Theories

In the current business environment, almost every book on leadership practice has its own take on what constitutes a good and effective leader. The major views of leadership that dominate much of our thinking today include:

Leadership Traits. The *leadership traits approach* reinforces the notion that leadership is an art rather than a science, that people are born with leadership traits, and that only great people possess them.[11] This approach emphasizes certain personality traits that contribute to the leadership process, including intelligence, alertness, insight, responsibility, initiative, persistence, self-confidence, and sociability.[12]

Trait theorists argue that you can spot a potential leader just by looks, manner, or level of education. Trait theory assumes that leaders share certain physical, psychological, and sociological characteristics that determine their effectiveness. This approach is used when a person is above average in height and good looks, intelligence or charisma, and in sociological characteristics, including educational level or socioeconomic class.

Leadership Skills. The *leadership skills approach* posits that leadership is a science, not an art, and that it comprises a set of skills and abilities that can be learned and developed. In this view, effective leadership depends on three basic personal skills: (a) technical, (b) human, and (c) conceptual.[13]

This style is useful if you have a technical skill or knowledge and proficiency in a specific activity, if you are able to get along with people and to work within teams, and if you are able to understand and better decide the measures that must be taken in a particular field of work.

Theorists behind this approach believe that great leaders are not born with innate leadership qualities, but rather must acquire the knowledge and abilities necessary for effective leadership.[14]

Leadership Style/Behavior. The *leadership style/behavior approach* focuses exclusively on what leaders do and how they act. In this approach, leadership is essentially composed of task behaviors and relationship behaviors (i.e., what leaders do and how they act). This leadership style is useful if you want to help group members achieve their objectives and if you want subordinates to feel comfortable with themselves, with each other, and with the situation in which they find themselves.[15]

Situational Leadership. The *situational leadership approach* tends to match leadership actions with leadership situations. For example, a supervisor will have to adapt and be flexible to accommodate the group's needs rather than staying in one mode.[16]

In this approach, leaders are challenged to use all of the basic traditional leadership styles when appropriate. This approach is useful if you are capable of being autocratic sometimes, and at other times variously democratic, or laissez-faire, depending on the situation.

Transformational Leadership. *Transformational leadership*, as its name implies, is a process that changes and transforms individuals and influences followers to accomplish more than is normally expected of them. In fact, it is one of the most well-known leadership theories within the so-called new leadership paradigm.[17]

Use the transformational leadership style if you want to inspire workers to find better ways of achieving a goal, or if you want to mobilize people into effective groups. It is also useful if you want to raise the morale, well-being, and motivational level of a group through excellent rapport. Transformational leaders are also good at conflict resolution.[18]

How to Lead and Manage People

Leadership skills—which involve motivating, inspiring enthusiasm, and building respect for people—are highly sought after by employers.[19] Yet the question of what makes a good leader has been widely debated. One thing that *is* clear that the ability to lead effectively relies on a number of key skills, which we'll discuss below. But it is also true that different leaders often have vastly different styles and characteristics. There is, in fact, no one right way to lead in all circumstances. One of the main characteristics of good leaders is their flexibility and ability to adapt to changing circumstances.

In my particular view, leading and managing skills are inextricably intertwined. You cannot lead people without knowing how to manage them, and you cannot manage people without knowing how to lead them. Knowing the difference and when to employ each set of skills are the keys to success in any organization.

Now that you've learned the difference between leadership and management and received an overview of the three basic forms of leadership styles, you're ready to learn the skills needed to lead and manage people. In my experience as a leader, I have learned that leading and managing people in organizations requires the following skill sets:

Skill No. 1: Mastery of Emotion—Emotional Intelligence. To lead and manage people, you must first and foremost learn to master your own emotions. In fact, both leaders and managers must always be upbeat to ensure that their workers continue to follow them.

Life coach Tony Robbins defines *emotions* as any feelings, such as joy, sorrow, fear, hate, and love. Robbins believes that the only reason anyone does anything is to change the way they feel.

If you want to make more money, lose weight, or buy a new item of clothing, you are doing it because of what you think it will give you, which involves some kind of emotion. (It is worth noting that you can always change your emotional state no matter how you are feeling presently.)[20]

There are three factors that determine what you feel, moment to moment, which Robbins and other psychologists call the *emotional triad*: At any time, your emotional state is controlled by your (a) physiology (your body), (b) your focus, and your (c) language or words. Using the emotional triad can keep leaders and managers emotionally stable.

Physiology. According to Robbins, emotion is created by motion: Whatever you are feeling right now is related to how you are using your body. If you start to feel emotionally down you might want to stand up, reach your arms up in a big swinging motion, and breathe in deeply; if that doesn't work, you could try to smile or march in place. These actions will help you return to your emotional equilibrium. This is because the way you use your body biochemically changes how you feel.

Focus. To feel happy, focus on things in your life that will make you feel happy. You may want to ask yourself questions like, "What am I happy about in my life right now?" You may also try remembering happy moments from the past, like a fun birthday, wedding, or graduation. Whatever you focus on, you will feel. When you're feeling down, change your focus, find reasons to be grateful, and picture your world as you would like it to be.[21]

Language. Your words and language patterns also change how you feel. If you say things like, "I feel really tired" or "This is too hard," you will literally feel tired or experience things as too difficult. This mentality simply does not empower you. All words have different emotional states associated with them. There are certain phrases you use that are disempowering, which will affect how you feel moment to moment. Awareness of your vocabulary, statements, phrases, and metaphors is thus crucial to controlling your emotional state. Use words or language that will encourage and empower you to move on, and pay attention to the words you repeat to yourself.[22]

The Emotional Triad

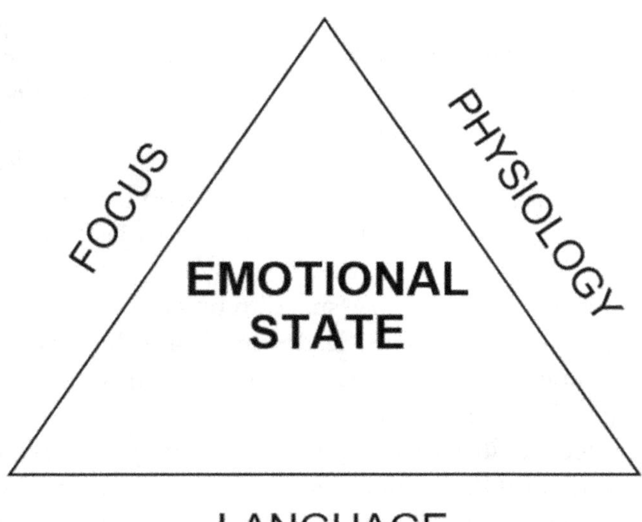

Skill No. 2: Serve First. If you want to lead and manage people successfully, be a "servant leader" and learn to serve first. That's because the business environment is changing, and leaders and managers must modify their traditional ways of doing business, which often are no longer cost effective.

Today, traditionally autocratic and hierarchical leadership and management models are yielding to a different way of working. That new manner of leading is based on teamwork and community. It seeks to involve others in decision making, is strongly based in ethical and caring behavior, and is attempting to enhance workers' personal growth. At the same time, it seeks to improve the caring and quality of institutions.[23] This emerging approach is called *servant leadership*.

The word *servant* is often construed to mean "personal or domestic attendant," i.e., people who serve or wait on others or people who perform household duties for others. On the other hand, the word *leader* has the connotation of a person who rules, guides, or inspires others—the head of an institution.

These two words are usually thought of as opposites. However, Larry Spears, CEO of the Spears Center for Servant-Leadership, argues that the basic idea of servant leadership is both logical and intuitive. For example, during the Industrial Revolution, leaders and managers tended to view people as objects; they considered workers as cogs within a machine. Yet in the past few decades, a shift in perspective has taken place. According to Spears, standard practices are rapidly moving toward the ideas put forward by Robert Greenleaf, Stephen Covey, Peter Senge, Max DePree, Margaret Wheatley, Ken Blanchard, and many others who suggest that there is a better way to lead and manage organizations.

I strongly believe in Robert Greenleaf's model of servant leadership. It begins with the natural feeling that one wants to serve—to serve *first*. Then that person makes a conscious choice to aspire to lead. Yet the servant leader is sharply different from one who is a *leader first*. That person may choose to lead based on a need to assuage an unusual drive for power or to acquire material possessions. The "leader first" and the "servant first" are two extremes, and between them are shades and blends that are part of the infinite diversity of human nature.

The difference manifests itself in the care taken by the servant-first leader to make sure that other people's highest priority needs are being served. The best test to determine if you, as a servant leader, are meeting your workers' needs is to ask the following questions: Do those being served grow as people? Do they, while being served, become healthier, wiser, freer, more autonomous, and more likely themselves to become servants?[24]

The good news is that in serving first, leaders and managers themselves grow as people; they become healthier, wiser, freer, more autonomous, and more likely themselves to become servants. Greenleaf asserts that this, in turn, often benefits the least privileged in society in that they, at minimum, will not be further deprived.[25]

To utilize this leadership style, Greenleaf suggests that leaders focus primarily on people's growth and well-being as well as the conditions in the communities to which they belong. While traditional leadership generally involves the accumulation and exercise of power by one at the "top of the pyramid," servant leadership is different. These leaders must be ready to share power, put others' needs first, and help people develop and perform at as high a level as possible.

There are ten core characteristics of servant leadership, which—with practice—will help anyone to lead and manage people effectively:[26]

1. Active Listening. Servant leadership requires leaders to actively listen to other people, not just be good at communication and decision making. Listening involves focusing on what the team is saying and using this information to guide the group toward its objectives.

An effective leader should also identify the things left unsaid. Leaders should regularly venture among team members and assess the mood in the room, as conflicts can often be sensed and unhappiness felt without someone having to voice it.

In order to improve your listening skills, focus on being attentive. You can further improve your attention skills by cueing into body language and by improving your ability to give and receive feedback.[27]

2. Empathy. Active listening and the ability to empathize go hand in hand. Since the focus of servant leadership is to serve others, you must be able to accept and recognize people's individual values and feelings. Even when someone is underperforming at work, a servant leader should be able to love and understand him or her as a person.

In a business environment, empathy is often hard to achieve, because the focus is on company objectives and performance. But with servant leadership, the focus shifts to the individual employee and his or her well-being. An empathic leader will not just accept any behavior or performance, but instead of simply dismissing the team member, the leader tries to understand the behavior.

To improve your ability to be empathic, when having a conversation, try to put your own viewpoint aside and openly listen to what the other person is saying. You need to be inquisitive and learn more about different ways of doing things. Instead of rejecting an idea or thought, learn more about it to understand where the person suggesting it is coming from.[28]

3. Healing. According to Spears, servant leadership emphasizes the individual's emotional health, together with mental and physical well-being. Servant leaders should focus on their potential to heal themselves and others.

In a business context, healing is achieved by ensuring that employees have enough support options available. This could mean access to counseling, provision of proper health care facilities, a strong health and safety culture, or focus on self-development through courses and training.

In order to improve your healing abilities, you should make the above resources a priority, but you can also help people achieve success by utilizing the approach most optimal to the situation.

It's important to ensure that you do not focus just on work-related topics in your conversations with people, but also get to know how they are doing. Make sure you read self-development guides and provide tips on what you have learned to your team. It's also vital to make sure you are doing well mentally and physically so that you have the strength to help others.[29]

4. Awareness. Spears stressed that servant leadership requires general awareness and self-awareness. Self-awareness, in particular, requires the leader to see his or her own emotions and behaviors in the context of how they affect the rest of the team. Through self-awareness, you become better at noticing what the people around you are doing and can therefore fix problems more quickly.

Self-awareness is tightly connected to the feedback culture within the organization. It is important that employees are able to provide feedback, not just about themselves and each other, but also about management and leadership.

The secret to awareness is taking a closer look inside yourself. Finding out about your strengths and weaknesses is crucial for understanding your inner self and how you affect others around you. You can learn more about yourself through personality tests, such as the Myers-Briggs Type Indicator. More importantly, however, good leaders seek feedback from the team to learn more about how they are perceived and how their actions influence others.[30]

5. Persuasion. According to Spears, servant leadership does not rely on authority to get things done. Instead, it uses persuasion to facilitate decision making. Servant leaders seek consensus rather than compliance, which is perhaps the biggest difference from traditional authoritarian models.

Greenleaf states that servant leaders should take a fresh look at issues of power and authority and that the ability of people to relate to one another creates a less coercive and more creative, supportive environment.

In large part, persuasion in business is characterized by an organization's need to "make its case." Servant leaders should involve employees in decision making and explain what the objectives are and why, as this can help influence workers to act in a positive manner.

There are a few ways to master the art of persuasion. You can improve your body language, your communication style, your ability to sense the right time to talk, and your ability to listen.

Finally, you should aim to be an expert in your field, as doing so guarantees that your team will look up to and feel inspired by you. Show enthusiasm and expertise in your actions, and you will undoubtedly inspire others.[31]

6. Conceptualization. Greenleaf noted that a servant leader is able to conceive of solutions to difficult problems that may not presently exist.[32] This conceptualization requires that the leader look beyond simple day-to-day realities. While it is important that leaders stay on top of daily operations and ensure they are efficiently implemented and achieved, leaders must also look beyond short-term objectives and develop a visionary strategy for the future.

The most efficient way to improve the ability to conceptualize solutions to business problems is through improvement in business acumen. You need to improve your understanding of your industry and your organization by reading relevant reports, books, and industry blogs. This can help you see where your industry and your organization are heading and better prepare you, as a leader, for the future.[33]

7. Foresight. Another point related to conceptualization is the idea of foresight. In other words, servant leadership requires the ability to foresee likely outcomes through an understanding of the past. There are three key points to foresight in leadership:

1. The ability to **learn** from past experiences
2. The ability to **identify** what is currently happening
3. The ability to **understand** the consequences of specific decisions

For both Spears and Greenleaf, foresight is tightly related to intuition. It is an area where leadership studies have not yet ventured in great detail. Spears, nonetheless, suggests that in order to improve foresight and become better at predicting the future, you should improve your analytical skills. This can be achieved by focusing on your decision-making process and by following up on the decisions you have made—in short, you need to develop a deeper understanding of the consequences of your decisions.[34]

8. Stewardship. *Stewardship* in servant leadership means taking responsibility for your actions and those of the team. The main assumption is to commit to serve others' needs first. For Greenleaf, this indicates that not only is the organization holding its trust in the leader, but the whole organization is there to serve the wider community. Additionally, stewardship requires openness as well as persuasion. It is not about controlling actions, but rather allowing yourself to be accountable.[35]

In order to infuse stewardship into your leadership, start by understanding your own values and how they guide you in your leadership roles. Furthermore, recognize how those values align with those of the organization and the team you are leading. Remember not to be afraid of pointing out when situations are not aligned with these values.[36]

9. Commitment to Others' Growth. According to Spears, the servant leadership model focuses on the intrinsic value of people outside of their contribution as employees.[37] Thus, the aim of a servant leader is to help people realize their potential beyond just the ability to do the job well. Servant leadership requires a commitment to helping people realize their personal and professional development potential as well as to support it. Greenleaf stated: "The secret of institution building is to be able to weld a team of such people by lifting them up to grow taller than they would otherwise be."[38]

To demonstrate your commitment to others' growth, you can set an example as a leader by investing in your own personal and professional development. If you are constantly seeking to grow, you provide motivation to the team around you to do the same.

In addition, you may also discuss personal and professional goals with your team. By understanding how they would like to develop, you can help provide the tools and routes for them to achieve these objectives. Learn more about how to grow your people and the benefits associated with this growth.[39]

10. Building Community. Finally, servant leadership relies on the development of a community and a sense of togetherness within the organization. With this in mind, business leaders can foster a sense of community by focusing on team building. By creating effective and caring teams, the organization as a whole will become more caring.

In order to support community building, you must ensure that different people within the organization interact with each other. Organizing social events and get-togethers is important. It is important to encourage diversity and the flow of opinions within the organization as much as possible.[40]

Skill No. 3: Solving Conflicts. To lead and manage people, it is crucial to understand that no two people think the same, no matter how much they have in common. This requires understanding that conflict will inevitably occur between people in the workplace. The only way of getting around it is to not "freak out" or feel threatened.

Moreover, sometimes it may be hard to get resolution to a conflict. Yet instead of seeing conflict as a threat, reframe it as a sign of growth for yourself and an opportunity to harness the skills needed to lead and manage people.

Generally, *conflict* refers to some form of friction, disagreement, or discord arising within a group when one or more members' beliefs or actions are either resisted or deemed unacceptable to one or more members of the group.[41]

Research professors Linda Putnam and Marshall Poole provide a more specific definition of conflict as "the interaction of interdependent people who perceive opposition of goals, aims, and values, and who see the other party as potentially interfering with the realization of these goals."[42]

Katherine Miller, a professor of organizational communicatons, highlights three general characteristics of conflict:

1. Incompatible goals
2. Interdependence
3. Interaction[43]

Incompatible goals arise when two or more people utilize different approaches to achieve specific goals. Incompatibility, however, is not a sufficient condition for organizational conflict to occur. Instead, conflict arises only when the organizational members' behaviors are *interdependent*. Furthermore, *interaction* involves the expression of incompatibility, and "highlights the importance of communication in the study of conflict."[44]

Additionally, conflict can arise at three organizational levels:

1. Between the organization's members, known as *interpersonal conflict*,
2. Between members of the same group, known as *intragroup conflict*, or
3. Between members of two or more groups, known as *intergroup conflict*.[45]

Miller notes that individuals seldom move suddenly from peaceful coexistence to conflict-ridden relationships. Rather, people move through phases as conflict develops and subsides. Business professor Louis Pondy defines five phases of organizational conflict:[46]

1. *Latent conflict*: Individuals interact in interdependent relationships conducive to developing incompatible goals.
2. *Perceived conflict*: One or more individuals perceive the situation to be characterized by incompatibility and interdependence.
3. *Felt conflict*: Individuals begin to personalize perceived conflict by focusing on the conflict issue and planning conflict management strategies.
4. *Manifest conflict*: Conflict is enacted through communication. Interaction may involve cycles of escalation and de-escalation as various strategies are used.
5. *Conflict aftermath*: The conflict episode has both short- and long-term effects on the individuals, their relationships, and the organization.[47]

Relational Factors. The relationship between the conflicting parties (e.g., supervisor–subordinate, colleague–colleague) appears to strongly impact the conflict management process. One important characteristic of the relationship between the conflicting parties is *power*, or the hierarchical position individuals occupy within an organization.[48]

Relational factors include (a) supervisor versus subordinate, (b) subordinate versus supervisor, and (c) colleague versus colleague. Conflict management styles can help you analyze how relational factors influence the conflict management process.

Conflict Management Styles Model. Management professor Kenneth Thomas described two dimensions of conflict management styles, *concern for self* and *concern for others*, and identified five conflict styles that fall at various points on his conflict grid.[49]

This model is useful in understanding how five relational factors influence conflict management processes: (a) competing, (b) collaborating, (c) avoiding, (d) accommodating, and (e) compromising.

Use the *competition style* when you believe you need to be high in self-concern, characterized by a drive to maximize individual gain at others' expense. In contrast, use the *collaboration style* when you need to construct solutions to conflict that meet the needs of all parties involved. You may use the *avoidance style* when you believe you need to be low in concern for self and want to disengage from the conflict. Use the *accommodation style* when you need to sacrifice self-interest to satisfy others' needs. Finally, use the *compromise style*, which straddles the midpoint between concern for self and concern for others, when you need to use compromise to arrive at a resolution to the conflict.[50]

Thomas's Conflict Management Styles Model

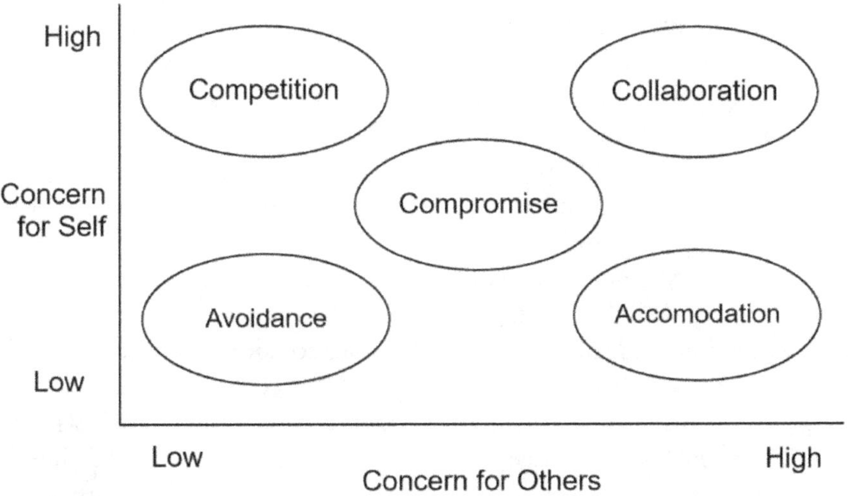

Putnam and Poole reviewed the existing research on hierarchical levels and conflict styles and recommend that you use (a) competitive styles when dealing with subordinates, (b) accommodation or collaboration when dealing with superiors, (c) accommodation or avoidance styles when dealing with peers, and (d) compromise styles when the conflict grinds into a deadlock, yet a resolution is necessary. At that point, a third party is normally involved to help mediate any necessary concessions.

It is also important to understand that, according to Thomas, no two individuals have exactly the same expectations and desires, which inevitably results in conflict. In fact, Thomas argues, conflict is a natural part of our interactions with others.[51]

Additionally, conflict in the workplace often occurs due to a lack of communication, which—if not confronted—can cause major problems for a business.[52]

Yet many employers mistake disagreements with conflicts; by contrast, disagreements are differences in opinion that could, but do not always, lead to conflict. Handling disagreements and other forms of possible conflict quickly can be healthy, but ignoring them may be destructive and could result in detrimental outcomes to organizations, including rapid turnover rates, loss of productivity, and absenteeism. The cost of turnover in the workplace can be extraordinary.

Researchers have found that 60 to 80 percent of all conflicts in organizations in the United States come from strained relationships between employees (i.e., relational factors).[53] Additionally, a typical manager spends 25 to 40 percent of his or her time dealing with workplace conflicts, amounting to one to two days out of every work week.[54] Further, Fortune 500 senior executives spend 20 percent of their time in litigation activities.[55]

Moreover, the number of employees seeking mental health consultation for work-related conflict increased from 23 to almost 30 percent in a three-year period in the early 2000s.[56] Workplace conflict is a decisive factor in more than 50 percent of employee departures,[57] and more than 50 percent of employers report being sued by an employee.[58]

Unresolved conflict represents the largest reducible cost in many businesses, yet it remains largely unrecognized.[59] To create a better chance for success in leading and managing your people, consider adopting the collaborative style in which both you and your followers win. Also make sure your organization adopts conflict management processes, such as mediation and arbitration, to reduce relational conflicts. Doing so will help you and your organization report a 50 to 80 percent reduction in litigation costs, a good reason to consider conflict management processes, indeed.[60]

Skill No. 4: Ethics. Both my experience in leading and managing people for many years and time spent researching this topic have afforded me the opportunity to clarify my perspectives about leaders and managers, specifically in the area of ethics.

Ethics are critically important in leading and managing people, and a lack of ethics can damage your reputation.[61] In other words, it is best to refrain from taking actions to make short-term profits that could put your business or personal reputation at risk.[62]

One important ethical guideline is the need to be authentic—putting into words what you experience with your followers[63] and doing what you say you will do.[64] Business consultant and author Peter Block asserts that "this is the most powerful thing you can do to have the leverage you are looking for and to build client commitment." Block suggests further that to be successful in leading and managing people, a person needs to influence rather than control followers.[65]

Some professional and ethical behaviors leaders and managers should commit to include getting involved; sticking to an assigned role; reaching out for responsibility; doing whatever it takes to get the job done; being a team player; being observant, honest, and loyal; really listening to the client's needs; and taking pride in your work.[66]

It is also important to make sure that your organization's mission statement, vision, values, and strategy are fully aligned at all times. If you adhere to these ethical principles, you will be effective in leading and managing your people.

Skill No. 5: Understanding Women, People of Color, and Foreign-born Leaders. I believe that leading and managing people is inherently different for women, people of color, and foreign-born leaders, because traditional notions of leading and managing are largely derived from a white, usually urban, male context, thus making traditional leadership behaviors potentially inappropriate and possibly ineffective for them.[67]

The measurement tools used for many leading and managing processes were developed primarily by European American males and may therefore contain substantial measurement bias when applied to other ethnic groups.

In addition, these leadership and management processes are often interpreted based on norms obtained mostly from European American male participants and, if used without consideration for a person's ethnic background, could lead to ineffective or risky leading and management of people in minority populations.[68]

Challenges Faced by Non-Mainstream Leaders and Managers. The prevalence of non-mainstream leaders and managers has steadily increased throughout the United States over the last two decades, but there are particular challenges they must deal with.

One of those many challenges is that the small things they say and do can make a difference in how mainstream people in the organization perceive them. For example, when noticing subtle differences, they might attribute these variations to personality, gender, or, worse, character flaws.[69]

Though the number of women, minority, and foreign-born leaders and managers has increased significantly, they often do not have the leadership development techniques to address their particular needs.

A unique challenge for them is that non-mainstream leaders and managers differ in their communication preferences and styles. One way of compensating for this difference is to master conflict management styles. Neglecting this issue can create conflict—socially, professionally, and intimately—especially between the sexes.[70]

Moreover, it should be noted that even the most progressive, modern organizations were created by and for white males and thus tend to have systems, policies, norms, and structures that favor that particular life experience.

In addition, leaders must be sensitive to the behaviors and values that tend to favor traits and characteristics traditionally associated with white maleness, regarding them as the "norm" at work, while undervaluing traits and characteristics traditionally associated with women, people of color, and foreign-born leaders and managers.[71]

If you are a woman leading and managing people, you must note that for the most part you will encounter gender-biased environments. In most organizations, the standards of success are measured in male terms and therefore, women are typically isolated from formal networks.

Furthermore, wage and salary structures are different for traditionally male work versus work that is considered traditionally female. In addition, while the "norms" are to accept certain male managers' behaviors, the behavior of female managers might be rejected within the same organization.

For example, different norms may apply to the demonstration of vulnerability.[72] Leaders and managers must therefore recognize that ongoing discrimination exists for women and minorities in managerial roles.

Adding New Leadership Skills Means Adapting to Change

After reading this chapter, you may notice a few competencies you want to add to your existing skillset in order to lead and manage people more effectively. That means learning to accept and effect change.

Change is one of the few things about which we can be certain. It can be positive and lead to rewards, but it can also be uncomfortable and awkward. One truth is that it is only when people are given an inspirational vision that they can accept change more easily.

Whether good or bad, change requires you to adjust and cope.[73] If you want to lead and manage people today and are not willing to accept change, you may struggle with the tasks set before you. You must recognize that change is necessary to improve the effectiveness of your leadership and management skills.

A prime example comes from the earlier discussion of non-mainstream leaders and managers. As was discussed above, research shows that leadership roles can be even more challenging for women, people of color, and foreign-born managers. Thus, some leadership models may be inappropriate and ineffective for women, Latinos/as, African Americans, Native Americans, Asians/Asian Americans, and other ethnic minorities.[74]

Additionally, foreign-born leaders and managers are faced with a multitude of problems when they lead and manage people in American organizations. The most important of these is the ability to recognize and make the changes necessary to assimilate into the organizational culture. Coming from a foreign culture whose values are different, leaders who lack trust in the business system could manage in such a way that leads to low morale and low productivity, potentially diminishing profits.

Fortunately, there is a general willingness on the part of foreign-born leaders and managers to change and assimilate.[75] However, this change often comes slowly and painfully. Nonetheless, with some coaching and mentoring, struggles and concerns during the change process can be minimized.

Finally, studies point to the fact that where culture is interwoven into the fabric of management philosophy, the results tend to be successful. When local culture is absent from the work environment and the leadership and management techniques are also alien to local workers, either wholesale failure or underperformance is a common business result.[76]

In other words, if foreign-born leaders and managers interweave their culture into their organizational management philosophy, they are more likely to be successful. At the same time, if they do not discard antiquated or culturally irrelevant ways of doing business, their struggles and concerns will be monumental and of serious consequence.

This is true for *all* leaders and managers.

Dr. Bennett Annan was born in Accra, Ghana, in West Africa and migrated to the United States more than thirty years ago. He holds an MS in Mechanical Engineering and worked as a mechanical and manufacturing/ engineering manager for twelve years. He then completed an MBA to enhance his managerial skills. He was the general manager of a medical center when he enrolled in the organizational leadership program for his Doctorate in Education at Pepperdine University to enhance his leadership skills.

Since 2009, he has been giving presentations on various aspects of managing and handling life's obstacles for three ministries at St. Rose of Lima Catholic Church in Simi Valley. In 2013, he realized he could do more for these ministries by going back to school at Phillips Graduate University, where he earned an MA in clinical psychology which allowed him to become a licensed marriage and family therapist. At Phillips, he also completed a Doctorate in Psychology with an emphasis in Organizational Management and Consulting, believing he could do more for organizations by understanding how organizations work.

NOTES

[1] Daviault, C., & Campbell, C. (2017). *Leading and managing people* [Online course]. Retrieved from https://oeru.org/oeru-partners/oer-foundation/leading-and-managing-people/
[2] Ibid.
[3] Drucker, P. F. (1996). Leaders are doers. *Executive Excellence, 13*(4), 8. Retrieved from http://www.worldcat.org/title/executive-excellence/oclc/42326528
[4] Bennis, W., & Nanus, B. (2004). Management vs. leadership. In *Management skills: A Jossey-Bass reader* (pp. 41–52). San Francisco, CA: Jossey-Bass.
[5] Martin, J. (1995). On the quest to become a leader. *Tribune Business Weekly, 6*(31), 1.
[6] Hersey, P., & Blanchard, K. H. (1988). *Management of organizational behavior: Utilizing human resources* (5th ed.). Englewood Cliffs, NJ: Prentice Hall.
[7] ResourcefulManager. (2016). *The resourceful manager's guide to leadership.* Malvern, PA: ResourcefulManager.
[8] Ibid.
[9] Ibid.
[10] Northouse, P. (2004). *Leadership theories and practice* (3rd ed.). Thousand Oaks, CA: Sage.
[11] Bass, B. M., & Avolio, B. J. (1994). *Improving organizational effectiveness through transformational leadership.* Thousand Oaks, CA: Sage.
[12] Northouse, *Leadership theories and practice.*
[13] Katz, R. L. (1974, September). Skills of an effective administrator. *Harvard Business Review.* Retrieved from https://hbr.org/
[14] Northouse, *Leadership theories and practice.*
[15] Ibid.
[16] Martin, On the quest to become a leader.
[17] Northouse, *Leadership theories and practice.*
[18] Spahr, P. (2015, October 30). *What is transformational leadership? How new ideas produce impressive results.* Retrieved from https://online.stu.edu/transformational-leadership/
[19] Skillsyouneed. (2017, November 14). *Leadership skills.* Retrieved from https://www.skillsyouneed.com/leadership-skills.html
[20] Robbins, T. (1992). *Awaken the giant within: How to take immediate control of your mental, emotional, physical and financial destiny.* New York, NY: Free Press.
[21] Ibid.
[22] Ibid.
[23] Spears, L. C. (2004). Practicing servant-leadership. *Leader to Leader, 2004*(34), 7–11.
[24] Greenleaf, R. K. (1977). *Servant leadership: A journey into the nature of legitimate power and greatness.* Mahwah, NJ: Paulist Press.
[25] Ibid.
[26] Spears, Practicing servant-leadership.
[27] Ibid.
[28] Ibid.
[29] Ibid.
[30] Ibid.
[31] Ibid.
[32] Greenleaf, *Servant leadership.*
[33] Spears, Practicing servant-leadership.

[34] Ibid.
[35] Ibid.
[36] Ibid.
[37] Ibid.
[38] Greenleaf, *Servant leadership*.
[39] Spears, Practicing servant-leadership.
[40] Ibid.
[41] Holt, M. (2017). Risks of not confronting conflict in the workplace. Retrieved November 14, 2017, from Retrieved from http://www.chron.com/
[42] Putnam, L. L., & Poole, M. S. (1987). Conflict and negotiation. In F. M. Jablin, L. L. Putnam, K. H. Roberts, & L. W. Porter, *Handbook of organizational communication*. Newbury Park, CA: Sage.
[43] Miller, K. (2015). *Organizational communication: Approaches and processes*. Stamford, CT: Cengage.
[44] Ibid.
[45] Ibid.
[46] Pondy, L. R. (1967). Organizational conflict: Concepts and models. *Administrative Science Quarterly*, 12, 296–320.
[47] Miller, *Organizational communication*.
[48] Ibid.
[49] Thomas, K. W. (1976). Conflict and conflict management. In M. Dunnette, *Handbook of industrial and organization psychology* (pp. 889–935). Chicago, IL: Rand McNally.
[50] Ibid.
[51] Thomas, K. W., & Kilmann, R. H. (1974). Thomas-Kilmann conflict mode instrument. Palo Alto, CA: Consulting Psychologists Press.
[52] Holt, Risks of not confronting conflict in the workplace.
[53] Dana, D. (2005). *Managing differences: How to build better relationships at work and home*. St. Louis, MO: MTI Publications.
[54] Ilgaz, Z. (2014, May 15). Conflict resolution: When should leaders step in? Retrieved from Washington Business Journal: https://www.forbes.com
[55] Ford, J. (2000, July). Workplace conflict: Facts and figures. Retrieved from http://mediate.com/articles/Ford1.cfm
[56] Shepell, W. (2002, November 15). Workplace trends linked to mental health crisis in Canada [Press release]. Retrieved from https://www.shepellfgiservices.com/newsroom/pr-nov152002.asp
[57] Johnston, E. (2011, July 5). Workplace conflict is expensive. CFR Mediation Blog [Web log post].
[58] Armour, S. (2001, March 27). Workers win more lawsuits, awards. *USA Today*. Retrieved from http://www.usatoday.com/
[59] Dana, *Managing differences*.
[60] Stipanovich, T. J. (2004). ADR and the "vanishing trial": The growth and impact of alternative dispute resolution. *Journal of Empirical Legal Studies* (1), 843–912.
[61] Greiner, L., & Poulfelt, F. (Eds.). (2010). *Management consulting today and tomorrow*. New York, NY: Routledge.
[62] Greiner & Poulfelt, *Management consulting today and tomorrow*.
[63] Block, *Flawless consulting*.

---

[64] Kouzes, J. M., & Posner, B. Z. (2002). *The leadership challenge* (3rd ed.) San Francisco, CA: Jossey-Bass.
[65] Block, P. (2011). *Flawless consulting: A guide to getting your expertise used* (3rd ed.). San Francisco, CA: Pfeiffer
[66] Ibid.
[67] Ruderman, M. N., & Ohlott, P. J. (2005). Leading roles: What coaches of women need to know. *Leadership in Action, 25*(3), 3–9.
[6868] Thyer, B. A., Padgett, D. K., & Royse, D. (2016). *Program evaluation: An introduction to an evidence-based approach*. Boston, MA: Brooks Cole.
[69] Hyun, J. (2012). Leadership principles for capitalizing on culturally diverse teams: The bamboo ceiling revisited. *Leader to Leader, 64*, 14–19.
[70] Ruderman & Ohlott, Leading roles.
[71] Ibid.
[72] Ibid.
[73] Byvelds, R., & Newman, J. (1997). Understanding change. *Factsheet, 91*(14), 57.
[74] Ruderman & Ohlott, Leading roles.
[75] Annan, B. (2008). *Immigrants in U.S.: Insights, views & approaches*. Los Angeles, CA: Sharp Image.
[76] Versi, A. (2004). A management revolution is needed. *African Business, 303*(13).

Image:
Highway sign by Gerd Altmann on Pixabay.

TWO

PRACTICAL TACTICS FOR UNDERSTANDING YOUR EMPLOYEES

by Melanie Gharapetian, PsyD

Employees are a company's greatest asset—they're your competitive advantage. You want to attract and retain the best; provide them with encouragement, stimulus, and make them feel that they are an integral part of the company's mission.
– Anne M. Mulcahy, former CEO of Xerox Corporation

Human behavior can be fascinating and complex. Individuals bring many differences to work, such as their values, personality, emotions, and knowledge. A challenge employers face in trying to run an effective organization is understanding individual employees and successfully matching the right employee to each job.

As a manager, you need to take time to get to know your employees, learn their capabilities, background, and interests. This helps build rapport and makes them feel valued in the organization.

Imagine if your boss doesn't know anything about you or never takes the time to talk with you. You might begin to feel that your boss doesn't care or doesn't recognize what you're doing for the company.

Taking the time to learn about your employees will not only help you determine the capabilities of your workforce, but it can also help improve individual job performance. Knowing what your workers' responsibilities are will help the company stay on track with its goals and gives you the

chance to help them in areas where they can improve as well as the opportunity to recognize them for their time and effort.[1]

Understanding the Individual

Values. Individuals have their own sets of beliefs and values. Values determine our priorities and influence our work and how we live our lives. We usually attain our values through life experiences and what we're taught. Values impact the choices we make, our perception of the world, and our behavior.[2]

In the workplace, people are most likely to work for a company or choose a career whose values align with their own. For example, people who value creativity are more likely to choose a job that is free-flowing, that allows them to think outside the box and come up with their own ideas. These individuals are less likely to work for a company that is by-the-book structured, because their values won't mesh.

The ideal recruitment process should begin with a company identifying its values and creating an accurate job description, including the required skills, experience, and characteristics needed to be successful in the position. During this process, it is also important for managers and recruiters to understand the individual attributes that are most important to succeeding within the company culture.[3]

To enable you as a leader to better understand the values of your employees, have them make a list that defines what is most important to them. Common work values include recognition for achievements, job security, compensation, leadership, and career growth. Individuals can rate each value on a scale of 1 to 10, "1" being the most important and "10" being the least.

At this point, you can evaluate this list and determine if each employee's needs and values are being met. Defining these values can ensure that you understand what is important to your team and help you address issues that may need further discussion.

Personality. We often talk about the personalities of the people around us. We hear people say, "He has such an easygoing personality." Or, "Her personality is so charming." These are descriptions of how we view people based on our perception of what personality means.

The term personality describes our thoughts, feelings, and the behaviors that make us unique. Our personality comes from within and remains relatively consistent, although it can evolve over time based on our life experiences and environment.[4]

Personality can have an impact on a person's performance and behavior at work and how he or she might react to various situations. Different personality traits can be best suited for different jobs and workplace cultures. To efficiently manage behavior in an organization, understanding the personalities of your employees is important in order to match people with jobs best suited for their personality.[5]

For example, if your company is looking for someone who is good at collaborating and working in teams, someone who prefers to work independently and doesn't like working in teams may not be a good fit in that specific job.[6]

Personality Assessments. During the initial screening of candidates, personality assessments can be conducted to evaluate how they think or how they would react in different scenarios to determine if they are a potential fit for a position. Employers can also assess their existing employees' personalities on the job to have a better understanding of who they are.

It is important to keep in mind that personality assessments are not highly scientific. However, they are useful to gain a general understanding of an individual's traits, qualities, or preferences.[7] There are many assessment options to choose from depending on what you are looking to achieve:

The Big Five Personality Traits. Many modern-day psychologists

Trait	Description
Openness	Being curious, original, intellectual, and open to new ideas.
Conscientiousness	Being organized, systematic, punctual, achievement-oriented, and dependable.
Extraversion	Being outgoing, talkative, sociable, and enjoying social situations.
Agreeableness	Being affable, tolerant, sensitive, trusting, kind, and warm.
Neuroticism	Being anxious, irritable, temperamental, and moody.

who study personality believe that there are five dimensions that make up the fundamentals of an individual's personality. There are many words that could be used to describe personality traits, but at some point researchers realized that certain words describing personality characteristics each related to a specific dimension.[8]

When these traits were grouped, five dimensions were identified to describe variations in human personalities: Openness, Conscientiousness, Extraversion, Agreeableness, and Neuroticism.[9]

People can identify with some traits more than others or can relate to some aspect of each dimension. Additionally, personality traits vary from person to person, but research suggests that both biological and environmental factors play a role in shaping personality.[10]

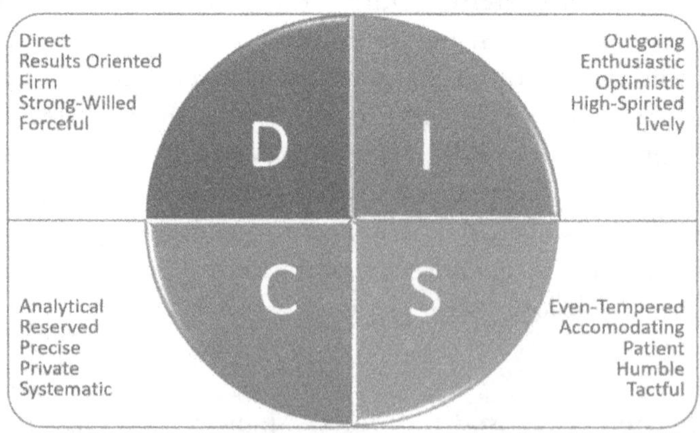

The **DISC Assessment** helps us learn more about others, ourselves, and how we deal with conflict. The assessment asks questions about how we respond to challenges, how we act in a team, how we respond to rules, and our overall preferences.

As a manager or employee, the DISC profile can help us improve our working relationships, learn how to become a better leader, respond to conflict appropriately, and be more effective when communicating with others.[11]

Myers-Briggs Type Indicator. The Myers-Briggs (MBTI) is a popular personality assessment that has been used over the last thirty years. The

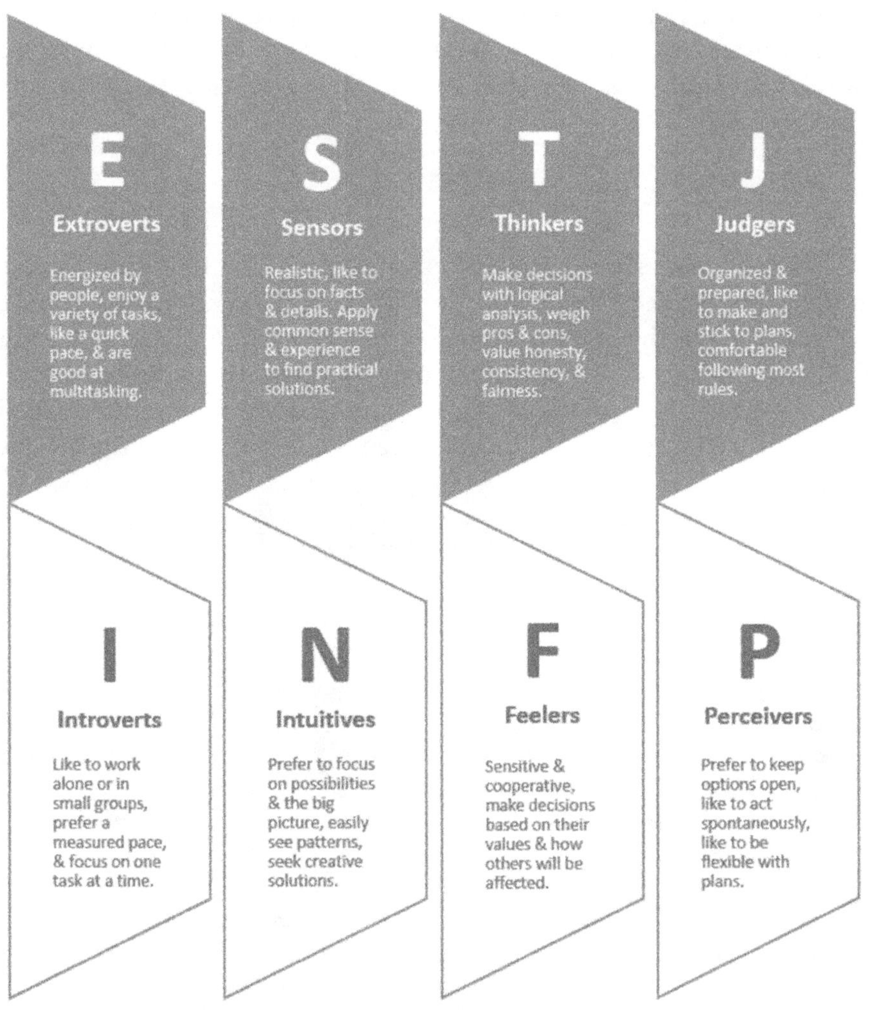

MBTI is a self-report questionnaire designed to quantify personality types. Each personality type is described in terms of a four-letter code.

The four dimensions classify individuals either as extraverted (E) or introverted (I), sensing (S) or intuitive (N), thinking (T) or feeling (F), and judging (J) or perceiving (P). Each individual is classified in terms of one of sixteen possible four-letter codes (such as ENTJ, ENFP, and ISFJ). Each type defines a specific set of behavioral traits and reflects attitudes and decision-making styles.[12]

Each type defines a specific set of behavioral traits and reflects attitudes and decision-making styles.[13] The assessment gives a general overview of personality preferences and behavioral traits that can help leaders understand how people perceive the world and how they make decisions. The assessment is not intended to measure ability or performance.

Understanding your own preferences can help you approach your work in a way that best suits your style and can help you learn how to adapt to the people around you.

Emotional Intelligence

To better understand and connect with employees, leaders must understand the importance of emotional intelligence (EQ) and make an effort to apply EQ skills in their daily interactions with their team. Emotional intelligence, in part, refers to people's ability to be aware of their own emotions and recognize the emotions of others. This is a critical interpersonal skill that is especially helpful in business. When we develop these skills, we can

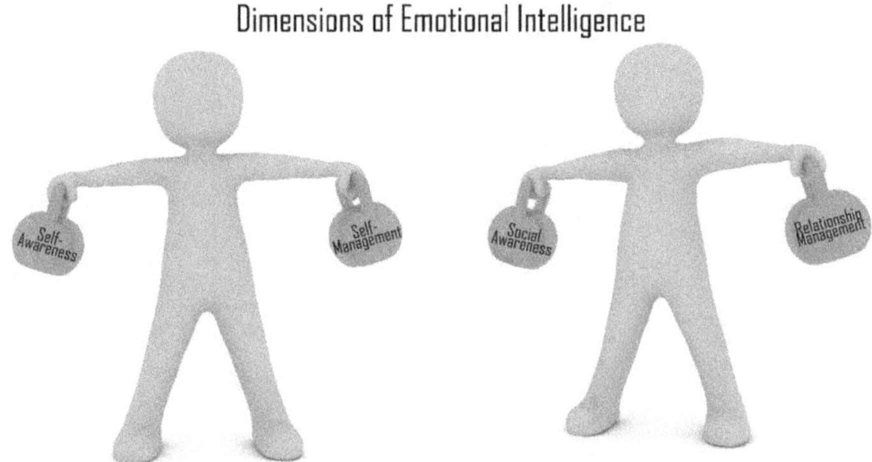

better control our behavior, perceive others' feelings, and manage relationships effectively.

EQ is a quality that is important at every level of someone's career, especially if the person wants to succeed and be well respected. Multiple studies have shown that when people feel respected, recognized, and understood, job performance and productivity increase. EQ is a competency that should be continually worked on and discussed at all levels in the workplace.

The Characteristics of Emotional Intelligence:

1. **Self-Awareness.** Recognize your emotions as they happen and don't let your feelings take over. Become aware of your strengths and weaknesses and be confident.

2. **Self-Regulation.** Think before you act and before making decisions. Control your emotions; be flexible and open to new ideas.

3. **Motivation.** Set clear goals, stay focused, and be positive. Shift away from negative thoughts as they occur and focus on the positive.

4. **Empathy.** Recognize how other people feel; identify their needs and viewpoints. Listen to what people have to say. Be honest and nonjudgmental.

5. **Social Skills.** Learn to communicate effectively, develop relationships, work well in teams, and be able to lead and inspire others.[14]

Employee Attitudes

Attitudes can refer to our feelings, beliefs, and mannerisms in response to someone or something. The way we act at work often depends on how we feel about being there.

Factors that relate to positive attitudes at work include being able to participate in a variety of tasks, receiving feedback, fair policies, good relationships between employees and managers, and non-stressful environments.

Some companies like to conduct attitude surveys or exit interviews as a tool to improve their organization. Attitude surveys can help leaders identify issues that employees are having, and exit interviews focus on getting feedback from employees who are leaving the company with the idea of reducing the turnover of current and future employees.

Moreover, managers can help influence a positive attitude at work by first using emotional intelligence to recognize the emotions of others. When problems occur, they can use those opportunities to learn and grow from an experience rather than letting it hinder them. Managers who model a positive attitude at work set a good tone for everyone else to follow suit.

Here are some helpful tips to encourage positive attitudes in the workplace:

- ✓ Hire people with positive attitudes and values that align with your company's mission, vision, and values.
- ✓ Communicate the behavior you want.
- ✓ Model the behavior you expect.
- ✓ Observe the attitudes of your employees.
- ✓ Evaluate the reasons behind the behavior.
- ✓ Reinforce the right behaviors consistently.
- ✓ Be a leader and inspire your team.[15]

Dr. Melanie Gharapetian graduated from Phillips Graduate University with a Doctorate in Psychology with an emphasis in Organizational Management and Consulting. She also earned a BA in Psychology from California State University, Northridge with a minor in Human Resource Management.

Throughout her career she has had experience in customer service management and training, organizational consulting, and teaching. In her interactions with people in the business environment, she has learned the importance of organizational structure and communication. Her business consulting objectives focus on helping improve people's motivation and performance by improving their work environment.

NOTES

[1] Gupta, A. (2010, April 26). Individual behavior in organization. Retrieved from http://practical-management.com/Organization-Development/Individual-Behavior-in-Organization.html
[2] Bauer, T., & Erdogan, B. (2012, December 29). Understanding people at work: Individual differences and perception. Retrieved from https://2012books.lardbucket.org/books/an-introduction-to-organizational-behavior-v1.1/s07-understanding-people-at-work-i.html
[3] Ibid.
[4] Cherry, K. (2017, July 20). What is personality and why does it matter? Retrieved from https://www.verywell.com/what-is-personality-2795416
[5] Gupta, Individual behavior in organization.
[6] Bauer & Erdogan, Understanding people at work.
[7] Cherry, What is personality and why does it matter?
[8] Ibid.
[9] Goldberg, L. R. (1990). An alternative "description of personality": The big-five factor structure. *Journal of Personality & Social Psychology, 59*, 1216–1229.
[10] Cherry, What is personality and why does it matter?
[11] Personality Profile Solutions (n.d.). DISC profile - How DiSC® Profiles work. Retrieved from https://discprofile.com/what-is-disc/how-disc-works/
[12] Boyle, G. J. (1995). Myers-Briggs Type Indicator (MBTI): Some psychometric limitations. *Australian Psychologist, 30*, 71–74.
[13] Ibid.
[14] Akers, M., & Porter, G. (2016, July 17). What is emotional intelligence (EQ)? Retrieved from https://psychcentral.com/lib/what-is-emotional-intelligence-eq/
[15] ERC. (2013, October 15). 8 ways to get the employee behavior you want. Retrieved from https://www.yourerc.com/blog/post/8-Ways-to-Get-the-Employee-Behavior-You-Want.aspx

Images:

Coworkers image by rawpixel on Pixabay.

Weight-lifter images by Peggy and Marco Lachmann-Anke on Pixabay.

THREE

PRACTICAL TACTICS FOR MOTIVATING YOUR EMPLOYEES

by Jamie Menendez-Adamski, PsyD, MA

Can you look introspectively at your life and ask yourself what it is that gets you through the day? When you wake up, what gets you going? If someone asked you what drives you to continue on each day, what would be your honest answer?

Each of us is different, and what motivates people to follow and achieve their goals comes from various needs. People are motivated by money, personal goals, or the desire to make a difference in their own life or someone else's.

Regardless of what drives you to reach your goals, motivation must be managed and balanced.

What is Motivation and Why Is It Necessary?

Employees who are happy are productive workers. But how do you motivate your workers to be productive and achieve the goals of the organization? As an organizational leader, you should always be thinking of ways to keep your employees productive and therefore reaching for your company's goals.

Motivation has been studied for decades. In fact, companies invest massive financial resources in rewards systems and in practices to attract, retain, and motivate employees. When those practices work, they improve individual, team, and organizational effectiveness.[1]

So, what exactly is motivation? One definition is that it is a general desire to accomplish a task. Employee motivation in particular is what helps employees complete tasks and meet goals.

Employee motivation is based on the conditions under which they are ready to dedicate their labor, time, and talents to their work. This often occurs by devising better techniques to get the job done, with—employers hope—a sense of eagerness and dedication.

Leaders in organizations have long recognized that one of their main

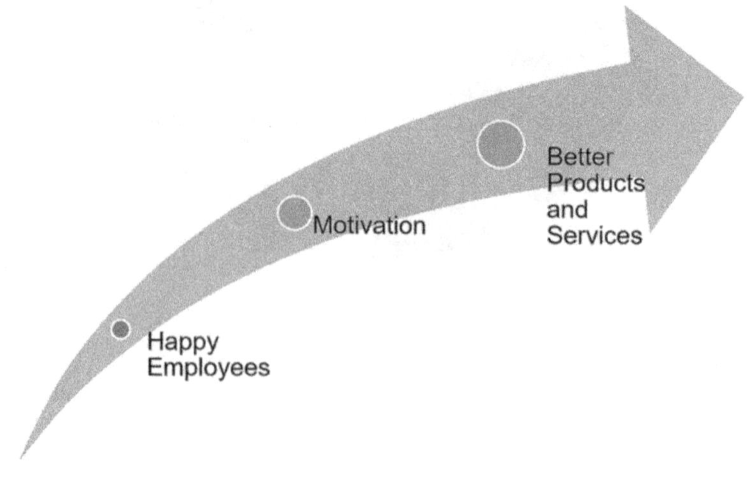

objectives is to motivate their team so that they are working together to reach company objectives. And, when employees feel engaged, they are more likely to work productively for the good of the company.

In those circumstances, employees can see that their efforts contribute to the success of the organization. Employees who are satisfied with their jobs make great impacts on the growth and outcomes of the organization.

When employees feel engaged in their work, they generate higher-quality products and services and have lower rates of turnover. In fact, a Gallup survey reported that "56% of disengaged and 73% of actively disengaged" workers seek new employment.[2]

Focusing on employee engagement can be of tremendous benefit to any company, as a low turnover rate saves your business the thousands of dollars it typically costs to hire and train new employees. It's always easier and more cost effective to groom your employees and provide opportunities for promotion from within your organization than it is to have to spend money searching for new employees and then even more on training them.

Being able to develop your team from the beginning is an effective way to prepare for the future. But the truth is that it's never too late to start motivating your employees.

Creating a Motivating Work Environment

Making sure the organization is providing a motivational work environment is key to having motivated employees.[3]

First, we must *examine* the work environment. The main questions here are: Is your organization promoting an ideal work environment for your employees? Do you provide a healthy workspace where all your employees can communicate, learn, and grow?

Leaders should consider hiring an outside business consultant who can investigate the strength of the company's ability to foster employee engagement.

Open Your Motivational Toolkit

Leaders in the workplace have used different types of assessments to determine how employees might be motivated in the workplace. These assessment tools, such as DISC[4] and Myers-Briggs,[5] can help determine employee personality types, which in turn can help leaders better understand employee behavior. Leaders can also use information from research as a tool to understand their employees or to determine how to increase an employee's performance.

Information from assessments, empirical research, the advice of experienced business professionals (for example, in hundreds of bestselling business books), and other tools can help improve the short- and long-term performance of your employees.

But tactics for improving employee motivation are always evolving, and people change over time. Therefore, as leaders, we must evolve with our employees and understand what matters to them and how they are motivated in the workplace.

What Drives Employees?

First, leaders need to recognize what drives their employees. Creating an environment where everyone feels that they are contributing to a common goal is a key principal in the success of any organization.[6]

Furthermore, leaders *must* develop an understanding of employee engagement, because that's what motivates employees to achieve your com-

pany's goals—your goals. Knowing what drives employee engagement is a key to successful employee motivation.[7]

Here are some key strategies that can help you better secure employee engagement:

- Communicate and promote a clear vision for your organization.
- Challenge your employees (in the right amounts).
- Allow decisions to be made by the team (don't micromanage).
- Provide the necessary resources to your employees so they can get the job done.
- Foster opportunities for career advancement within your organization.
- Remind employees that management is dedicated to their best interests and well-being.
- Establish clear communication of expectations and professional behaviors.[8]

Communication

Communication is essential in any organization whose leaders want it to be successful. Clear channels of communication can encourage organizational efficiency. A lack of clear communication can actually lower morale.[9]

Additionally, by offering opportunities to your employees to voice their concerns, ideas, and opinions you are keeping open the lines of communication with your employees. When listening to your employees, you are showing them that their input matters to the organization and to you, their leader.

To get started, follow these simple steps to ensure that your organization's expectations are clearly communicated:

- Identify and communicate your organizational mission, vision, and values.
- Publish rules and policies.
- Educate all employees on these rules and policies.
- Design and communicate a professional code of conduct.
- Schedule regular meetings with employees so they can provide input and ideas.

Employee Empowerment

Empowering your employees is also essential to motivation. When you give your employees the ability to have input into how they do their jobs, they feel connected to the organization's mission, vision, and values.

Leaders who ask for employee input and get their suggestions about how to improve their performance will feel like they are being heard. And it is important to *ask*—they may not share the information otherwise.

Furthermore, performance-oriented employees need recognition and praise when they achieve their goals. Pointing out that they didn't meet their goals is, in fact, counterproductive, and doing so is likely to reduce future work performance. Instead, managers should help employees develop strategies to achieve their goals.

Having trust in your employees is also essential. Giving them the authority to make decisions to a certain point without asking permission gives employees the incentive to continue working.

In fact, as a leader you should take your employee's advice and implement it. Doing so allows employees to know that you trust them and that their opinions are important.[10]

Incentives

Incentives can motivate employees, and they do not have to be expensive or even money-related.[11] For example, incentives can include an extra day off, gift cards, or tickets to a movie.

Other rewards are both financial and nonfinancial, such as appreciation, job security, and promotions. Programs that highlight your employee's successes can be a significant investment toward accomplishing your organization's goals.

Be sure to acknowledge everyone who has contributed to getting a task done, including those employees whose jobs are not easily quantified. And don't forget—making sure that employees understand the importance of the rewards programs you choose to implement and how they work is essential to the success of any employee incentives program.

Opportunities for Advancement

Employees are motivated when they know that they are working toward a goal. For many employees, their personal goals include career advancement. If they believe that there is no possibility for moving up in your company, then they will tend to think that they are in a dead-end job with no opportunities ahead of them.

By providing opportunities for growth and training, employers can ensure that their employees not only have the possibility for advancement, but also have the *ability* to do so.[12] In other words, you should provide employees with the skills they need to climb the ladder. Furthermore, providing the possibility for advancement can help build your organization's reputation, especially among your potential new hires.

Leading by Example

You cannot expect your employees to have excitement for your organization if they don't see it first in you, their leader. Leading by example can get your employees on board and working with you to achieve the same goal.[13]

When company leaders demonstrate that they are trying to make the target together—with their employees—their subordinates will work harder and will be much more willing to accomplish organizational objectives. Being excited about working together can motivate employees and show them that they have a purpose in the organization.

Teamwork

Encourage teamwork among your employees. Teamwork is a great motivator. Working together and seeing everyone's hard work pay off is a great feeling. As a team, your people will be even more motivated to accomplish the tasks and goals your leadership has set for your organization.[14]

Trust

Teams that have the trust of their leaders can communicate more effectively and more easily accomplish their collective goals. However, it's only when employees feel that leaders are looking out for their best interests that they feel trust within the organization.

Trust is an essential motivational tool. Without it, morale is often low. With it, employees are motivated to work toward excellence, because they trust they will also reap the rewards of their efforts.[15]

In summary, motivating your employees can be accomplished in many different ways. Getting to know your employees and understanding what drives them is essential to choosing the correct way to increase motivation.

Keeping the level of motivation high can be challenging, but when your employees are motivated, your organization's goals become the goals of your employees, and success often follows.

Keep in mind these seven key points when working to motivate your employees:

- Communication
- Employee Empowerment
- Incentives
- Opportunities for Advancement
- Leading by Example
- Teamwork
- Trust

Dr. Jamie Menendez-Adamski earned a Doctorate in Psychology with an emphasis in Organizational Management and Consulting from Phillips Graduate University. She also earned a Master's in Human Development with an emphasis in Leadership and Human Services from Pacific Oaks College.

For more than fifteen years, she has worked in the field of early education with children months old to age five. She currently owns and runs a rewarding family childcare program. In that capacity, she has worked with the Los Angeles Universal Preschool funding agency, providing preschool for forty-eight four-year-olds each year. She has also worked with the Early Head Start program.

She believes that every child should have access to a quality early childhood education program. Her passion as a business consultant is to increase the competency and capacity of the efforts of those working in early childhood education.

NOTES

[1] Conley, C. (2007). *PEAK: How great companies get their mojo from Maslow.* San Francisco, CA: Jossey-Bass; Mathis, R. L., Jackson, J. H., Valentine, S. R., & Meglich, P. A. (2017). *Human resource management* (15th ed.). Boston, MA: Cengage.
[2] Moody, K., & O'Donnell, R. (2018, April 2). Enhancing engagement in the 5-generation workforce [Web log]. Retrieved from https://www.hrdive.com/news/enhancing-engagement-in-the-5-generation-workforce/519244/
[3] Amabile, T. M. (1993). Motivational synergy: Toward new conceptualizations of intrinsic and extrinsic motivation in the workplace. *Human Resource Management Review, 3*(3), 185–201.
[4] Discprofile.com. (n.d.) DiSC overview. Retrieved from https://www.discprofile.com/what-is-disc/overview/
[5] The Myers & Briggs Foundation. (n.d.) Take the MBTI® instrument. Retrieved from https://www.myersbriggs.org/my-mbti-personality-type/take-the-mbti-instrument/home.htm?bhcp=1
[6] Mathis et al., *Human resource management.*
[7] Ibid.
[8] Staren, E. D. (2009, July/August). Optimizing staff motivation. *Physician Executive Journal,* 74–77.
[9] Hatten, T. S. (2016). *Small business management: Entrepreneurship and beyond* (6th ed.). Boston, MA: Cengage.
[10] Mathis et al., *Human resource management.*
[11] Ibid.
[12] Noe, R. A. (2017). *Employee training & development* (7th ed.). New York, NY: McGraw Hill.
[13] Brooks, I. (2009). *Organisational behaviour: Individuals, groups and organisation* (4th ed.). Essex, England: Pearson.
[14] Noe, *Employee training & development.*
[15] Brooks, *Organisational behaviour.*

Images:

Circle of Hands by Gerd Altmann on Pixabay.
Evaluate Arrow Circle by John Hain on Pixabay.
Team Arrow image by Daniel Mena on Pixabay.

FOUR

PRACTICAL TACTICS FOR MANAGING ORGANIZATIONAL DILEMMAS

by Bennett Annan, PsyD, EdD, MBA, MS, MA, LMFT

This chapter presents a case study as an example of how employing an ineffective leadership style can adversely affect an organization. Dr. Annan presents solutions for this leadership dilemma—which systemically is an organizational *dilemma—that can be adopted by leaders who would like to work at improving the effectiveness of their organization. The story is based on his own experience. The solutions are based on his experience as a business leader and consultant and on research.*

If leaders and managers are to be successful in the workplace, they must master the management of organizational dilemmas—the ability to correctly identify dilemmas that exist within an organization's functioning. According to Art Dykstra, former CEO of Trinity Services, a *dilemma* is generally defined as a situation involving opposing choices.[1]

A Case Study in Organizational Dilemma

The most challenging experience of my career thus far was when the foreign-born president of the clinic where I worked as the general manager engaged in a dispute with me about how to run case management meetings and the clinic as a whole.

The clinic's staff of some twenty workers had already been having problems interacting with her because of her authoritarian style of management. This clash between management style and organizational culture had resulted in repeated acts of employee insubordination, a trend that was steadily rising. Despite these circumstances, the company was still reporting profits overall, but those numbers had been dwindling for a few years. Something needed to be done to curb this undesirable situation.

I approached the president with a request to meet with her to resolve these issues. In our first meeting, she was adamant that others should change, and our meeting ended abruptly. No resolution was achieved; instead, she demanded that I resign if I did not like her style of management or her interactions with employees.

Why Leadership Matters. When an organization is not functioning effectively, it is critical that leadership issues are addressed first. According to Edgar Schein, a former professor at the MIT Sloan School of Management and an organizational development expert, "Leadership and culture are conceptually intertwined."[2] Schein asserted that leadership functions in

the creation and management of organizational culture.

In the case of the president of the clinic, because she was a new leader in that company, she needed to be fully conscious of the impact her leadership style, behaviors, and personal characteristics would have on the company's culture. In a case such as this, a clash between the existing organizational culture and the new leader's style can influence management practices between leaders and subordinates, and that impact may be detrimental to the organization.

I thus persisted in seeking opportunities to speak with the president. After a few informal meetings with her, it became apparent to me that the use of her native management style and culture, which is characteristic of many foreign-born professionals, triggered antagonistic feelings in many of her American workers.[3]

A Business Approach Based on Psychology

Keeping in mind that two of my degrees are in psychology, one in marriage and family therapy and another in organizational psychology, I decided a person-centered approach based in psychological theory and practice would work best in addressing this organizational dilemma.

Psychologist and theorist Carl Rogers maintained that there are three characteristics for a growth-promoting climate whereby people can realize their inherent potential: (a) congruence, (b) unconditional positive regard, and (c) empathic understanding.[4]

Congruence means that the leader is genuine and authentic. *Unconditional positive regard* involves basic acceptance and support of a person, regardless of what the person says or does. *Empathy* means understanding accurately what someone is feeling—what we might call stepping into his or her shoes.

Favoring Rogers' approach means that I tend to shy away from assessments and tests. I also shy away from analyzing case histories.[5]

What matters instead is the individual's *self*-assessment. I believe people are trustworthy by nature and that they have the capacity to understand and resolve their own problems. People are also innately resourceful and capable, and they can understand what is making them unhappy. Based on these beliefs, I encourage people to reflect on their experiences, which requires nonjudgmental listening and acceptance in order to promote change.

First, it was clear that the president's leadership style was lacking in congruence, because she had not established clear rules, which is typical of leaders with an authoritarian style.[6] Leaders who expect team members to follow their rules must first ensure that guidelines are clearly stated and that each person on the team is fully aware of them. Unfortunately, authoritarian leaders often fail to do that. The president was also unreliable, and inconsistent leaders can quickly lose the respect of their teams when they don't follow through and enforce the rules.

Additionally, the president's authoritarian leadership style also lacked unconditional positive regard for others, which can impair group morale. People tend to feel happier and perform better when they feel they're making positive contributions to the group's future. Since autocratic leaders typically don't allow input from team members, followers start to feel stifled and dissatisfied.

Autocratic leaders often don't listen to team members. While leaders might not change their mind or implement a team member's advice, employees must feel that they can express their concerns. Instead, these leaders can often make team members feel ignored or even rejected.[7]

Finally, the president's authoritarian leadership style lacked empathy, since she did not provide the group with the knowledge and tools they needed. Leaders who fail to ensure that employees have the education and abilities to perform the tasks set before them end up with demoralized subordinates, and that affects the bottom line: profits.

Implementing Change

In subsequent meetings with the president, I consciously displayed all three of Carl Rogers' techniques with the hope of implementing change:[8]

Congruence. Quite often, people will say one thing, but their body language is reflective of something else; others are aware of this, which may

impact trust and openness in relationships.[9] For example, I may say "I understand where you're coming from" to someone but have a confused look on my face. People typically can see this confusion and may feel uncomfortable expressing their feelings from that point forward. Thus, I must be aware of my body language and what it is saying while also remaining in the present moment.

Whenever confusion arose, I needed to address this with the president. And it was very important to put the president at ease to ensure the continuation of trust.

Unconditional Positive Regard. To provide unconditional positive regard, I needed to be accepting, respecting, and caring toward the president.[10] This did not mean that I had to agree with everything she said or did but that I saw the president as doing the best she could. I demonstrated that by expressing concern rather than disagreement. Unconditional positive regard allowed the president to express what she thought without feeling judged and helped to facilitate the change process by showing her that she could be accepted.

Empathy. I expressed empathy and showed my understanding of the president's emotions, which allowed her to open up further. Empathy is different from sympathy in that sympathy often involves feeling sorry for someone, whereas empathy demonstrates understanding.[11]

Here's an example showing the difference:

Statement: *I feel as though no one cares about me and that I'm all alone.*
Empathetic Response: *So, you're feeling alone at the moment and as if no one cares.*
Sympathetic Response: *I'm sorry that you feel that way.*

Non-Directiveness. Finally, I chose to be nondirective, allowing the president to be the focus of meetings without giving my advice or implementing my strategies or activities.

According to Rogers, change can occur through a relationship in which the other party is able to feel like "a separate person, in which the experience going on within . . . is empathically understood and valued, and in which he is given the freedom to experience his own feelings and those of others without being threatened in doing so."[12]

My goal was to cultivate a relationship in which "the other will discover within himself the capacity to use that relationship for growth and change."[13]

Strengths and Limitations of the Person-Centered Approach

Strengths. The Rogerian approach offers a perspective that is up-to-date and optimistic; many aspects of this approach are also relevant to a multicultural perspective.[14] In addition, this approach provides a strategy that can be employed by many individuals, leaders, and managers, given its emphasis on leader-employee relationships. That is important, considering that research has substantiated the importance of leader-employee relationships in organizations.

Further, employees are more likely to have a positive experience in engagement with their leaders and managers when the focus is on the employees and their problems.[15] Individuals feel they can express themselves more fully when they are being listened to and not judged. Finally, the Rogerian approach empowers people, as the responsibility is on the individual to make decisions.

Limitations. One caveat of the Rogerian approach is that it may lead individuals to be supportive of others without challenging them. Users of this approach may also find it difficult to allow others to find their own way. Moreover, this approach can be ineffective in facilitating resolutions to the dilemma if the recipient is nondirective and passive.

Some theorists have argued that the person-centered approach is simplistic and unrealistically optimistic; it does not draw on developmental, psychodynamic, or behavioral therapy and is thus limited in facilitating an overall understanding of others.[16]

We all know that in many instances, listening and caring may not be enough. This approach may not be appropriate for those who are not motivated to change or for those with significant psychopathology. More importantly, this approach can fail to prepare others for the real world due to the unconditional positive regard for the individual. Finally, this approach lacks techniques to help others solve problems.

When to Apply Other Solutions

When I work as a consultant to help businesses overcome organizational dilemmas (among other things), I need to keep in mind that I am "in a position to have some influence over an individual, a group, or an organi-

zation" but with "no direct power to make changes or implement programs."[17] To be a successful consultant, I also must have interpersonal skills. In addition, the ability to identify and verbalize issues around trust, feelings, and responsibility is an important dimension to consulting success.[18]

Leaders and employees can use the same techniques with their subordinates and coworkers—as appropriate.

A Person-Centered Foundation. In my very first meeting and during the course of any professional consulting engagement with my clients, I use Rogers' techniques of congruence, unconditional positive regard, and empathy. This is because a consultant's major duty is to influence change and be viewed as trustworthy within the organizational setting. Consultants must be able to influence clients' behaviors through the formation of positive interpersonal relationships. That is often true of leaders and sometimes may be the only way a subordinate may have to impact a boss's behavior.

I use this approach the most, because if clients are asking for assistance, they must have a business problem to solve. The best strategy to instill confidence in other people is to listen and pay close attention to what they are saying. The Rogerian approach helps in accomplishing that goal.

Solution-Focused Approach. During the course of a professional consulting engagement, if I realize my client is focusing on the problem rather than the solution, I use the solution-focused approach developed by psychotherapists Steve de Shazer and Insoo Kim Berg.[19]

In this approach, I act more as a collaborator, being there to help others achieve their goals. I use indirect methods, such as the use of extensive questioning about previous solutions and exceptions. I keep in mind that the other person is the expert and that I should take a stance of "not knowing" and of "leading from one step behind" through solution-focused questioning and responding.

In addition, I listen for and absorb my clients' words and meanings regarding what is important to them, what they want, and related successes. From there, I can formulate and ask the next question by connecting to clients' key words and phrases.

It is through this continuing process of listening, absorbing, connecting, and the client responding that consultants and clients together co-construct new and altered meanings that build toward solutions and change.[20]

This approach may not be employable if you are the subordinate, but it can be an effective approach for leaders to use with their employees.

Cognitive Behavioral Approach. During the course of a consulting engagement, if I realize my client is hanging onto the past and showing difficulties in making a change, I can employ cognitive behavioral techniques. I break each problem down into its separate parts, and together with the other person, we examine thoughts, feelings, and behaviors to assess whether they are unrealistic or unhelpful and how those characteristics affect each other. I then help my client to work out how to change unhelpful thoughts and behaviors.

After I have identified what the client can change, I sometimes recommend "homework" so the client can practice these changes in everyday life. I help clients develop the skill of questioning self-critical or upsetting thoughts and replacing them with more helpful (and more realistic) ones.

Thus, I help clients recognize when they are about to do something that will make them feel worse and help them consider alternatives that are more helpful. Ensuring that clients continue to practice and develop these skills makes it less likely that the problems will return.

This is an approach that may work better for consultants and leaders but can also work with willing coworkers.

Systemic Approach. *Systems thinking* is the process of understanding how various pieces influence one another within a larger system. I use this approach for my professional consulting work, because to understand clients, we must understand the systems in their environment. People cannot truly be understood in isolation.[21]

I find this approach very important because no organizational culture can be understood without using the tools of systems thinking. These tools include brainstorming, examining structure, graphing linkages and variables over time, and looking at archetypes.[22]

Many of the core components of systems thinking are an ideal fit for professional consulting and the business environment. A systems approach in which the big picture is kept in mind is rapidly becoming one of the most popular and effective methods of problem-solving when facing organizational dilemmas.

Determining What Fits

There is no single psychological theory that can fit all professional consulting situations.[23] However, the use of a suitable approach is critical to employing an effective solution to your organizational dilemma. It is important to take care when selecting a psychological approach to fit the situation, but it is possible by using these approaches to facilitate creative solutions to serve your workplace situation.

A Resolution to an Organizational Dilemma

You may be wondering how (or if) the organizational dilemma with the clinic president was ultimately resolved. I was eventually able to indicate to her that engaging with employees, raising their level of motivation, increaseing employee morale, and connecting with her employees using participative management—all of which are characteristic of a transformational management style—would help solve the problem.[24]

One benefit of my personality type, according to the Myers-Briggs Type Indicator (MBTI), is that I am tactful in making suggestions.[25] I was, therefore, able to convince the president to see the problem and persuade her to begin the change process from authoritarian to participative management. In time, the president became aware of her responsibilities, her capability to influence, and her effectiveness at motivating employees in ways that support the greater good rather than her own self-interests.[26]

Six months later, the president was pleased with my counseling efforts and pleasantly surprised at the change of attitudes in her employees. In fact, a year later she appointed me to head the clinic's counseling department. I considered this to be an implied compliment for my counseling efforts.

There was no question that the problem had to be resolved in order to sustain the company's image as well as bottom-line profits. This effort required me to believe in myself and in what I thought was good for the company, because I was convinced it would help improve the company's overall organizational culture. And it did.

Dr. Bennett Annan was born in Accra, Ghana, in West Africa and migrated to the United States more than thirty years ago. He holds an MS in Mechanical Engineering and worked as a mechanical and manufacturing/engineering manager for twelve years. He then completed an MBA to enhance his managerial skills. He was the general manager of a medical center when he enrolled in the organizational leadership program for his Doctorate in Education at Pepperdine University to enhance his leadership skills.

Since 2009, he has been giving presentations on various aspects of managing and handling life's obstacles for three ministries at St. Rose of Lima Catholic Church in Simi Valley. In 2013, he realized he could do more for these ministries by going back to school at Phillips Graduate University, where he earned an MA in clinical psychology which allowed him to become a licensed marriage and family therapist. At Phillips, he also completed a Doctorate in Psychology with an emphasis in Organizational Management and Consulting, believing he could do more for organizations by understanding how organizations work.

NOTES

[1] Dykstra, A. (2011, Fall). Leadership: The management of organizational dilemmas. *Perdido Magazine*. Retrieved from http://perdidomagazine.com/leadership-management-organizational-dilemmas/
[2] Schein, E. (1992). Organizational culture and leadership. In J. T. Wren (Ed.), *The leader's companion: Insights on leadership through the ages* (pp. 271–281). New York, NY: The Free Press.
[3] Hofstede, G. (2001). *Culture's consequences: Comparing values, behaviors, institutions and organizations across nations*. New York, NY: Sage.
[4] Rogers, C. (1961). *On becoming a person*. New York, NY: Houghton Mifflin.
[5] Rogers, C. (1967). *Person to person: The problem of being human, a new trend in psychology*. New York, NY: Real People Press.
[6] Cherry, K. (2018, February 16). *What Is autocratic leadership? Key characteristics, strengths, and weaknesses of autocratic leadership*. Retrieved from Verywellmind.com: https://www.verywellmind.com/what-is-autocratic-leadership-2795314
[7] Ibid.
[8] Rogers, *On becoming a person*.
[9] Seligman, L. (2006). *Theories of counseling and psychotherapy: Systems, strategies, and skills* (2nd ed.). Upper Saddle River, NJ: Pearson.
[10] Ibid.
[11] Ibid.
[12] Rogers, *On becoming a person*.
[13] Ibid.
[14] Seligman, *Theories of counseling and psychotherapy*.
[15] Corey, C. (2005). *Theory and practice of counseling & psychotherapy* (7th ed.). Belmont, CA: Thomson Learning.
[16] Seligman, *Theories of counseling and psychotherapy*.
[17] Block, P. (2011). *Flawless consulting: A guide to getting your expertise used* (3rd ed.). Hoboken, NJ: Pfeiffer.
[18] Ibid.
[19] de Shazer, S., & Berg, I. K. (1993). Making numbers talk: Language in therapy. In S. Friedman (Ed.), *The new language of change: Constructive collaboration in psychotherapy* (pp. 5–24). New York, NY: Guilford.
[20] Ibid.
[21] Brown, J. H., & Christensen, D. N. (1986). *Family therapy: Theory and practice*. Monterey, CA: Brooks/Cole.
[22] Kim, D. (n.d.) Palette of systems thinking tools. Retrieved from https://thesystemsthinker.com/palette-of-systems-thinking-tools/
[23] Stivers, C. (2015, April 10). Solution focused brief therapy basics: Meet Insoo Kim Berg and Steve de Shazer [Blog post]. Retrieved from https://thefamilytherapyblog.com/2015/04/10/solution-focused-brief-therapy-basics-meet-insoo-kim-berg-and-steve-de-shazer/
[24] Northouse, *Leadership theories and practice*.
[25] Imam, A., Hinton, F., Gran, J., Willetts, J., Pepper, K., Denton, K., & . . . Lightburn, S. (2005). *Making good business better: An ENFJ profile*. Retrieved from http://www.qed-consultancy.co.uk/soe/enfj.html
[26] Wynne, L. C., McDaniel, S. H., & Weber, T. T. (1986). *Systems consultation: A new perspective for family therapy*. New York, NY: Guilford Press.

Images:

Another Way image by Gerd Altmann on Pixabay.
Conflict image by www_slon_pics on Pixabay.
Crossed Arms image by vontoba on Pixabay.
Doors image by Arek Socha on Pixabay.

Culture eats strategy for breakfast.
— Peter Drucker, Management Consultant, Author

Customers will never love a company until the employees love it first.
— Simon Sinek, Author of *Start with Why*

Culture is to recruiting as product is to marketing.
— HubSpot's Culture Code

Culture is simply a shared way of doing something with a passion.
— Brian Chesky, Airbnb Co-Founder/CEO

Determine what behaviors and beliefs you value as a company,
and have everyone live true to them. These behaviors and beliefs should be
so essential to your core, that you don't even think of it as culture.
— Brittany Forsyth, Shopify VP of Human Relations

PART TWO

PEOPLE PRACTICS IN ORGANIZATIONAL CULTURE

FIVE

PRACTICAL TACTICS FOR MANAGING CORPORATE CULTURE

by Alice Nkore, PsyD, MBA

The Hazards of Ignoring Corporate Culture

Corporate culture (also known as organizational culture) has become vitally important today because it is closely linked to the effectiveness of businesses and nonprofits.[1] Researchers believe that corporate culture can either act as a catalyst for reaching corporate goals or just as easily get in the way of everyday efforts toward attaining business objectives.[2]

There has been a recent shift toward thinking about organizations as human, living systems, making culture an important part of how owners and managers design their companies.[3] For example, if an organization's culture clashes with the values of its community, the business must adapt or it will not be able to make a valuable social contribution.[4]

What Exactly is Corporate Culture?

Corporate culture includes the expectations, experiences, philosophy, and values that hold the organization together. It is expressed in the organization's self-image, inner workings, interactions with the outside world, and future expectations, as seen through the eyes of its employees.[5]

Another definition is as "a pattern of shared basic assumptions that the group learns as it solves its problems . . . which has worked well enough to be considered valid and . . . [is] taught to new members as the correct way to perceive, think, and feel in relation to those problems."[6]

Cultural anthropologist Margaret Mead defined organizational culture as a form of learned behavior, a set of beliefs, habits, and traditions common to any group of people that are learned by other people who enter that society.[7] This definition translates to what is commonly referred to in today's business world as "the way we do things here." While Mead's definition describes how employees behave, corporate culture also defines what employees should and cannot do.[8]

There is still another way of looking at corporate culture. It exits at two levels. On the surface are visible artifacts and observable behavior—these include the ways people dress and act, office layouts, symbols, control systems, and power structures. Invisible elements represent the second level, which are the underlying values, assumptions, beliefs, and thought processes operating unconsciously to define the culture.[9]

What we see.	Behaviors, systems, processes, policies.
What we say.	Ideals, goals, values, aspirations.
What we believe.	Underlying assumptions.

Psychologist Bruce Peltier believes that "behavior is a response to the demands of the system" and that organizational culture indirectly becomes the system that guides behavior. It is a well-designed corporate culture that makes it possible for leaders to implement and periodically measure their success in terms of employee performance in relation to team and organizational goals.[10] Whether such goals are being met can actually be measured—with the help of the Organizational Culture Assessment Instrument (OCAI), a validated research tool developed by Kim Cameron and Robert Quinn. OCAI can help to determine if a business's culture is addressing organizational needs and supporting overall strategy.[11]

Furthermore, "Corporate culture continues to attract attention, particularly as companies merge and economies evolve, especially across national boundaries."[12] This means that when two organizations with different cultures merge, it is important that management create shared cultural values to provide a framework to harness and direct employees' behavior.[13]

Finally, corporate culture can also be understood by examining Abraham Maslow's hierarchy of needs theory, which describes the need for a *sense of belonging*.[14] Employees constantly seek the approval and affection of their peers in order to fit into a particular social group. Maslow highlights a contradiction in two goals of belonging: "growth" and "safety." These always pull in opposite directions, yet individual employees feel compelled to satisfy both goals simultaneously.

While most traditional organizations are designed to provide the first three levels of Maslow's hierarchy of needs—food, shelter, and belonging—corporate culture is the channel through which the need for inclusion, within the organization, is met.[15]

How Important Is Corporate Culture to Your Business?

Culture provides people with a sense of identity for their organization and generates a commitment to beliefs and values that are larger than they are alone.[16] Additionally, a strong corporate culture has a positive effect on business performance.[17]

Strong cultures are also thought to exist in businesses that display a close fit between themselves and the environment, that possess a rich and complex system of shared values, and that have a well-specified and routine set of social norms and rituals.[18]

A wide range of research recognizes corporate culture as a key driver of business performance in general.[19] When aligned with mission, strategy, leadership, and a good plan for change management, a strong organizational culture can drive positive business outcomes and be a powerful differentiator. But when there is significant misalignment between business and personal values, and the organizational culture is based on self-interest rather than a common good, most business initiatives will fail.[20]

An article on corporate culture in *Harvard Business Review* outlined eight culture styles and how they impact organizational performance:

> Properly managed, culture can help business leaders achieve change and build organizations that will thrive in even the most trying times. [There are] eight distinct culture styles:

> (a) caring, focused on relationships and mutual trust, (b) purpose, exemplified by idealism and altruism, (c) learning, characterized by exploration, expansiveness, and creativity, (d) enjoyment, expressed through fun and excitement, (e) results, characterized by achievement and winning, (f) authority, defined by strength, decisiveness, and boldness, (g) safety, defined by planning, caution, and preparedness, and (h) order, focused on respect, structure, and shared norms.
>
> These eight styles fit into an "integrated culture framework" according to the degree to which they reflect independence or interdependence (people interactions) and flexibility or stability (response to change). The culture styles can be used to diagnose and describe highly complex and diverse behavioral patterns in a culture and to model how likely an individual leader is to align with and shape that culture.[21]

It's an Advantage. In his book *The Advantage*, Patrick Lencioni argued that the single greatest advantage any company can achieve is through an effective corporate culture.[22]

Yet most leaders ignore organizational culture even though it is a tool that is simple, free, and available to anyone who wants to use it to achieve their business goals.[23] That makes understanding corporate culture, the dynamics of the business, and how to lead within it vital for management seeking to initiate change directed toward growth and improvement.[24]

When organizational culture aligns with mission, strategy, and vision, a business will not only be able to succeed but will also tend to operate more efficiently, including internationally.[25] Additionally, corporate culture allows leaders to work either individually or in teams to continually develop effective business initiatives.

Research has demonstrated that over time, if a leader's efforts are valued and well-received, they can begin to shape culture through both conscious and unconscious actions. A truly influential leader is one who sets new cultures in motion and imparts values and assumptions that can persist for decades.[26]

What Business Leaders Need to Know

That culture plays a pivotal role in organizational success and failure cannot be ignored. Companies such as "Google, online retailer Zappos, and Southwest Airlines are believed to be successful primarily based on their culture, while other companies are said to have cultures that put them at a competitive disadvantage."[27]

Furthermore, managers play a fundamental role in creating and promoting positive cultures within their organizations.[28] In such cultures, employees flourish by being role models, ensuring that strategic objectives are aligned with personal development plans and that collaboration exists within and among departments.

A major difficulty for any leader is to step outside the culture and to start evolutionary processes that adapt to the needs of the organization.[29] This ability to perceive the limitations of the current culture and then develop a new one is the leader's ultimate challenge.[30]

How Corporate Culture Is Born

Cultures arise within organizations based on history and experiences, starting with the founders and those members of the organization who have shared in its growth and have developed assumptions about the world and how to succeed in it.[31]

Leading effectively means that leaders and managers must strive to create a culture that reinforces the organization's mission and makes the business successful in its environment.[32]

Organizational culture evolves in six ways:

1. A **general evolution** in which a business naturally adapts to its environment.
2. A **specific evolution** of teams or sub-groups within the business to their different environments.
3. A **guided evolution resulting from cultural insights** on the part of the leader.
4. A **guided evolution that encourages teams** to learn from each other and empowers selected hybrids from subcultures that are better adapted to current realities.
5. A **planned and managed culture change** through creation of parallel systems of steering committees and project-oriented task forces.
6. A **partial or total cultural destruction** through new leadership due to mergers and acquisition that eliminates the carriers of the former culture (turnarounds, bankruptcies, etc.).[33]

Types of Corporate Culture

This section considers two schools of thought related to corporate culture. The first is based on the work of organizational theorist Richard Daft, who explains corporate culture on two levels: (1) the visible culture: symbols, and (2) the invisible culture: underlying values and assumptions.

Daft defines four types of organizational cultures based on the extent to which a business's competitive environment requires flexibility or stability and the extent to which the strategy focus and strengths are internal or external:

1. **Adaptability culture**, characterized by a strategic focus on the external environment through flexibility and change in order to meet customer needs.
2. **Mission culture**, characterized by an emphasis on a clear vision of organizational purpose and goals, such as profitability and market share, without the need for rapid change.
3. **Clan culture**, characterized by a focus on the involvement and participation of employees and on rapidly changing expectations from the external environment.
4. **Bureaucratic culture**, characterized by an established hierarchy that helps to maintain a stable business environment.[34]

The other school of thought is based on Kim Cameron and Robert Quinn's model of four types of organizational culture:

1. **Clan culture**, which is similar to an extended family with its leader seen as the parental figure.
2. **Adhocracy**, which has a constantly changing structure due to the need to be creative and come up with new ideas; it is characterized by risk-taking, especially on the part of the leader.
3. **Market culture**, which is market-driven and highly competitive; in this culture, a successful leader is one who attains the largest market share of the industry.
4. **Hierarchy**, which is formal and highly structured; an effective leader in a hierarchical culture is one who establishes policies and procedures that lower costs.[35]

Possessing an effective organizational culture is the most powerful factor in the success of businesses that have maintained a competitive advantage.[36] Yet any of the types of organizational culture listed above can be successful, depending on the needs of the external environment and if the culture represents the innermost assumptions and ideals of the group of people that comprises the organization.[37]

What Role Does Culture Play in Business?

A strong organizational culture should provide the following:

1. Reduce collective uncertainties.
2. Create social order.
3. Build community.
4. Initiate a collective identity and commitment.
5. Establish a vision for the future.[38]

Daft argues it another way: Culture serves two essential functions in organizations: (1) to integrate members so that they know how to relate to one another, and (2) to help the organization adapt to the external environment. Culture guides employees in decision making in the absence of written rules and policies while enabling the organization to deal with challenges and take advantage of external business opportunities.[39]

The Right Culture Contributes to Success. With the right organizational culture, employees can focus on improving their skills, gaining competence, developing capabilities, learning from their mistakes, and working toward task mastery. Effectively managing this combination of factors only works if managers and executives take an interest in the opportunities for growth that result from fostering a positive organizational culture, which in turn can lead to improved productivity, efficiency, and effectiveness.[40]

Moreover, managers should also pay attention to their own unique organizational culture, as it can be an effective tool to attract high-quality staff and distinguish a business from its competition.[41]

In fact, one study about the relationship between dimensions of organizational culture and organizational belonging revealed that "there is a significant correlation between organizational belonging and variables of personal innovation, responsibility, leadership, coordination and managerial support."[42]

BUT: Also Consider the Downside. Unfortunately, organizational success does not automatically arise from the existence of organizational culture, and the issue of "fit" needs to be considered when hiring new employees. That's because "fit" relates to the alignment of individual values with those of the organization.[43]

And, sadly, the possibility exists that an organization's culture can actually "provide a better fit for employees willing to engage in unethical behavior, a good example being when organizational culture in the finance industry is indeed unique and partly to blame for promoting the kind of malfeasances that brought down the global financial system" such as occurred in 2007–2008.[44]

When making hiring decisions, organizations should not just evaluate candidates based on cultural fit alone, but should also anticipate "enculturability," that is, how quickly employees are likely to adjust to a new culture and perform to their best ability.

These ways of looking at cultural fit deepen a manager's understanding of the contribution staff members make and the role they are likely to play in the organization's future success.[45]

In a 2017 study by Zafar Acar and Pinar Acar, the authors claimed that various types of corporate culture "may contribute to organizational success depending on the needs of external environment and strategic orientation of the organization."[46] That suggests that managers who work to adapt corporate culture in a way that reinforces business strategy will ensure that the organization is much more likely to succeed.

Strategies for Interacting in Other Nations

1. National Culture Impacts Corporate Culture. National culture to some extent influences organizational culture. Managers who want to be effective must gain a better understanding of the culture in any country in which they work to determine which perceptions are dominant.

There are six dimensions of culture to consider:

a) Power distance (egalitarian versus hierarchy).
b) Individualism versus collectivism.
c) Feminine versus masculine.
d) Uncertainty avoidance (comfortable with ambiguity versus anxiety from ambiguity).
e) Long-term goals versus short-term goals.
f) Restraint versus indulgence.[47]

2. Understanding Other Cultures Is Important. Understanding other cultures applies to consultants, managers, and employees who are responsible for working in unfamiliar environments, as when an organization operates in different geographical locations or countries.[48]

Business professor Timothy Hatten suggests that "the most important cultural factors . . . are language, religion, education, and social systems." For example, if employees accept responsibilities that put them in another culture, they should first ask, "How do these factors differ from those in my country?"[49]

Hatten argues further that managers and employees are the face of the business and that leaders should make conscious choices to provide the means to allow their employees to succeed. In situations where employees are sent overseas, specialized training can help them adjust to cultural differences and help them perform their work better.[50]

3. Know the Consequences of Culture Shock. The term *culture shock* is often used when describing negative experiences from exposure to another culture.

"Culture shock can be described as the wave of emotions an expatriate employee or manager feels immediately upon entering a foreign country." In fact, due in part to employees not being able to adapt to the culture, an estimated 16–40 percent of expatriate assignments end in failure, with some estimates reaching as high as 70 percent.[51]

Yet few people realize that the effects of culture shock can be much

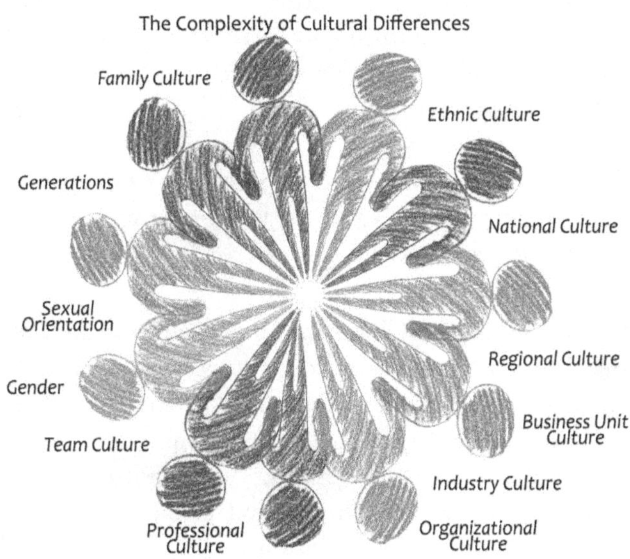

deeper and more prolonged if it is not dealt with effectively.[52] Organizations as well as individuals incur a cost for failing to effectively address the negative impacts of culture shock.

British business consultant Ian Brooks outlined the following consequences of culture shock:

- The pressure experienced in the first few months may force the new global manager or employee to leave the organization.
- Quitting can be a major loss for both the individual and the organization.
- The individual could develop psychological problems.
- The organization will incur the cost of replacing the employee and may lose revenue due to that worker's departure.
- An employee may later suffer the effects of reverse culture shock: "*Reverse culture shock* occurs when a consultant, manager/employee who has been overseas for some years, and has adapted well to his or her new culture, is faced with returning to the home country."[53]

The Future of Corporate Culture

Executive consultant Anthony Coe conjectures that the future of organizational culture will be one of collaboration and analytics. In other words, those who work to change the culture of their organizations will lean toward a clan or adhocracy culture and away from a traditional bureaucratic culture with its rules, policies, and procedures.[54]

Additionally, with the explosion of new tools in information technology and the lightning-fast transmission of knowledge in the media, cultural change has become a phenomenon. Therefore, "no organization in the twenty-first century would boast about its constancy, sameness, or status quo compared to ten years ago."[55]

A Quest for the Right Culture. At the same time, having a certain kind of culture, being a certain kind of culture, and wanting a certain kind of culture have become common demands in the workforce worldwide. Millennials and the upcoming Gen Z, for example, will target working for a specific type of organization, depending on its culture.[56]

Most managers today are shifting away from a bureaucratic culture due to the desire for greater flexibility among a young workforce.[57] More than ever, organizations are starting to take a comprehensive look at employee health and well-being and how organizational culture can promote these in what workplace strategy expert Leigh stringer referred to as "strategies for creating a healthy workplace."[58]

How to Succeed in an Unfamiliar Culture

One way to help employees and managers succeed as they work inside foreign cultures is to help them develop cultural competencies. These can include:

- The ability to build relationships and trust, especially in high-context cultures. Asian, Arab, and African cultures exemplify high-context in that there is far more nonverbal communication, while the United States is an example of a low-context culture in which "what you say is what you mean."
- Linguistic ability. A minimal level is often sufficient, as it shows respect and demonstrates interest in the people in the other culture.
- The ability to cope with uncertainty.
- Incorporating cultural empathy through understanding of a variety of different cultures.
- Adopting a strong sense of self, including the ability to be self-critical.
- Exercising a good sense of humor, which is a stress reliever and is important for building relationships.
- Developing the ability to respond to a variety of cultures simultaneously.[59]

Tips for Global Leaders

Business consultant and professor Nancy Adler suggests that consultants, leaders, and employees should recognize that certain values are universally accepted regardless of environment or location. Adler advises that global consultants, leaders, and employees apply the following concepts and principles in order to be successful within another culture:

- A global manager needs to have an attitude toward continuous development and improvement through education about self and other cultures.
- There is worldwide appreciation for organizations and leaders who

work toward saving the environment by following the principles of corporate social responsibility.

- Leaders who advocate for their company's talent and promote employee growth are respected by employees in every culture.
- A leader is expected to promote the "log cabin to president" philosophy, the belief in no barrier to development for anyone who wants to rise to the top if they possess the right skills.
- The most effective leaders enable employees to make decisions and perform independently. They avoid micromanagement, because it shows lack of trust and frustrates most employees.
- Good leaders let workers problem-solve first before soliciting outside help, allowing employees to develop their own skills.
- Global leaders adopt an outlook for short-term and long-term benefits. They simultaneously keep a big picture perspective while still achieving short-term goals.
- A global leader embraces an open-door policy to allow accessibility and free communication between management and employees.[60]

Global Managers Can Help Employees Adjust to New Cultures

Leaders who expect to send employees to other countries to work should consider the following advice from GE CEO Jeff Immelt: "A good global leader has an appreciation for how people do their work in a local culture." Immelt noted that a leader also has the responsibility to help those coming from outside to adapt to the new culture. Immelt offered additional advice about what leaders should do as they begin to think globally:

- There are no universally accepted ways to manage organizations; the appropriate approaches depend on the prevailing situation.
- Have a mandatory orientation about organizational culture prior to an employee's arrival in a foreign country.
- Demonstrate your understanding of the potential impact of cultural differences through the organization's various communication systems.
- Encourage a support system of senior employees to new employees to reduce anxiety.
- Offer internal counseling services to deal with psychological issues.
- Engage external consultants to assess whether corporate culture is a good fit for employees and if it will support organizational strategy.[61]

Recommendations for a Workforce Entering a Foreign Culture

Success in a foreign culture will depend on the following tips based on my (Dr. Nkore) personal experience living, studying, and working in a foreign culture:

- Research the new culture ahead of time.
- Focus on opportunities rather than on cultural differences.
- Ask those who have been through the same experience for their "secrets for success" in the new culture.
- Be adaptable.
- Understand that a cross-cultural perspective is more applicable today than it was years ago.
- Be aware of cultural biases and mental models, which can be obstacles to success.
- Avoid making assumptions about people and situations.
- It is better not to impose your own cultural values upon others; your values may not be applicable to other cultures.
- Remain open-minded and receptive to positive elements that could be transferable from other cultures.
- Allow sufficient time to adjust to the new culture. Push through any

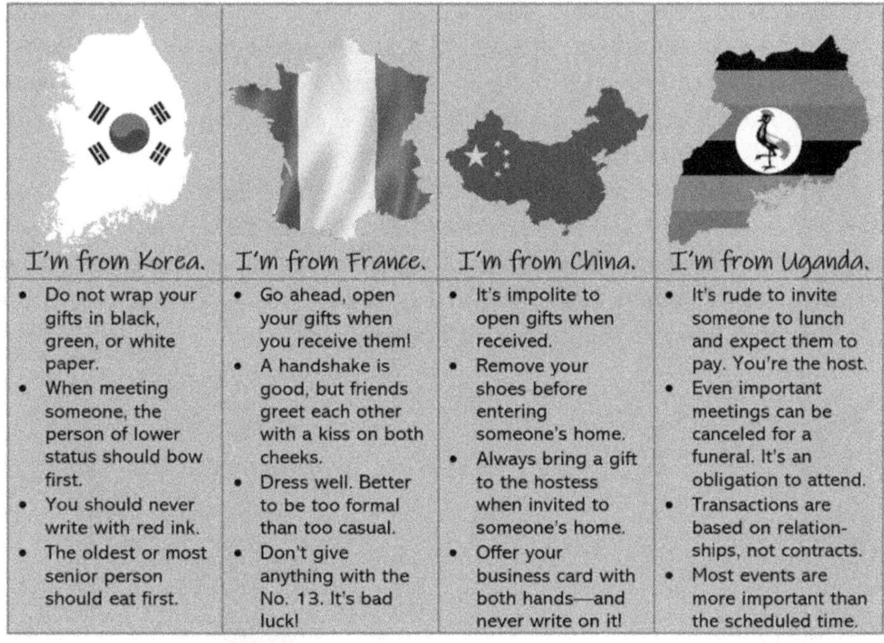

temporary anxiety in confronting the unknown, and eventually embrace the new culture.

- From experience, I recommend staying three months minimum in a new culture before making the decision to quit and go home.

When we attempt to understand an organization, we must consider not just the overall culture but also the presence of subcultures and how they are aligned. We should also know that organizational culture provides stability, meaning, and predictability. Corporate culture also shapes the strategy and behaviors that ensure an organization's growth and continuity within its environment.

Alice Nkore was born and raised in Uganda. She came to the United States as an international student. In addition to earning a Doctorate in Psychology with an emphasis in Organizational Management and Consulting, Dr. Nkore holds an MBA from the University of Dallas in Texas and a BA in Social Sciences from Makerere University, Uganda. She has worked with many organizations, including Walt Disney World Supply Chain Management and is currently a management and leadership consultant with the Institute of African Leadership based in Simi Valley, California.

Before enrolling in the doctoral program, Dr. Nkore was looking to acquire skills in the practice and profession of consulting, specifically in the areas of training and development, executive coaching, strategic planning, and change management so she could offer her clients tangible and relevant solutions to their personal, professional, and business problems. Her consulting focus is to develop individuals who in turn will be in a position to organize, manage, and transform organizations, whether that organization consists of their family, their community, a business, or a government.

Her goal is to make sense of complex issues and make them accessible and easily understood by common people so they are not left behind in the current wave of global transformation. She strongly believes that learning and knowledge acquisition can and should be a basic human right. Dr. Nkore has authored one book: Seeds of Ambition: Putting Together the Pieces of Your Life.

NOTES

[1] Belias, D., Velissariou, E., Kyriakou, D., Gkolia,, A., Sdrolias,, L., Koustelios, A., & Varsanis, K. (2016). The advantages of organizational culture in Greek banks. *Journal of Management Research* , 123–134.
[2] Cameron, E., & Green, M. (2015). *Making sense of change management.* London, UK: Kogan Page Limited.
[3] Block, P. (2011). *Flawless consulting: A guide to getting your expertise used* (3rd ed.). San Francisco, CA: Pfeiffer.
[4] Drucker, P. F. (1995). *Managing in a time of great change.* New York, NY: Penguin.
[5] *Business Dictionary.* (n.d.). Organizational culture. Retrieved from: http://www.businessdictionary.com/definition/organizational-culture.html
[6] Schein, E. H. (1988). *Organizational culture.* Retrieved from dspace.mit.edu: https://dspace.mit.edu/bitstream/handle/1721.1/2224/SWP-2088-24854366.pdf?sequenc
[7] Mead, M. (1951). *Cultural patterns and technical change.* Paris, France: UNESCO.
[8] Bower, M. (2003, May). *The company philosophy: "The way we do things around here."* Retrieved from https://www.mckinsey.com/global-themes/leadership/company-philosophy-the-way-we-do-things-around-here
[9] Daft, R. L. (2013). *Organization theory & design* (11th ed.). Mason, OH: Cengage.
[10] Peltier, B. (2010). *The psychology of executive coaching: Theory and application* (2nd ed.). New York, NY: Routledge.
[11]Cameron, K. S., & Quinn, R. E. (2006). *Diagnosing and changing organizational culture.* San Francisco: Wiley Publishers; Suderman, J. (2012). Using the Organizational Cultural Assessment (OCAI) as a tool for new team development. *Journal of Practical Consulting,* 52–58.
[12] Peltier, *The psychology of executive coaching.*
[13]Daher, N. (2016). The relationships between organizational culture and organizational innovation. *International Journal of Business & Public Administration,* 1–15.
[14] Maslow, A. H. (1968). *Toward a psychology of being.* New York, NY: Van Nostrand Reinhold.
[15]Conley, C. (2007). *PEAK: How great companies get their mojo from Maslow.* San Francisco, CA: Jossey-Bass.
[16] Daft, *Organization theory & design.*
[17] Deal, T., & Kennedy, A. (1982). *Corporate culture: The rites and rituals of corporate life.* Reading, MA: Addision-Wesley.
[18] Brooks, I. (2009). *Organisational behaviour: Individuals, groups and organisation* (4th ed.). Essex, England: Pearson.
[19] Prowle, M., Kalar, M., & Barrow, L. (2016). New development: Value for money (VFM) in public services—the importance of organizational culture. *Public Money & Management,* 547–552.
[20]Van-Eerven Ludolf, N., do Carmo Silver, M., Simoes Gomes, C. F., & Oliveira, V. M. (2017). The Organizational Culture and Values Alignment Management Importance for Successful business. *Brazilian Journal of Operations & Production Management,* 272–280.
[21] Groysberg, B., Lee, J., Price, J., & Cheng, J. Y. (2018). The leader's guide to corporate culture. *Harvard Business Review,* 44–52.

[22] Lencioni, P. (2012). *The advantage: Why organizational health trumps everything else in business.* San Francisco, CA: Jossey-Bass.
[23] Schmidt, M., & Slaughter, R. (2017). A strategic leader's guide to transforming culture in large organizations. *JFQ: Joint Force Quarterly*, 60–65.
[24] Schein, E. H., & Schein, P. (2016). *Organizational culture and leadership* (5th ed.). Wiley.
[25] Rose, A. (2018, 04 13). *The impact of organizational culture on strategy implementation.* Retrieved from: https://yourbusiness.azcentral.com/impact-organizational-culture-strategy-implementation-17367.html
[26] Groysberg et al., The leader's guide to corporate culture.
[27] Srivastava, S. B., & Amir , G. (2017). Language as a window into culture. *California Management Review*, 56–69.
[28] Draper, J., & Clark, L. (2016, Feb). Managers' role in maximising investment in continuing professional education. *Nursing Management – UK*, 30–36.
[29] Schein (1988), *Organizational culture.*
[30] Schmidt & Slaughter, A strategic leader's guide to transforming culture.
[31] Schein, E. H. (1996). Three cultures of management: The key to organizational learning. *Sloan Management Review*, 9–20.
[32] Daft, *Organization theory & design.*
[33] Cameron & Green, *Making sense of change management*; Schein (1996), Three cultures of management.
[34] Daft, *Organization theory & design.*
[35] Cameron & Quinn, *Diagnosing and changing organizational culture.*
[36] Ibid.
[37] Daft, *Organization theory & design.*
[38] Cameron & Quinn, *Diagnosing and changing organizational culture*; Trice, H., & Beyer, J. (1993). *The cultures of work organizations.* Englewood Cliffs, NJ: Prentice-Hall.
[39] Daft, *Organization theory & design.*
[40] Mehmood, Q., Melvyn, H. R., Samina, N., & Tim, V. (2016). Authentic leadership and followers' in-role and extra-role performance: The mediating role of followers' learning goal orientation. *Journal of Occupational & Organizational Psychology*, 87.
[41] Mărăcine, M. S. (2012). Organizational culture - basic element of organization performance. *Young Economists Journal/ Revista Tinerilor Economisti*, 149–155.
[42] Tabatabaee, S. M., Koohi, A., Ghandali, A., & Tajik, T. (2016). The study of relationship between organizational culture and organizational belonging in employees of Varamin County Office of Education. *International Education Studies, 9*(5), 183–192.
[43] Hoorn, A. V. (2017). Organizational culture in the financial sector: Evidence from a cross-industry analysis of employee personal values and career success. *Journal of Business Ethics*, 451–467.
[44] Ibid.
[45] Srivastava & Amir, Language as a window into culture.
[46] Acar, A. Z., & Acar, P. (2017). Organizational culture types and their effects on organizational performance in Turkish hospitals. *EMAJ: Emerging Markets Journal*, 18–31.
[47] Brooks, *Organisational behaviour.*
[48] Hatten, T. S. (2016). *Small business management: Entreprenuership and beyond* (6th ed.). Boston, MA: Cengage.
[49] Ibid.

[50] Ibid.
[51] Sims, R. H., & Schraeder, M. (2004). An examination of salient factors affecting expatriate culture shock. *Journal of Business & Management*, 73–87.
[52] Marx, E. (1999). *Breaking through culture shock: What you need to succeed in international business.* London, UK: Nicholas Brealey.
[53] Brooks, *Organisational behaviour.*
[54] Coe, A. (2014, Sept. 19). The past, present and future of organizational culture. Retrieved from: https://www.linkedin.com/pulse/20140919235425-28613081-the-past-present-and-future-of-organizational-culture/
[55] Cameron & Quinn, *Diagnosing and changing organizational culture.*
[56] Schein, E. H. (1985). *Organizational culture and leadership.* San Francisco: Wiley.
[57] Daft, *Organization theory & design.*
[58] Moore, A. (2017, November). 2017 trends. *Talent Development Magazine.* Alexandria, VA: ASTD.
[59] Schneider, S. C., & Barsoux, J.-L. (2003). *Managing across cultures.* Harlow: Financial Times Prentice Hall.
[60] Adler, N. (1997). *International dimensions of organizational behavior* (3rd ed.). Cincinnati, OH: South-West College Publishing.
[61] Immelt, J. I. (2016, May 20). The world I see: Jeff Immelt's advice to win in time of anger about globalization. Retrieved from: https://www.ge.com/reports/the-world-i-see-immelts-advice-to-win-in-the-time-of-globalization/

Images:

Chinese Flag Map image by GDJ on Pixabay.
Circle of People image by Gerd Altmann on Pixabay.
French Flag Map image by Tumisu on Pixabay.
Iceberg image by MoteOo on Pixabay.
Korean Flag Map image by GDJ on Pixabay.
Ugandan Flag Map image by GDJ on Pixabay.

SIX

PRACTICAL TACTICS FOR MANAGING CHANGE AND RESISTANCE

by Sherman L. Mitchell, II, PsyD, MAIOP, MPA

Jane has been a manager in a customer service company for twelve years. She arrives at work on Monday and is told by the district manager that she will be trained on a new computer system that allows customers to check in without standing in line. The CEO is excited about this new technology, boasting that it will improve customer satisfaction. The day it is launched, longtime customers are confused and employees, including Jane, are frustrated and unsure about why they were not forewarned before implementation. To top it all off, Jane and the majority of employees and customers hate the new system.

Does this situation sound familiar? Whether you're a manager or employee, you have experienced some form of organizational change, and if you're looking for a handy how-to guide for unlocking the key to managing organizational change and resistance, look no further.

This chapter provides a roadmap for managers to implement practical steps for increasing success in change efforts. Whether the change is planned or unplanned, it is clear that it alters the experience, schema, and routine of the individuals involved. It creates a circumstance where there are winners (often those who are in favor of the change) and losers (those who are not) in terms of whether people will cope or resist.

In examining the relationship between the change process within an organization and the positive acceptance of those changes by its employees, it's important to note the role that the brain plays in human behavior. Research on neuro-leadership affirms that leaders use the prefrontal cortex in their decision making, problem solving, and influencing others, specifically as they facilitate change.[1]

When it comes to the study of organizational change and the amount of participation and involvement that employees demonstrate during the change process, the role of positive psychology and mindfulness are areas requiring further exploration. The idea behind positive psychology is that in order for employees to have a positive experience with organizational change, organizational leaders must find ways that enable them to thrive within the work setting. Studies of positive psychology have found that people have an increased desire to feel connected to something larger than themselves in the workplace.[2] Employees essentially want to feel that their role in the organization has purpose and meaning.

Research also suggests that the limbic brain shapes how people view situations in ways that may be different from what was intended.[3] Your employees' behavior is often dictated by their perception of how a proposed change will affect them.

Understanding this reality can help leaders assist employees in participating in the change process, such as by providing them with a more positive outlook and by positively supporting change efforts. Knowing how employee behavior affects change can better position organizational leaders to implement systems that allow change efforts to last.

The WeRInvolved model by Dr. Sherman Mitchell (2017) is a catchy reminder of steps to follow as you implement change. The WeRInvolved change process not only focuses on the introduction to the proposed change, but how to engage your employees in the change process, increasing the likelihood that your change initiative will be supported, implemented, and therefore stick.

A paraphrase of an assertion by Charles Darwin is that "It is not the strongest of the species that survives, nor the most intelligent, it is the one that is *most adaptable to change*"[4] [emphasis added]. At some point, every organization will experience change in response to both internal and external stimuli. The concept of change is at the forefront of all societal development, including the organizational landscape. In order to remain relevant and competitive in this landscape, organizations are tasked with developing techniques and other innovative ways to implement change that are acceptable to their employees while maintaining their organizational efficiency.

Being mindful of why change initiatives are unsuccessful provides opportunities for change management consultants to assist organizational leaders with the tools necessary to facilitate successful change processes by refocusing and shifting their thoughts toward practical options for implementation. In addition, the most effective consultations require a thorough knowledge of how a culture of change is facilitated and what tools are used for managing effective change strategies.

The first WeRInvolved step is derived from the knowledge that when it comes to implementing organizational change, managers may forget the importance of ensuring that employees understand the purpose for the recommended change and how it will contribute to organizational effectiveness.

Often, because the vision or change strategy is so clear in the minds of organizational leaders, it is assumed that employees will understand it in the same manner. Yet forgetting to communicate the purpose may affect the success or failure of implementation. This discrepancy has created the need for leaders to facilitate the planning and execution of the first step in the change process, which is to "explain the purpose of the change."

Step #1: What Are the Purpose and Benefits of the Change?

The objective of this step is to communicate, across the organization at both the management and employee level, why the change is needed. Employees should be . . .

- Informed about the department's or organization's reason for the proposed change.

Step 1. What is the purpose for the change?

Prepare organization about why the change is needed.

Discuss who will be impacted by the change.

- Enlightened about the impact the change will have on the organization's bottom line.
- Told why the change is needed in order to improve business.
- Informed about what effects this change will have on employees, departments, customers, and day-to-day processes.
- Department leaders should check the status of their employees' understanding of the proposed change initiative.
- Organizational leaders, in this step,

create opportunities for each department to review whether the purpose of the change was successfully communicated.

- Organizational leaders should articulate a forecast for short-term and long-term benefits.

Step #2: Each Person Contributes to the Discussion Regarding the Recommended Change

The objective of this step is to communicate with those responsible for gaining the full participation of everyone who needs to be involved in the change efforts.

To better grasp the second WeRInvolved step, it is first helpful to understand how an organization, i.e., a system, works. Each member in the organization is essentially playing a role in the whole unit. This aspect of organizations can be compared to Murray Bowen's family systems theory, which focuses on human functioning and "the potential of human growth and change."[5] Bowen is widely known for being the father of family systems theory, which depicts the family as a unit in which each member is able to function interdependently with one another.

As we reflect on the role we assume in our homes, we should also remind ourselves of the experiences of many in the workplace. Within our families, experiences may sometimes include feelings of having very little influence and even less power. Often, parents and other adult figures create the rules and expectations, and our role as a child is to follow and abide by the rules they set forth.

Analogously, organizational leaders habitually diminish the role of employees by expecting the members of their organization to just do what is expected of them. Family systems theory can be applied to employees as an integral part of the organization for which they work. The family system can be used by organizational leaders as a basis for learning empathy for employees and for understanding their roles within the organizational system.

To assist leaders in these efforts, the WeRInvolved model provides guidelines for effectively communicating the organization's purpose for change and for understanding the impact change efforts may have on members of the system, i.e., employees.

- Determine who will be responsible for deciding which employees

Step 2. Each person has an opportunity to participate or gets to have input.

Prepare informal qualitative and quantitative data in preparation for the change.

Have regular meetings to communicate expectations.

and managers will participate in the change process.

- Create opportunities for employees and managers to give feedback, utilizing the following means: meetings, interviews, focus groups, questionnaires, and observations.
- Determine how much support is needed by employees during the change process.
- Provide opportunities for employees and managers to give recommendations about how to improve the process.
- Provide training and ongoing support for new skills and behaviors required by the recommended change.

Step #3: Resistance Should Be Examined as Change Efforts Are Reemphasized

The third WeRInvolved step comes from the understanding that within organizations, successful change implementation is oftentimes impeded when leaders are met with resistance from employees. The objective of this step is to manage employee resistance to change efforts in order to gain full participation.

When it comes to initiating change, leadership teams often neglect to consider the impact that such changes will have on their people.[6] Furthermore, organizational leaders often "neglect the role of individuals' change history in shaping responses to organizational change interventions."[7]

As a result of these oversights, employees' reaction or lack of involvement goes unnoticed until the change efforts fail. In fact, many change management theorists suggest that failed change efforts are a result of not designating specific employees to support the project and mitigate resistance. An important truth in managing change is that creating a solid coalition to move change efforts forward becomes as vital as the change initiative itself.

It's important for leaders to understand that since change often brings discomfort or uncertainty, it is natural for humans to create a mental framework or schema in order to understand or rationalize it. A schema is "a cognitive structure that represents organized knowledge about a given concept or type of stimulus."[8]

Festinger's cognitive dissonance theory[9] explains how people's minds are connected to the way they think, feel, and behave. Research also demonstrates how people experience negative thoughts, emotions, or behaviors that are difficult for them to alter.[10]

Yet, from the behavioral point of view, even if there is perceived resistance, employees will be supportive of change efforts when they perceive some benefit.[11] It is essential that managers recognize that employee hesitance to participate in the change process may be because they are harboring old feelings and do not see the change effort as being worthwhile.

According to research, the way to reduce employee resistance is to include them early on via communication about what will take place during the change initiative. Doing so helps employees understand the rationale behind the change, which helps to reduce anxiety and uncertainty.[12] Early inclusion also helps employees to see the vision from the leader's perspective, which prevents them from jumping to conclusions and thereby lending a favorable feeling toward the change process.[13]

Once employees have the information they need, their participation in the process gives them a shared sense of meaning and ownership in the change and, as a result, increases their commitment and weakens their resistance.

Step 3 of WeRInvolved incorporates actions that will mitigate employee resistance:

Step 3. Reemphasize the change efforts and prepare for resistance.

Prepare informal qualitative and quantitative data in preparation for the change.

Have regular meetings to communicate expectations.

- Create awareness about the feelings behind people's hesitation about the proposed change.
- Use goals to ensure that the change is sustainable.
- Check the status of new change efforts and short-term accomplishments.
- Address the concerns of employees who may be experiencing hesitation or reluctance about the change.
- Ask the question: Are newly identi-

fied expectations being met?
- Revisit training opportunities and provide support for new skill requirements.
- Provide measures for determining whether change efforts support the organization's purpose for change, measure perceptions, and identify benefits and any resistance that may be stalling the overall initiative.

The greater your employees' participation in the proposed organizational change, the weaker their resistant thoughts. Studies have shown that there is a positive link to benefits to the organization when employees are involved in change. Some of the benefits of employee involvement include the influence of creativity and innovation among employees and an immediate return on the company's investment.[14]

There are five theories applicable to understanding all change efforts: (1) social cognitive theory evaluates the individual's experience to change and the effect(s) of self-efficacy; (2) organizational citizenship behavior examines the trust level of employees based on experience and positive confidence in response to organizational efforts; (3) a sense of ownership is the result of employee participation, which increases the likelihood that the change initiative is viewed favorably; (4) attachment behavior results from behavioral systems that correlate to change acceptance and maintaining relationships; and (5) role theory and leader-member exchange theory (LMX) suggest that engagement is the cornerstone of solidifying an employee's work role as commonly assessed in organizational change efforts.

Bandura's social cognitive theory[15] is widely supported in that a person's individual experience with change is a direct causation of their observation(s). Organizational citizenship behavior theory holds that desired behavior outcomes are linked to support for organizational change. An example of behavior that exhibits negative support for organizational change would include introducing counterproductive measures to impede the change process.

Step # 4: Getting Involved Takes a Concerted Effort from All Levels of the Organization

A great deal of research has been devoted to examining the employee's participation and involvement in change initiatives in organizations as well as the rationale behind the employee's decision to participate. Based on the findings, employee nonparticipation manifests as different forms of resistance, including thoughts of resistance, resistant behavior, and feelings of resistance.

The objective of this step is to communicate with all the people who should be involved in helping the organization gain full participation in your company's change efforts:

Step #4. Ensure involvement happens before, during, and after the change effort.

Communication from top management should encourage employee involvement.

Your employees are your biggest asset, so include them in your change efforts.

- Is the vision for the change being articulated in a manner that supports both the proponents and the opposition?
- Are you providing for involvement and support from key people?
- Are you cultivating a climate of support by embracing ideas from your employees and managers during the change process?
- What protocols have been established for feedback, both support and criticism for the change?
- Have employee surveys and focus group results been shared with all constituents?
- Once those questions have been answered, review the process with supporters and champions of the change and meet with those who are struggling with the change concept.
- Revisit previous steps if needed.

One of the most important concepts that all organizational leaders should understand is that *employee involvement is needed and beneficial to the change process.* Studies have shown a direct link between organizational benefits and employee involvement. Employees who are more involved usually demonstrate more creativity and innovative ideas in the workplace, which may increase organizational productivity and an immediate return on the company's investment.[16]

Data captured from interviews of organizational leaders in various industries reveal their perspectives on employee involvement in the change process. When a culture of employee involvement is cultivated in organizations, it instills confidence in the employees, and that sense of confidence encourages employees to problem solve and take reasonable risk.[17]

Examinations of several longitudinal, meta-analytic, peer-reviewed studies that consisted of more than 800 subjects across multiple industries confirmed a correlation between employee involvement and perceived support as a critical variable that affects the outcomes of the change process. When organizations create an environment that nurtures employee involvement, it instills confidence in the employees. That sense of confidence encourages employees to take on reasonable risks and solve problems independently.[18]

By involving all necessary stakeholders, leaders are essentially helping employees understand the rationale behind the change, which helps to reduce anxiety and uncertainty.[19] Executives can also assist employees in seeing the company's vision from the leader's perspective, reducing the likelihood that employees will jump to conclusions and, thereby, lending a favorable feeling to the change process.[20]

Sometimes managers forget the importance of the humanistic side of change, which includes thoughts, feelings, and—ultimately—an individual's behavior, all of which may affect the success or failure of the change implementation.

Research has unearthed some practical implications for implementing change. Studies have demonstrated the benefits of gaining a better understanding of how employees experience change, that change efforts are hindered if employees are not engaged, and that employee participation in change efforts has a great impact on change initiatives.

Although there may be other ways to increase the likelihood of successfully implementing change, leaders can easily implement the WeRInvolved model, which provides simple but effective guidelines for managing organizational change.

Dr. Sherman L. Mitchell, II, had a desire to understand organizational theories and human involvement in the workplace, which led to him attain a Doctorate in Psychology with an emphasis in Organizational Management and Consulting, a Master's in Organizational Psychology, a Master's in Public Administration, and a Bachelor of Arts in Sociology with an emphasis in Criminology and Corrections.

He has worked in the nonprofit sector for more than twenty years at the administrative, supervisory, and executive levels, dedicating his attention to assisting organizations and leaders in effective organizational management, with strategies for introducing effective organizational change initiatives, and in engaging employees in the change process, increasing the likelihood that the change will be supported, implemented, and, therefore, stick.

NOTES

[1] Siegel, D. J. & McCall, D. (2009). Mindsight at work: An interpersonal neurobiology lens on leadership. *Journal of Neuro Leadership, 2*, 23–34.
[2] Rheem, D. (2017). *Thrive by design: The neuroscience that drives high-performance cultures.* Charleston, SC: Forbes Books.
[3] Ibid.
[4] Megginson, L. C. (1963). Lessons from Europe for American Business. *Southwestern Social Science Quarterly, 44*(1): 3–13.
[5] (Bowen, 1978, p. 393)
[6] Peltier, B. (2010). *The psychology of executive coaching: Theory and application* (2nd ed.). New York, NY: Routledge/Taylor & Francis.
[7] Fuchs, S., & Prouska, R. (2014, September 2014). Creating Positive Employee Change Evaluation: The Role of Different Levels of Organizational Support and Change Participation. *Journal of Change Management, 14*, 361–383.
[8] Fuchs & Prouska, p. 361.
[9] Festinger, L. (1957). A theory of cognitive dissonance. Redwood City, CA: Stanford University Press.
[10] Garcia-Cabrera, A. M., & Garcia-Barba, F. H. (2014). Differentiating the three components of resistance to change: The moderating effect of organization-based self-esteem on the employee involvement-resistance relation. *Human Resource Development Quarterly, 25*(4), 441–469.
[11] Ibid.
[12] Ibid.
[13] Ibid.
[14] Greenberg, J., & Baron, R. A. (2000). *Behavior in organizations: Understanding and managing the human side of work* (7th ed.). Upper Saddle River, NJ: Taylor & Francis.
[15] Bandura, A. (1977). *Social learning theory.* Englewood Cliffs, NJ: Prentice Hall.
[16] Greenberg & Baron, *Behavior in organizations.*
[17] Gravenkemper, S. (2016). Employee involvement: practitioner perspectives. In M. J. Grawitch & D. W. Ballard (Eds.), *The psychologically healthy workplace: Building a win-win environment for organizations and employees.* Washington, DC: APA.
[18] Grady, V. M., & Grady III, J. D. (2013). The relationship of Bowlby's attachment theory to the persistent failure of organizational change initiatives. *The Journal of Change Management*, 13, 206–222; Gravenkemper, Employee involvement; Garcia-Cabrera, & Garcia-Barba, Differentiating the three components of resistance; Judge, W. Q., Hu, H. W., Gabrielsson, J., Talaulicar, T., Witt, M. A., Zattoni, A., et al. (2015). Configurations of capacity for change in entrepreneurial threshold firms: Imprinting and strategic choice perspectives. *Journal of Management Studies, 52*, 506–530.
[19] Garcia-Cabrera, & Garcia-Barba, Differentiating the three components of resistance.
[20] Ibid.

SEVEN

PRACTICAL TACTICS FOR CHANGING YOUR COMPANY CULTURE

by Shari Scott, PsyD, MA

This chapter tells a story rather than giving itemized suggestions to implement. The narrative is primarily about the Xerox Corporation, which experienced the worst kind of difficulties and yet bounced back because its leaders were willing to work hard at changing its internal culture, primarily as an adaptation to external change.

It's worth noting that sometimes learning from story—or by example—is just as effective as learning from a list of tactics.[1]

A Story of Change

A company's internal culture and its flexibility, or ability to change, are essential elements for its success and well-being. In fact, a company with a culture that willingly accepts change and adapts to it is poised to meet the demands and expectations of both society and its stakeholders and is far more able to position itself to outrank others in its industry.

Defining Culture and Change. One definition of organizational *culture* is as "an organization's shared norms, values, and traditional ways of doing things." And organizational *change* can be defined as "a shift in the organization's strategy, culture, tasks, technologies, mission, vision, and the attitudes and skills of the employees."[2]

In seeking to understand and use these principles, it is important to note that changing an organization's culture and trying to modify employee behaviors to align with that culture can be difficult—and it takes *time.*

Responses to Corporate Change. When changing the culture of an organization, some employees (and perhaps some leaders) may decide that the direction of the company is no longer something they want to be a part of, and they will seek employment elsewhere. That may mean losing key employees.

That's why it's vital for leadership and management to work together with employees as they move company culture in the desired direction, because getting buy-in from employees is the only way those workers will embrace the change.

What follows is a story about one company that changed its corporate culture and did so effectively.

Xerox: An American Success Story

Established in 1906, the Xerox Corporation had by 1959 become the first plain paper photocopier manufacturer. Before the turn of the twenty-first century, Xerox was the envy of the copier-printer industry, enjoying soaring stock prices and fast-rising earnings. It was so successful that the verb "to xerox" is still listed in dictionaries as a synonym for making a photocopy.

Then, just as a new century dawned, the copier-printer giant nearly plummeted into an abyss; its disintegrating sales and profits forced its leaders to seriously contemplate filing for federal bankruptcy protection.[3]

Resistance to Change. During its heyday, the Xerox culture was hierarchal. It was a regimented and well-regulated place to work. Procedures and processes governed how employees performed their work, and the long-term goals of the organization were designed to maintain efficiency, predictability, and stability.

In short, the culture at Xerox was not amenable to change, and it was effectively paralyzed by its bureaucracy. For nearly twenty years prior to this crisis point, the company had experienced several restructures, cost cutting measures, and reinvigorations. But because the leadership and corporate culture remained the same, there had not been much progress.

Decisions were made by Xerox leadership that greatly influenced its overall strategy, size, internal and external environments, and company culture. One result was that the culture became highly political and dysfunctional, which caused Xerox leaders to lose sight of the company's strategic goals.[4]

A Breath of Fresh Air. In 2001, Anne Mulcahy became the first woman appointed as chief executive officer of Xerox. When she took over, the company was facing financial ruin. Expenses were at an all-time high because of substantial investments in manufacturing and infrastructure combined with poor pricing strategies and a high product inventory. As a result, its margins were too low to return the company to profitability.

To add insult to injury, the Securities and Exchange Commission had commenced an investigation into the company's billing and accounting practices, alleging irregularities and fraud.

When Mulcahy accepted the CEO position, she boldly disclosed to the company's shareholders that drastic actions were necessary to salvage and turn the organization around and that the current business model was not sustainable.

Although Mulcahy was advised to declare bankruptcy, she instead focused her immediate attention on restoring Xerox to its former glory. She began that journey by talking with employees and customers and by implementing severe cost-cutting measures. Notably, Mulcahy rejected the notion to reduce costs for research and development.[5]

By the time Mulcahy announced her retirement in May 2009, she was admired for having engineered one of the most extraordinary corporate recoveries in recent history. She was acclaimed for paying off the company's enormous debt, for reinvigorating its products and technology, and for growing its sales—astronomically—to more than $17 billion.

Mulcahy described herself as a "representative of the remarkable achievements of Xerox employees" when she became the first woman CEO designated by her peers to receive *Chief Executive* magazine's "CEO of the Year" award.[6]

What Does It Take to Implement Change? An organization can be influenced to enact change when it is enabled in the following six areas: (1) it institutes policies that are supportive of the change, (2) it encourages a receptive corporate culture, (3) it avails itself of its influential stakeholders, (4) its employees have skills that are adequate for their roles, (5) managers employ various management styles, (6) and its executive leadership team has a clear vision.[7]

In the case of Xerox, Mulcahy was able to "shift the organization's strategy, culture, tasks, technologies, mission, vision, and the attitudes and skills of its employees," which mirrored the definition of what it takes to effect change (as stated earlier in this chapter).

Because of Mulcahy's influence, Xerox was able to sustain the necessary changes that brought about its restoration and renewed success.

The Influence of Leadership in Cultural Change

One definition of leadership is "one person influencing another to willingly work toward a predetermined goal or objective."[8] Leadership has also been described as a system or method that a person uses to inspire a team of individuals to accomplish a common goal.[9] Scholars generally agree that leadership is primarily the influence of one person on another in order to accomplish an agreed upon objective.

Leadership in the context of organizational change has been described by researchers as "the process of diagnosing where the workgroup is now, and where it needs to be in the future, and formulating a strategy for getting there. Leadership also involves implementing change through developing a base of influence with followers, motivating them to commit to and work hard in pursuit of change goals, and working with them to overcome obstacles to change."[10]

Trendsetting Leadership. When Mulcahy took the helm at Xerox, its leadership model evolved within the context of organizational change. She was the kind of leader who was able to gain the trust of her employees and stakeholders by utilizing values that demonstrated a significant level of authenticity.[11]

Research about leadership has demonstrated that it is the *genuine* actions of a leader that are always essential, especially in a time of crisis. In other words, authentic behavior is necessary in order to persuade stakeholders to adopt a different stance. The leaders must genuinely believe in what the business can deliver within its new circumstances.[12]

The realities and possibilities of whatever crisis is at hand, along with its casualties, must be communicated honestly by an authentic leader. In the case of Xerox, Mulcahy was brutally honest with the leaders of the company, its shareholders, and its employees. Although she attempted to minimize the impact of the change, she also did what was necessary to rescue Xerox.[13]

When Mulcahy retired from Xerox, she turned the reins of the company over to Ursula Burns. As CEO, Burns was the second woman to lead the Xerox Corporation. She also became the first African American to lead a Fortune 500 company since July of 2009. She had earned the highest position at Xerox after thirty years of dedication, hard work, self-confidence, and advancement within the company.[14]

Burns served as CEO of Xerox from 2009 to 2016 and as its board chair from 2010 to 2017.[15] Under her leadership, the organization continued to soar to new heights. She was also considered a leader who effectively implemented and sustained organizational change.

Burns' philosophy of leadership was brute honesty. She understood that many employees who had spent several years with the organization genuinely felt like it was a family, and she liked to remind employees that real families are frank with each other. Burns determined that it was the responsibility of the company's leaders to encourage truthfulness among its employees so that there would be no fear of repercussion for expressing a perspective that might be considered unpopular.[16]

As late as 2017, Xerox sustained a vibrant leadership team that was admired around the globe for its ability to uphold the organization's culture and to adapt to changing environments. The *2017 Global Citizenship Report* indicated that the company's executives were measured by the following values: collaboration, results, empowerment, and discipline.[17]

In 2018, Xerox again suffered some setbacks, and as of July 2019 had announced its intent to undergo a holding company reorganization. Yet as of this writing, it remains a Fortune 500 company with billions in annual revenue.[18]

Research That Informs Change

According to the *Xerox 2017 Global Citizenship Report*, the company was committed to fostering an organization in which its culture was conducive to change and responsive to changing environments, both nationally and internationally.

Because of its recovery within the previous decade, leadership realized the importance of employee/management relationships. Xerox leaders believed that to sustain recovery it was essential to continue to construct a culture that employees would be pleased to be a part of, a company attentive to its customers, and an organization based on accountability.[19]

In July 2017, the company conducted a culture survey to serve as a reference point for measuring how employees saw Xerox. It received a 70 percent response rate from employees worldwide in fifty nations speaking nineteen languages. The results were used by the leadership team to assist in guiding actions designed to strengthen and advance company culture.[20]

What It Means for Employees. Researchers have amassed convincing validation for the assertion that organizational culture and a company's ability to change can have substantial positive and negative impacts on individual and organizational outcomes. This is especially true when weaknesses and suggestions for improvement remain unaddressed.[21]

The areas that affect individual employees specifically are career fulfillment, reliability, and premature job departure, as well as significant organizational outcomes, such as customer satisfaction, product quality, and economic performance.[22]

Xerox specifically has remained in alignment with these observations from research regarding trends in organizational culture and change management. The company continues to solicit feedback from its employees and stakeholders and has indicated it is determined to respond in a positive manner to the ever-evolving tech industry.[23]

The Future of Leadership and Cultural Change

One of the trends companies such as Xerox should consider as we move further into the current century is a new kind of leadership that foments a fresh take on company culture.[24]

Servant-Leadership. This relatively new model is known as servant-leadership. Servant-leaders emphasize empowering others, being attentive to the needs of all stakeholders, and, of course, serving others. Research now indicates that these values and principles are useful and can help improve a company's performance. Therefore, servant leadership should

continue to be modeled and taught to current and future leaders.[25]

A study published in 2013 listed obstacles that thwarted servant leadership practices in organizations. These included organizational culture, an apprehension to change, and a lack of knowledge regarding the servant leadership model. The study also provided insight into the potential impact these barriers could have on a manager's ability to practice servant leadership in the organization.[26] If a leader is not given the flexibility to utilize servant-leadership as a tool, there could be negative impacts to the work environment, including creating a culture in which employees experience a sense of displacement.

Although predominant business practices have historically dictated that the primary goal of an organization is to be profitable, researchers continue to emphasize the necessity of embracing people-centered leadership methods; the servant leadership model is one such approach.[27]

An Effective Leadership Style. Researchers studying leadership models have recognized the importance of incorporating the most appropriate and effective methodologies. Leaders who do so move their organizations toward achieving desired results. These scholars also noted that for an organization to thrive in today's market, management must know the principles, styles, and models of leadership that are implemented and practiced throughout the company.[28]

Furthermore, the study of organizational barriers related to servant leadership practices may assist servant leaders in all sectors of business to be better equipped to handle the multitude of challenges that companies face today. That's because the servant leadership model requires a partnership between team members and leaders. The recipe for a leader's success includes being able to connect with employees, to affirm their worth and value to the organization, and to empower them for achievement.[29]

People-Centered Change. The servant leadership model offers a follower-centric style that can effectively bring an organization through any phase of change that it may experience. During organizational change, a follower-focused approach should be emphasized, because it is essential to allow team members to grow and develop throughout the change process.

Moreover, the servant leadership model is an optimal leadership style. Its focus on the growth and empowerment of team members is ideal for introducing and implementing change.[30]

First, servant-leaders seek to mitigate any anxiety that employees and team members may have during an organizational transformation. Servant-leadership also models for the team that the motivation for change is unselfish. A servant-leader is conscientious about why transformation is essential and seeks to ensure that the change will be beneficial and not harmful to employees.

In other words, servant-leaders don't enact change for the sole benefit of making a profit or for personal career advancement. The unselfish characteristics of the servant-leadership model permit the leader to focus on transformations that will benefit, advance, sustain, and further develop the team members, employees, and the organization.[31]

The very nature of servant-leadership is a focus on others. This kind of leadership allows employees to provide services to the organization to the best of their abilities, which in turn benefits its overall culture and profitability.

Companies like Xerox would do well to follow this unique trend in servant-leadership, which will take it and other companies into the future in a way that provides for a more effective, and *ethical*, organization.

Dr. Shari Scott is a native of Southern California. Her professional career has included more than twenty-five years of administrative, management, and program implementation experience along with an extensive background in fiscal and grant management. She has worked with children, adolescents, adults, and families as a social worker within the Department of Children and Family Services and currently serves as the Direc-

tor of Community Outreach Services for Greater New Light Baptist Church in Los Angeles, overseeing the development and implementation of community services and outreach ministries. She earned a Doctorate in Psychology with an emphasis in Organizational Management and Consulting from Phillips Graduate University and a Master's Degree in Psychology from the University of the Rockies.

Dr. Scott has worked as a volunteer in a nonprofit office, practicing servant-leadership. She has also authored two books in which she candidly shares her life experiences with the hope that others who have encountered emotional, verbal, or sexual abuse will gain insight and, ultimately, freedom from their harmful effects. She is passionate about servant-leadership; her business consulting focus is in teaching nonprofit and business leaders and managers this effective and important leadership style.

NOTES

[1] Rossiter, M. (2002). *Narrative and stories in adult teaching and learning.* Columbus, OH: ERIC Publications.
[2] Dessler, G. (2001). *Management: Leading People and organizations in the 21st century* (2nd ed.). Upper Saddle River, NJ: Prentice Hall.
[3] Feinstein, C. (2015). Organizational crisis: The courage to reinvent in the face of adversity. *Feature Edition, 2015*(2), 19–37.
[4] Ibid.
[5] Daft, R. L. (2011). *The leadership experience* (5th ed.). Mason, OH: South-Western Cengage Learning.
[6] Ibid.
[7] Bowers, B., Nolet, K., & Jacobson, N. (2016). Sustaining culture change: Experiences in the green house model. *Health Services Research, 51 Suppl 1*, 398–417.
[8] Dessler, *Management.*
[9] Hussain, S. T., Lei, S., Akram, T., Haider, M. J., Hussain, S. H., & Ali, M. (2018). Kurt Lewin's change model: A critical review of the role of leadership and employee involvement in organizational change. *Journal of Innovation & Knowledge, 3*(3), 123–127.
[10] Ibid.
[11] Feinstein, Organizational crisis.
[12] Ibid.
[13] Ibid.
[14] Haile, S., Emmanuel, T., & Dzathor, A. (2016). Barriers and challenges confronting women for leadership and management positions: Review and analysis. *International Journal of Business & Public Administration, 13*(1), 36–51.
[15] Britton, D., & Ndubuizu, R. (2016). Ursula Burns: Restructuring an American icon at Xerox. *Junctures in Women's Leadership: Business.*
[16] Ibid.
[17] Xerox Corporation. (2017, January 31). 2017 Global Citizenship Report. Retrieved from https://www.xerox.com/corporate-citizenship/2017/Xerox-2017-Global-Citizenship-Report.pdf
[18] Xerox Corporation. (2019, July 25). Xerox To Complete Holding Company Reorganization. Retrieved from https://www.news.xerox.com/news/Xerox-to-complete-holding-company-reorganization
[19] Xerox Corporation. 2017 Global Citizenship Report.
[20] Ibid.
[21] Chatman, J.A., & O'Reilly, C.A. (2016). Paradigm lost: Reinvigorating the study of organizational culture. *Research in Organizational Behavior, 36*, 199–224.
[22] Ibid.
[23] Xerox Corporation. (2017). Xerox ranks among nation's best in measures that matter most to people and communities. Retrieved from https://www.news.xerox.com/news/Xerox-named-one-of-Amercias-Most-JUST-companies
[24] Baldomir, J., & Hood, J. P. (2016). Servant leadership as a framework for organizational change. *International Leadership Journal, 8*(1), 27–41.
[25] Keith, K. (2014). The ethical advantage of servant leadership [White paper]. Retrieved from https://toservefirst.com/pdfs/The-Ethical-Advantage-of-Servant-Leadership.pdf

---

[26] Savage-Austin, A.R., & Guillaume, O.D. (2013). Servant leadership: A phenomenological study of practices, Experiences, organizational effectiveness and barriers. *International Journal of Business and Social Research*, (4), 68.
[27] Ibid.
[28] Ibid.
[29] Ibid.
[30] Baldomir & Hood, Servant leadership as a framework for organizational change.
[31] Ibid.

Images:
Cogwheels image by Gerd Altmann on Pixabay.
Hands image by John Hain on Pixabay.

EIGHT

PRACTICAL TACTICS FOR ENHANCING WORKPLACE DIVERSITY

by Brandy Reid, PsyD, LMFT

Diversity is a buzzword that has recently been in the spotlight more than ever before. But it's more than just a term—it is in reality a foundation for developing awareness and sharpening professionalism.

Diversity is a social framework that allows us to put a box around not only what makes us unique but what also ties us together.[1] The main benefit to the workplace in understanding diversity is that it helps people become well-rounded professionals.

So, why do so many professionals and individuals, in general, struggle with the concept of diversity and all its elements? It's simple—it's confusing! And topics that are confusing can scare people away from learning and understanding more about others and themselves.

Diversity also brings up questions about our values, our identity, and whether we are or will be accepted by the majority. It's human nature to want to fit into the same general mold as the peers you are surrounded and inspired by. Yet taking the risk to expand your understanding of diversity is not only important, it is necessary.

This chapter defines various forms of diversity, examines the role diversity has played in U.S. history, explores diversity in organizational culture, discusses communication about diversity, explains how leadership development can exist through diversity, and uncovers how to strategically apply the concepts of diversity within your organization.

Defining Diversity

Due to misrepresentation and miseducation, the term "diversity" is sometimes loosely thrown around at work and elsewhere. Since many people are unclear about what they are truly saying or doing in the name of diversity, it is important that we operationalize the concept and define all its varied elements.

In the past, diversity simply meant "variety" in terms of the existence of multiple versions of something, but in the 1980s and 1990s, diversity became coded language for "minorities"—even more so for "blacks"—within organizations.[2]

A newer definition comes from David Livermore, a social scientist specializing in cultural intelligence: diversity primarily refers to those who are visibly diverse or are underrepresented because they have the most potential to create conflict yet who also have potential to enhance opportunities for developing innovative solutions for businesses.[3]

Understanding both the literal and social-contextual definitions is important. Yet the most anodyne definition of "diversity" is as a social construct. It is a term that can be used in various contexts with the aim of underscoring the varied expressions of people in a given setting. That is how diversity is defined for the purposes of this discussion.

With that in mind, the most commonly understood forms/categories will be used for this chapter. For example, race, ethnicity, nationality, and culture are typically used interchangeably. However, there are significant differences in these terms despite their threads of similarity,[4] and in fact, clarity about these categories helps employers create alliances and can be an essential asset in building employee rapport and loyalty.[5]

Yet as we explore the various facets of diversity, it is also vital to remember that embracing the wholeness of people, which also includes their diverse identifications, allows organizations to get the best out of their employees.[6] Further, it must be understood that these elements are only parts—not the sum—of the person you are engaging with. When the sum of a person is considered, beyond more than just their work ethic in a company, the individual's wholeness can be embraced and thus utilized to bring out the best in the work they produce.[7]

Race. Historically, the idea of race emerged with European expansion and with modern conceptions of human interaction. Throughout various contexts, race was considered a social construct used to categorize individuals for economic advantage, segregation, and identification.[8]

A more modern concept of race is as a category developed through interpretation of diversity in the human family with the primary function of attaching meaning to observed differences. This idea of race is founded on varied perceptions of these differences between human groups related to variations in melanin, facial features, hair texture, and culture.[9]

By contrast, the U.S. Census Bureau reflects a different standard when defining race. It adheres to the 1997 Office of Management and Budget (OMB) standards on race and ethnicity and documents racial identification in terms of a social definition rather than through the lens of biological, anthropological, or genetic factors. Each U.S. Census category reflects markers primarily related to ancestral geographical origins to determine a person's race.[10]

The U.S. Census Bureau uses five categories for racial identification:[11]

1. **White** = A person having origins in any of the original peoples of Europe, the Middle East, or North Africa.

2. **Black** or **African American** = A person having origins in any of the black racial groups of Africa.

3. **American Indian** or **Alaska Native** = A person having origins in any of the original peoples of North and South America, including Central America, and who maintains tribal affiliation or community attachment.

4. **Asian** = A person having origins in any of the original peoples of the Far East, Southeast Asia, or the Indian subcontinent, including, for example, Cambodia, China, India, Japan, Korea, Malaysia, Pakistan, the Philippine Islands, Thailand, and Vietnam.

5. **Native Hawaiian** or **Other Pacific Islander** = A person having origins in any of the original peoples of Hawaii, Guam, Samoa, or other Pacific islands.

Notably, race designation throughout the Americas is used as a marker with reference to geographical origin and cultural traits; however, the use of cultural traits is not used consistently, because the boundaries of racial groups are not universally agreed upon.[12]

Ethnicity. Ethnicity, which is under the umbrella of race, often refers to geographic origin; however, in many contexts it tends to emphasize language and cultural heritage.[13] Ethnicity refers more to elements related to identity, which can include nationality, regional culture, ancestry, and language. With this understood, the following are examples of ethnicity: African American or black American, Latin American, Hispanic, Afro-Latino, Asian, Muslim, Jewish, Caribbean, European, African, or white American.[14]

Culture. Culture is the set of shared attitudes, values, goals, and practices that characterizes an institution, community, or organization.

Nationality. Nationality is representative of where a person was born or has citizenship. It is common to claim more than one nationality.

Gender Identification. Gender identification is viewed as fluid and on a spectrum. Gender is born out of biology, role expression, or identity within the self. Gender identity categories can include male, female, agender (genderless), androgyne, bigender, genderqueer/non-binary, gender bender, transgender or hijra (a term used in South Asia and India), intersex, and pangender.

Sexual Orientation. Sexual orientation refers to the sexual attraction one has to another person, and it can also be considered fluid and on a spectrum. Sexual orientation can be categorized as any of the following: heterosexual, homosexual, asexual, bisexual, or pansexual.

In recent years there has been more research to examine the LGBQ experience in the workforce. A 2018 study indicated that 91 percent of Fortune 500 companies have a non-discrimination policy, while at the same time 13–63 percent of LGBQ individuals have experienced some form of discrimination in the workplace.[15]

Another research study examined measurement scales regarding the treatment of LGBQ community members versus heterosexual individuals in the workplace. In this study, LGBQ employees reported experiencing much more incivility associated with their sexual orientation than their heterosexual peers.[16] Yet this research also suggested that there may be different interpretations of treatment between male and female members identifying as LGBQ. Additionally, gay and bisexual employees—unlike their heterosexual or lesbian counterparts—view supervisor support in both positive and negative ways regarding leadership and communication styles.[17]

Generation. Generational diversity can be best understood as differences between the various generations. There are many timelines that identify one generation from another; the following seems to be the most accepted:[18]

1. **The Depression Era** (born: 1912–1921; coming of age: 1930–1939).
2. **World War II** (born: 1922–1927; coming of age: 1940–1945).
3. **Post-War Cohort** (born: 1928–1945; coming of age: 1946–1963).
4. **Boomers I**, or **Baby Boomers** (born: 1946–1954; coming of age: 1963–1972).
5. **Boomers II**, or **Generation Jones** (born: 1955–1965; coming of age: 1973–1983).
6. **Generation X** (born: 1966–1976; coming of age: 1988–1994).
7. **Millennials**, or **Generation Y**, or **Echo Boomers** (born: 1977–1994; coming of age: 1998–2006).
8. **Generation Z**, or **Digital Natives** (born: 1995–2012; coming of age: 2013–2020).

Religion. Religious diversity can be best understood as the religious ties that become a part of a person's identity and culture. Many religious identities have become more cultural than actual forms of spiritual practice. The main categories of religious diversity in the United States include Atheist/Agnostic/Nonaffiliated, Catholic, and Christian, with small minorities of those who consider themselves Buddhist, Hindu, Jewish, or Muslim.[19]

Recognizing and Incorporating Diversity in Business

What does the issue of diversity mean for business?

It means that leaders, and those who wish to develop staff or other leaders in their business, must not let what is seen on the outside confuse their expectations of the person within the workplace.

Among socialized human beings, there are various subtle or subconscious expectations placed on individuals based on their diversity identification. When an individual does not fit within the prevailing paradigm, the result may be confusion or tension within the organizational culture. Being unaware of these hidden expectations limits leaders' perceptions of and influence on their team or the company as a whole.

Nonetheless, diversity is becoming more celebrated, honored, and respected among individuals and in society in general. Still, the question of why to acknowledge diversity remains for many corporations. The importance of this ever-changing and complex dynamic called "diversity" cannot be understood without digging into the history of how this social framework was built and how we have been socialized into it, because then the essence of the purpose of diversity is lost.

Historically, America has always embodied elements of diversity, and through the years this country has prided itself on being a melting pot where

there can exist opportunities for a better life. Yet it goes without saying that the diversified America we know today hasn't always been harmonious. This reality has often led to the distortion of the contributions from diverse people and has skewed the appreciation for diversity overall.

As America progresses, we can only hope these notions progress as well. Why? Because they simply must in order for business to thrive.

Diversity, Communication, and Organizational Culture

Usually, the idea of diversity in organizational culture is in the context of having a mix of genders, races, ethnicities, sexual orientations, etc., in a setting where there is no discrimination based on these traits. In an organizational context, diversity refers to equality of opportunity and employment without any bias because of one's traits.

However, despite all efforts to make this an actualization in the common workplace there are still many barriers to diversity. These barriers relate to societal mindsets and personal psychological discomfort with having people from diverse backgrounds working alongside one another.[20]

In fact, in most workplaces, diversity is a taboo subject, seen as something that should not be discussed in professional settings. Many might think having a conversation about diversity would create division and tense feelings amongst individuals; however, it is possible it may do the opposite.

Throughout my years as a licensed therapist and organizational leader, it has been my experience that the confrontation of uncomfortable feelings can be one of the most freeing of experiences. That is because uncomfortable feelings are often rooted in a distortion or in fear. Once the fear is removed or the distortion is unraveled then there is opportunity for strong growth and progress toward identifying a problem.

It can be argued that a shift in perspective is needed in order to face the discomfort of addressing diversity rather than avoiding it.

Leadership and Diversity

Within leadership in organizations, diversity is often defined in terms of gender diversity. Typically, the concepts of leadership and management are more closely associated with men than with women. When research on leadership has been conducted, it was often through the lens of white men and with white men in mind as the audience of their work. This same research has affected our perspectives on leadership today.[21]

For example, we remain influenced by a traditional perspective about what makes someone a good leader, which is frequently defined as someone who is strong, charismatic, and decisive. These characteristics are traditionally seen as male rather than female. When women possess these qualities, they are often described in relation to men.

Yet as the minds of individuals stretch to see the wholeness of women in roles of leadership and there is more visual representation of women in these roles, then these respected roles will also embody a shift in mentality surrounding the concept of leadership.

A study published in 1993 by British researcher Judi Marshall suggested that female values and male values are not owned by each sex—both sexes have access to them. This allows men and women to be both the same and different.[22]

Then a 1990 meta study by Alice Eagly and Blair Johnson on management and leadership styles found that although women often adopted more democratic and participative styles compared with men, in general men were no more task oriented than women, and women were no more interpersonally oriented than men. The differences were, in fact, few.

While it appears that diversity in leadership is closely tied to gender diversity, despite these studies, it is important that the conversation also transcend gender to encompass all varieties of diversity.

Strategies for Applying Diversity Principles in the Workplace

Diversity isn't just an American issue but one that stretches across the globe, meaning that organizations that are growing within the global marketplace should embrace diversity as a top priority.[23] Moreover, although diversity is a set of values and skills most do not acknowledge, it can be the difference maker when attempting to gain partnerships and business opportunities.[24]

What that means in practical terms is that diversity training is needed for everyone! Diversity is necessary in order to see the world through the lens of those we are business with or would like to be in business with. It isn't just a business fad or a form of political correctness. It is the fabric of your business comprised of those you employ and those you want to engage in business as partners or customers.

The following are specific recommendations for ways to enhance the diversity of your workplace:

1. Leaders can utilize assessment tools to understand where their company currently stands or tools pertaining to diversity projects or initiatives. One tool developed by this writer (Dr. Reid) based on research and professional experience is the Remove the F.EA.R. model, which helps leaders better understand how employee morale is affected by false information, including false beliefs about diversity:

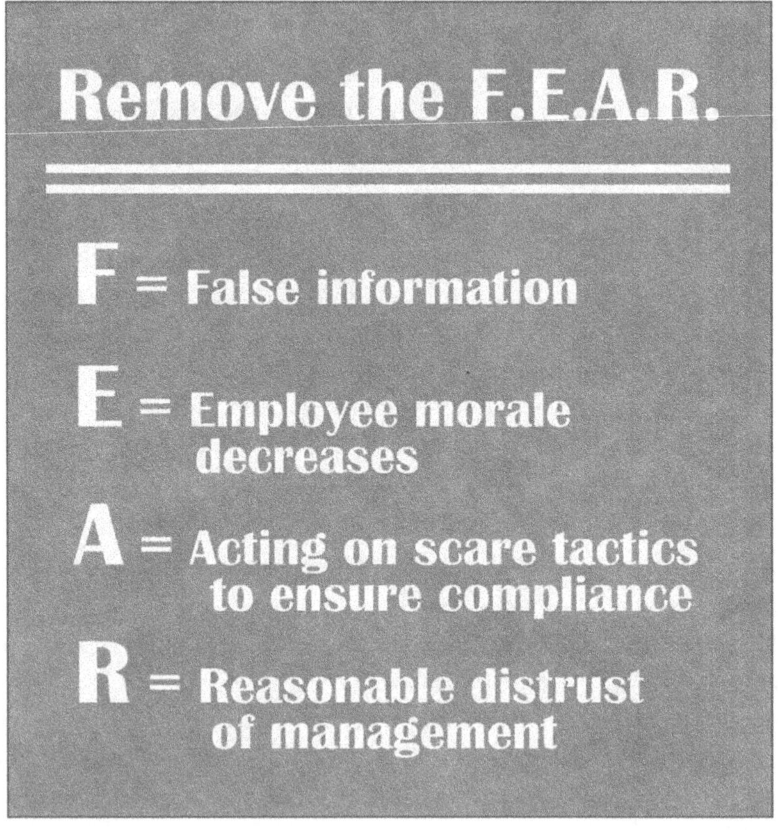

2. Set a standard that evokes true diversity within your company and that redefines your organizational culture so that it is more accepting of the principles of diversity.

3. Cement employee relationships through improvements in recruitment and by increasing morale, enhancing retention, and developing company pride. Utilizing the diversity of those in the company will improve these measures if done in a genuine fashion. People

innately feel when something is an obligation rather than a passion within an organization. Plus, in order to better productivity, there must be investment at all levels to show that your company embraces the wholeness of and not fragmented parts of the principles of diversity.

4. Recognize the specific areas of diversity that can be enhanced in your company.

5. Detail a measure of your progress toward diversity initiatives based on the actions to be implemented.

6. Make the necessary adjustments in a timely manner that is paced with the flow of your company.

7. Communicate progress and milestones along the way, and your employees will be able to process what these achievements mean for each person and for your company.

Dr. Brandy Reid, LMFT, is a licensed therapist with twelve years of experience and a demonstrated history working in community mental health and private practice. She is currently the clinical director at a group private practice agency and serves on the board of directors for Seed House Project. Dr. Reid is also a business consultant and can provide executive coaching services and training pertaining to company culture as well as diversity and inclusion.

Dr. Reid graduated with a BA in Sociology with a minor in Pan African Studies from California State University, Northridge, in 2008. She then went on to obtain her MA in Clinical Psychology with a specialization in Marriage and Family Therapy from The Chicago School of Professional Psychology in 2011. She also earned a Doctorate in Psychology with an emphasis in Organizational Management and Consulting from Phillips Graduate University in 2019.

Dr. Reid currently hosts two podcasts and is a bestselling author. She plans to open a resource and development center for LA youth and transitional age young adults, with an ambition to eventually expand it to other countries. Dr. Reid lives in Los Angeles, California.

NOTES

[1] Brown, D. K. (2011). *Social blueprints: Conceptual foundations of sociology*. New York, NY: Oxford University Press.
[2] Thomas, R. R. (1996). *Redefining diversity*. New York, NY: AMACOM.
[3] Livermore, D. (2016). *Driven by difference: How great companies fuel innovation through diversity*. New York, NY: AMACOM.
[4] Appelbaum, N, P. (2008). Race and ethnicity. In J. Kinsbruner, & E. D. Langer (Eds.), *Encyclopedia of Latin American History and Culture*, (2nd ed.), *5*. New York, NY: Scribner, pp. 462–476.
[5] Brooks, I. (2009). *Organisational behaviour: Individuals, groups and organisation*. Upper Saddle River, NJ: Pearson.
[6] Ibid.
[7] Thomas, J. R. (1992). *Beyond race and gender: Unleashing the power of your total workforce by managing diversity*. New York, NY: AMACOM.
[8] Appelbaum, Race and ethnicity.
[9] Ray, S. G. (2011). Race. In Ian A. McFarland (Ed.), *The Cambridge Dictionary of Christian Theology* (pp. 427-428). Cambridge, England: Cambridge University Press. Retrieved from http://link.galegroup.com.ezproxy.lapl.org/apps/doc/CX1542600446/GVRL?u=lapl&sid=GVRL&xid=dcd28e06
[10] U.S. Census Bureau. (2018, January 23). About race. Retrieved from https://www.census.gov/topics/population/race/about.html
[11] Ibid.
[12] Appelbaum, Race and ethnicity.
[13] Ibid.
[14] Buchanan, S. (2013). Ethnicity. In P. L. Mason (Ed.), *Encyclopedia of Race and Racism* (2nd ed., Vol. 2, pp. 119–124). Detroit, MI: Macmillan.
[15] Cox, J., Stanziani, M. R., Coffey, C. A., & deLacy, R. L. (2018). LGB Q&A: An investigation of the influence of sexual orientation on professional practice among LGBQ-affiliated forensic mental health professionals. *Professional Psychology: Research and Practice*, *49*(4), 255–263.
[16] Pizer, J., Mallory, C., Sears, B., & Hunter, N. (2012*). Evidence of persistent and pervasive workplace discrimination against LGBT people: The need for federal legislation prohibiting discrimination and providing for equal employment benefits*. Los Angeles, CA: The Williams Institute, University of California.
[17] Periard, D. A., Yanchus, N. J., Morris, M. B., Barnes, T., Yanovsky, B., Osatuke, K. (2018, March). LGB and heterosexual federal civilian employee differences in the workplace. *Psychology of Sexual Orientation and Gender Diversity, 5*(1), 57–71.
[18] Fleck, P. J. (n.d.) Understanding students of this generation [PowerPoint presentation]. Retrieved from https://advising.mst.edu/media/administrative/ugs/documents/Understanding%20Students%20of%20This%20Generation.pdf
[19] Pew Research Center. (2015, May 12). America's changing religious landscape. Retrieved from https://www.pewforum.org/2015/05/12/americas-changing-religious-landscape/
[20] Brooks, I. (2009). *Organisational behaviour.*
[21] Ibid.

[22] Marshall, J. (1993.) Patterns of cultural awareness as coping strategies for women managers. In S. E. Kahn and B. C. Long (Eds.), *Work, Women and Coping: A Multidisciplinary Approach to Workplace Stress*, (pp. 90–110). Montreal, Canada: McGill-Queen's University Press.
[23] MSG Management Study Guide. (n.d.). Introduction to organizational diversity. Retrieved from http://managementstudyguide.com/organizational-diversity.htm
[24] Bradberry, T., & Greaves, J. (2009). *Emotional intelligence 2.0.* San Diego, CA: TalentSmart.

Images:

Faces Collage image 1 by Gerd Altmann on Pixabay.
Faces Collage image 2 by Gerd Altmann on Pixabay.
Faces Collage image 3 by Gerd Altmann on Pixabay.
I'm Different image by Gerd Altmann on Pixabay.
F.E.A.R. Model text and image by Brandy Reid, copyright 2019, may only be used by permission of the author.

It is impossible for a business to not have a direction . . . you may as well decide it.
— Fritz Shoemaker, Author of *ChEQmate*

Communication and communication strategy is not just part of the game; it is the game.
— Oscar Munoz, United Airlines CEO

Fitting in is a short-term strategy; standing out pays off in the long run.
— Seth Godin, Businessperson, Author

The best marketing strategy ever: Care.
— Gary Vaynerchuck, Entrepreneur, Author

In a company that truly manages by its values,
there is only one boss—the company's values.
— Unknown

PART THREE

PEOPLE PRACTICS
IN
STRATEGIC PLANNING

NINE

PRACTICAL TACTICS FOR BUSINESS PLANNING

by Greg Hilsenrath, PsyD

What is strategic business planning? It's a map to—or blueprints for—where you want to take your business (or nonprofit). A strategic plan provides the path an organization will take in the future and the building blocks it will use, whether company leaders stick with the plan or find the need to deviate from it down the road.

From decision making and time management to project management and people management to conducting organizational surveys and questionnaires to determining return on investment, there's no doubt business planning can be complicated.[1] Yet—despite the need for sophistication in the process—most successful organizations practice it regularly.

In fact, today's organizations will not be able to compete on a global scale without a strategic plan that encourages innovation and builds customer loyalty. Furthermore, today's marketplace creates the need for working in teams, quickly managing change, and communicating more efficiently. Just participating in the planning process can enhance critical company communications.

What are some other benefits? During strategic planning, risks are assessed and predictions calculated. Using the tools needed to measure current performance and future risks indicates a commitment to efficiency that can build a foundation for growth.[2] Yet it's also important to keep in mind that participation from all areas within the company is needed for leadership to be able to build an effective plan.[3]

Think of constructing a strategic plan the same way you would build a house. It helps to start at the beginning and follow a set of steps that will help you end up with the kind of "home" that works best for your company "family."

Start Your Strategic Planning House with a Solid Foundation

As leaders begin the strategic planning process, it is vital to lay the foundation. This includes defining the scope of the plan, identifying outcomes, setting goals and objectives, and determining timelines for completion as well as for all the steps in between.[4]

Perhaps the most critical step in building a solid foundation is assembling a team that works well together and can deliver.[5] Teammates need to share a common goal and be on the same page about how the business should run. Building a team early with members that share values will help ease decision making throughout the process.[6]

Who Are We, What Are We Doing, and Where Are We Going?

Determining your company's mission, vision, and values statements is an essential part of building a strategic foundation and developing an effective strategy.[7] It is only after defining the mission, vision, and values of the organization that leaders can set strategic objectives that align with the company's long-term goals and then translate those strategies into implementation and evaluation.

If you already have these statements, the strategic planning process is a perfect time to reevaluate them. The outcome of that evaluation will determine whether any revision of the vision statement, mission statement, objectives, or approach is required.[8]

Think of mission, vision, and values as the first concept sketch of your house after you've told the architect what you value in a home, its purpose, and your vision about what it should look like.

The questions about your organization that are answered by mission, vision, and values statements are as follows:

Who Are We? Values are permanent, passionate, and distinctive, and they are an essential part of developing strategy. Core values are part of the tactical foundation. They are beliefs that guide conduct, drive activities, and set goals. Values establish the why, the what, and the beliefs not only of company leadership, but also of all your employees.[9]

What Are We Doing Here? Developing a mission statement is part of determining the company's core purpose, the underlying "why" we work so hard and "why" the business exists. A mission statement declares the organization's purpose and highlights the customer needs the business is working to fulfill.[10]

Management expert Peter Drucker reminds business leaders to "Keep it short. Your mission should fit on a T-shirt." Your mission statement should also serve as a guide for day-to-day operations and act as the foundation for future decision-making.[11]

Where Would We Like to Be in a Few Years? A vision statement is the organization's long-term goals and ambitions—said concisely. A vision statement is designed to inspire and motivate by providing a picture of the organization's future. It also provides an authenticity check for leaders, who compare their objectives and plans to the vision. If a course of action does not move your company toward its vision, a change of direction may be necessary.[12]

Scan Your Environment

When choosing a location for a new home, you look at potential building sites, the neighborhood, and potential advantages and disadvantages of the locale. Leaders should do the same for their organization, not just in terms of location, but in terms of their business model and strategies.

That's why scanning the business environment should be the next step in the strategic planning process.[13] It's important to gather information about the industry, competitors, economy, government, laws, and customer demographics.[14]

When conducting an environmental scan, several methods should be used to collect data, including communicating with leaders inside and outside the organization. Another example is through conducting focus groups.[15]

Collect the Right Data Before You Analyze It

Bayard Winthrop, who introduced a Web-only sweatshirt brand in 2012, provided hundreds of potential customers with prototypes and asked them what they thought. He asked "How did the fabric feel? Was it too rough? Too soft? Too clingy?"[16]

He did it to determine whether there was market demand for the product and to see if the product needed modifications. Winthrop says, "Without soliciting such detailed feedback from your most likely customers you will never know if your idea is a good one. We did everything from putting imagery up on the website to making a hundred sweatshirts and getting them into people's hands."[17]

A SWOT analysis is used to scan a business internally (strengths, weaknesses) and externally (opportunities, threats).[18] A SWOT can help leaders determine how to use company resources more efficiently, improve business operations, discover new business opportunities, identify potential risks, and choose a competitive strategy.[19]

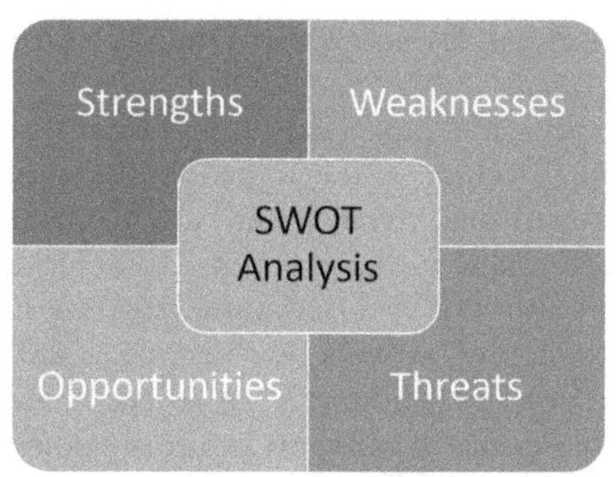

A more comprehensive and primarily external environmental scan is the PESTLE analysis, which was first conceived in a simpler form in 1967 by Francis Aguilar, a pioneer in business planning.[20] The acronym refers to six factors: Political, Economic, Social, Technological, Legal, and Environmental.[21]

Political factors may include "changes in government" and the resulting changes in policy. Economic factors may include "changes in public spending, interest or exchange rates, and the climate for business investment." Social factors may include "changes in lifestyles, attitudes, buying habits, or demographic[s]." Technological factors may include "new [tech] products and services or research and development activity." Legal factors may include "new legislation" or regulatory policy, and environmental factors may include the "impact of green policies." The PESTLE scan is designed to help businesses identify potential external threats and opportunities prior to planning and decision making.[22]

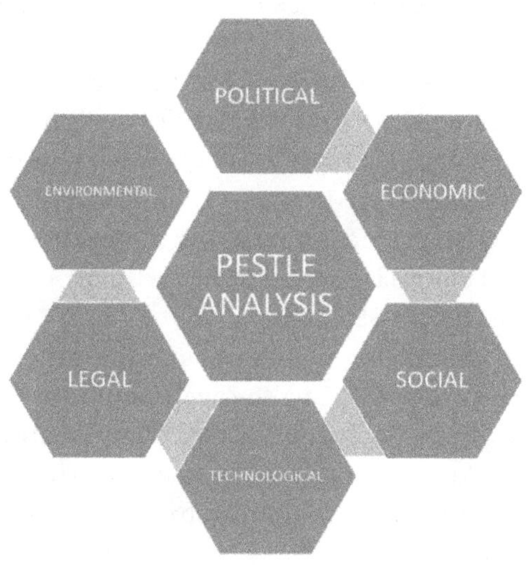

Once the data is collected, tools and tables provide a way to examine and analyze it.[23] There are also tools available that can help determine the validity and reliability of your collected data.[24]

Collecting the right data is like researching what you need for your home on the internet or getting referrals from friends. Who's the best architect? Who is a reliable, cost-efficient contractor? What are the best materials? How does radiant in-floor heat compare to a forced-air system? Having the right data helps you make better decisions.

What Do We Need to Get Started? What Are the Risks Once We Do?

Before implementing a strategic plan, it's important to rank what you need in order to get to your goal(s). In setting strategic priorities for an organization, planners should first ensure that priorities are in alignment with the organization's mission, vision, and values. In order to achieve alignment, planners must weigh the importance of revenue generation, research and development, public perception, competitive advantage, employee satisfaction, customer satisfaction, and more. Those decisions are made by asking specific questions about what a company is already doing well and where it needs to improve.[25]

Compare prioritizing your business needs in terms of working within a budget while you're building your home. What materials are you going to choose? What does the climate and environment require? What is the most important to you, and what can you afford?

It's also important to recognize the potential risks of what you're attempting to accomplish. Doing so will help leaders as they define the tactics they plan to pursue. Yet—it's not possible to eradicate all risks. In fact, there is a time when taking risks will help an organization grow. Without risk, an organization can become stagnant, and stagnation prevents growth. It is vital for leadership to calculate each risk and understand the various aspects of how risk can affect the organization—but risk is *inherent* in doing business.[26]

Risk can be positive, but unnecessary risks can prove disastrous. The idea is to identify disparities within the processes you are considering. A new venture may "look good on paper," but careful analysis may identify a potential for disaster. To lessen risk, consider backup plans for possible scenarios and prepare for alternative outcomes. There is no strategy that will eliminate all risk, but for many organizations an acceptable level of risk can be constructive.[27]

Managing risk is an ongoing process, and leadership must be proactive in its approach to the well-being of the organization. For this reason, the planning process should identify and address risks within the business market and industry landscape. Any strategic plan should include specific training in risk management for its leaders to ensure the organization remains healthy.[28]

Think of identifying risks in terms of where you are deciding to build your home. You might choose to live in Los Angeles, where there are frequent fires, floods, and earthquakes. But being in that area—let's say you work in the entertainment industry and need to live where it is centralized—may be worth the risk.

Designing Business Tactics That Work

For a book with the word "tactics" in its subtitle and in the title of every chapter, it's important at some point to define the term. There is a distinction between strategy—i.e., your business plan—and tactics, which are actions that support your plan.[29] Strategic planning consultant Victoria Duff gives examples of business tactics by comparing computer giants Microsoft and Apple:

> Microsoft's tactic was to be a software manufacturer and make its operating system available to computer manufacturers for use in their personal computer products, then sell the owners of PCs software to run on that operating system. Apple's tactic was to keep its operating system proprietary and manufacture its own brand of computers. Both companies have achieved their strategic goals of growing to become leaders in the internet and computing industry, but there are significant differences in their product strategies and tactics.[30]

After assessing risk, it is vital to design and validate tactics to use in implementing your strategic plan. Yet any business value must be proven, and implementing a test of your new tactics is a smart way to validate them.[31] Doing so is important for the organization's future. If there is no validation of business tactics, there is likely to be some loss of confidence among stakeholders, employees, and customers. Validation gives the people in your organization an assurance that the new strategy will work. That's why the validation process needs to be identified clearly in the business plan.[32]

In some plans, tactics might be the most important step. In this case, leadership should develop a series of phases to meet the plan's goals and then obtain all necessary resources.

Focusing Your Business Tactics and Resources. Prioritizing tactics and resources will help you present your case when gaining the commitment of key stakeholders and create alignment with your organization's needs and objectives. Every organization should focus on gaining buy-in from stakeholders, as plan ownership is critical for success. Without buy-in, the plan will not be valid, and reaching for goals becomes frustrating.

If any additional resources are needed, a strong case must be made to justify the requirements and how they relate to your company's mission and to your developing strategic plan. Leadership must also agree on what resources (customer, business, learning, or financial) will be used to validate your tactics.[33]

At this point in the process, the plan is starting to show tangible value. It is time to examine whether the organization's goals are laid out clearly within the plan. What should your goals be? They are simply facts taken from your business's mission statement that tell you how your company will benefit from what you're producing or from your business activities.[34] If your goals are inadequate, now is the time to reevaluate that area of the strategic plan. Organizational goals should spell out changes, restructuring, or other internal deviations needed to meet planned objectives.[35]

Working out your business tactics can be compared to deciding on a timeline for building your home and determining when you'll need which resources to complete it. You know you'll run into snags along the way, so always be ready to adapt your tactics to fit each situation that arises.

Campaign and Maintain

Communicate and Document Your Strategic Plan. If your strategic plan is going to fail, it will likely be because you haven't communicated the plan and the process to your stakeholders. Documenting and communicating your company's strategy, setting the plan down in some written form, and publicizing it throughout your company needs to be useful, ongoing, and practical. Documenting your company's strategic plan also provides a valuable marketing tool, sets a trail for audits, and provides an organized way to track your progress.[36]

Put your significant support information in your plan's appendices. These should include the specific action plans necessary to carry out business tactics and highlights from your analysis of the data. This is where your SWOT analysis should go, as it will support budgeting later on. This documentation will also help you determine later whether your strategic plan is working efficiently. A glossary to explain acronyms, industry-specific words and phrases could also be valuable.[37]

The plan should include a signature page that lists key members of the planning committee, senior managers, board members, and those who ultimately will be held accountable for the goals, objectives, and outcomes of the strategic plan. It will be important to ask for input from your departments and leaders so they can contribute to the structure of the final version of your business plan.[38]

When all the detached parts of the plan have been combined into your written strategic plan, a strategy can be developed for communicating the plan to your stakeholders. (Be sure to keep plan documents separate from classified communications to ensure that sensitive information does not become public.)[39]

Think of communicating your plan as a campaign—much like political or marketing campaigns. When communicating your plan to your constituents, it's best to practice K.I.S.S., defined as Keep It Simply Simple or in a rougher version, Keep it Simple, Stupid. Some simple communications can be managed with question-and-answer sessions or with a simple fact sheet. Other more complicated issues are more problematic. For those matters, further documentation and communication should be designed to mitigate any negativity.

Communicating your strategic plan is similar to what you might do after you're done building a home. If you're a builder and you want to sell, you design a public marketing campaign. If you're a homeowner and you want to let people know that you've moved (or because you want to show off your new home), you might send out formal announcements or invite everyone you know to a housewarming party so they can see it themselves. And, of course, you'll want to keep all the documentation you've accumulated dur-ing the building process for your records, for legal purposes, and especially if you ever plan to do it again.

Maintain Your Strategic Plan. Always consider a strategic plan as a living document—albeit a blueprint—that needs to respond to the changes that occur both inside and outside the organization. That is why there is never a last step in the development process, at least not if the plan remains in effect. Strategic planning then becomes a long-term process that updates strategy and objectives and gives leaders the ability to be constantly aware of results and next steps.[40]

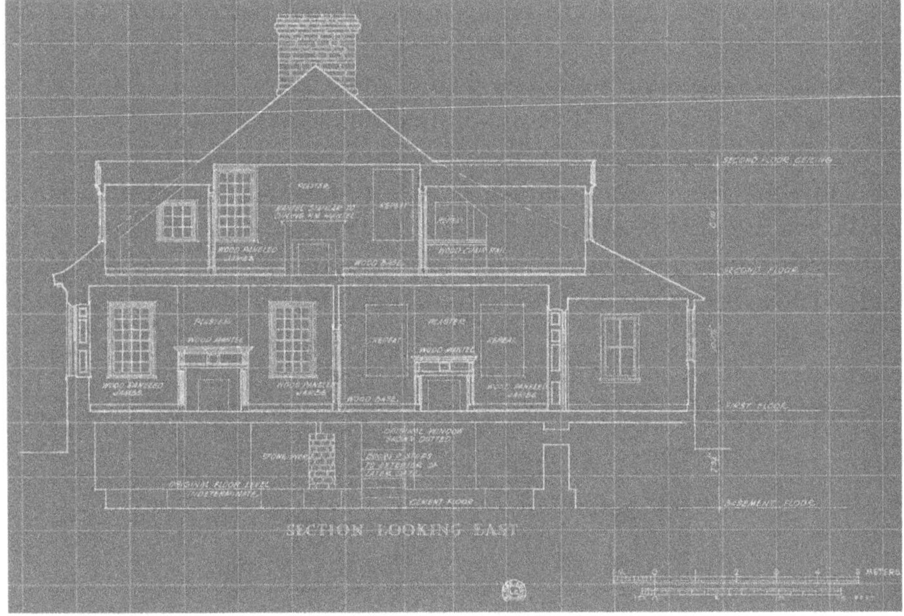

In fact, those responsible for ensuring strategy implementation should meet periodically to reconsider the business environment. Strategy experts suggest that maintenance reviews should occur at least every six months.[41]

Maintaining the plan does not always take an enormous amount of time. If a complete overhaul is needed, however, it may take as much time as developing a new strategy. How long maintaining the plan takes will depend on how much the plan changes since first developed or last updated. If change is minimal, with the same customer demographics, the same types of products and services, and the same mission, maintenance should focus mostly on new goals and tactics. However, if your company's mission has changed, a large-scale strategic planning effort will be necessary.[42]

There are two basic methods for scheduling a strategy review. The first is to schedule it like any other task. The second method is to identify a set of maintenance triggers and review them on a scheduled basis. If your organization is in a dynamic industry or is a small business, you are probably better off using the trigger method. Regularly looking at internal and external triggers will signal when one or more components of the strategic plan will need to be updated.[43]

External factors are changes that occur outside of the organization that might affect its strategy. Examples include economic changes, geopolitical disturbances, or technology changes that can change customer expectations. These types of changes will most likely require a review of the whole strategy.[44]

There are also internal triggers—changes that take place within the organization—that can create a call for a strategy review.[45] For example, corporate reorganization will affect any strategic plan; economic changes influence goals and objectives; and changes in organizational systems, processes, or procedures have an impact on the tactics, the order of their importance, the evaluation metrics, and potentially the evaluation instruments themselves.[46] It's also important to ensure that the strategy continues to link to your business's mission and values.[47]

It's easy to compare maintaining a strategic plan to maintaining your house once it's built. If you've ever owned real property, you know that maintaining it is a never-ending process.

Now You're Home, but Will You Stay There?

There is an incredible amount of information available on the strategic planning process. Most articles and books lay out steps for a process. Yet A. A. F. Goudt, who conducted a study about the perception of the strategic process among venture capital professionals and tech venture teams, interviewed an investor who argued that, "Every business plan is wrong." That's because people cannot predict the future. As reality moves forward, the plan will always change, and the key to adaptability is preparation.[48]

Goudt went on to say, "Change will always come; have open channels to communicate that inevitable change . . . A planning process continuously watches the difference between the plan and actual results, preparing for why and how the plan will be wrong is the key to a new business or venture of any kind."

And, like a house that continually needs to be maintained and updated, "A good business plan is never finished."[49]

Dr. Greg Hilsenrath holds a Doctorate in Psychology with an emphasis in Organizational Management and Consulting from Phillips Graduate University in Chatsworth, California. He also earned an undergraduate degree in Economics from the University of Maryland. He has more than twenty years of sales and consulting experience in a career focused primarily on federal government contractors and their efficiency in selling to federal agencies. He has led unique, challenging, and exciting projects for hundreds of federal employees with the objective of implementing new technology.

Yet he moved to California to help young adults dealing with addiction, stuck in undesirable situations, and unsatisfied with their lives. He has worked with young adults and teens struggling with low self-esteem, poor physical condition, and lack of life education. He has also examined the relationships between insurance companies, government, and the trillion-dollar substance abuse industry with the hope of improving the rehabilitation process and lessening the epidemic of substance abuse.

Dr. Hilsenrath considers himself a "compassionate life strategist." He has spoken at seminars and conferences on behalf of the federal government about ways to improve efficiency and manage change. His passion is to find the most efficient, least expensive way to fix and solve problems and show growth in every person and project.

Dr. Deborah Jackson contributed to this chapter.

NOTES

[1] Barksdale, S., & Lund, T. (2006). *10 steps to successful strategic planning.* Alexandria, VA: American Society for Training and Development.
[2] Mosley, J. E., Maronick, M. P., & Katz, H. (2012). How organizational characteristics affect the adaptive tactics used by human service nonprofit managers confronting financial uncertainty. *Nonprofit Management and Leadership, 22*(3), 281–303.
[3] Dyson, R. G. (2004). Strategic development and SWOT analysis at the University of Warwick. *European Journal of Operational Research, 152*(3), 631–640.
[4] Mathieu, J. E., & Rapp, T. L. (2009). Laying the foundation for successful team performance trajectories: The roles of team charters and performance strategies. *Journal of Applied Psychology, 94*(1), 90.
[5] Basadur, M. (2004). Leading others to think innovatively together: Creative leadership. *The Leadership Quarterly, 15*(1), 103–121.
[6] Ries, E. (2011). *The lean startup: How today's entrepreneurs use continuous innovation to create radically successful businesses.* Redfern, Australia: Currency Press.
[7] Khanzadi, M., Dabirian, S., & Taheriattar, R. (2012). Using hybrid method for strategic planning of construction contractor companies. *Journal of American Science, 8*(1), 513–524.
[8] Kaplan, R. S., & Norton, D. P. (2008). Mastering the management system. *Harvard Business Review, 86*(1), 62.
[9] Wenstop, F., & Myrmel, A. (2006, November 1). Structuring organizational value statements. Management Research News, Vol. 29 No. 11, pp. 673-683.
[10] Kaplan & Norton, Mastering the management system.
[11] Drucker, P. F. (2008). *The five most important questions you will ever ask about your organization.* San Francisco, CA: Jossey-Bass.
[12] Ibid.
[13] Mathieu & Rapp, Laying the foundation for successful team performance trajectories.
[14] Costa, J. (2007). Scanning the business environment. *Handbook of Hospitality Strategic Management*, 15.
[15] Sawyerr, O. O., Ebrahimi, B. P., & Thibodeaux, M. S. (2000). Executive environmental scanning, information source utilization, and firm performance: The case of Nigeria. *Journal of Applied Management Studies, 9*(1), 95–115.
[16] Mount, I. (2013, March 6). Clothing companies trying to find more direct paths to customers. *The New York Times.* Retrieved from https://www.nytimes.com/2013/03/07/business/smallbusiness/clothing-companies-try-to-sell-directly-to-consumers.html
[17] Ibid.
[18] Ibid.
[19] Hill, B. (2019, March 12). Why perform a SWOT analysis? Retrieved from https://smallbusiness.chron.com/perform-swot-analysis-5050.html
[20] Aguilar, F. J. (1967). *Scanning the business environment.* London, England: McMillan.
[21] The Toolkit Project. (n.d.) The PESTEL analysis: Augment the PEST analysis by bringing legal and environmental factors into consideration [Web site]. Retrieved from http://thetoolkitproject.com/tool/the-pestle-analysis#sthash.IQNEMgAe.lQjw3BYR.dpbs
[22] Evans, C. & Richardson, M. (2007). Assessing the environment. *British Journal of Administrative Management, 60*, 1–3.

[23] Ibid.
[24] Wheelen, T. L., & Hunger, J. D. (2011). *Concepts in strategic management and business policy.* New York, NY: Pearson.
[25] Barksdale & Lund, *10 steps to successful strategic planning.*
[26] Maynard, A. D. (2006, July 1). *Nanotechnology: A research strategy for addressing risk* (Pen 3). Washington, DC: Nanotechnology, Woodrow Wilson International Center for Scholars.
[27] Ibid.
[28] Ibid.
[29] Duff, V. (2019, February 6). What are business tactics & strategies? Retrieved from https://smallbusiness.chron.com/business-tactics-strategies-5148.html
[30] Ibid.
[31] Trimi, S. & Berbegal-Mirabent, J. (2012, December). Business model innovation in entrepreneurship. *International Entrepreneurship and Management Journal, 8*, 449.
[32] Motwani, J. (2003). A business process change framework for examining lean manufacturing: A case study. *Industrial Management & Data Systems, 103*(5), 339–346.
[33] Bryson, J. M. (2011). *Strategic planning for public and nonprofit organizations: A guide to strengthening and sustaining organizational achievement* (Vol. 1). Hoboken, NJ: Wiley.
[34] Vetting Tactics, Tools and Resources in Strategic Planning. (n.d.) Retrieved from https://www.universalclass.com/articles/business/vetting-tactics-tools-and-resources-in-strategic-planning.htm
[35] Poister, T. H., & Streib, G. (2005). Elements of strategic planning and management in municipal government: Status after two decades. *Public Administration Review, 65*(1), 45–56.
[36] Barksdale & Lund, *10 steps to successful strategic planning.*
[37] Huang, H. C. (2009, January). Designing a knowledge-based system for strategic planning: A balanced scorecard perspective. *Expert Systems with Applications, 36*(1), 209–218.
[38] Mosley, Maronick, & Katz, How organizational characteristics affect the adaptive tactics used by human service nonprofit managers
[39] Huang, Designing a knowledge-based system for strategic planning.
[40] Ketokivi, M., & Castaner, X. (2004, September 1). Strategic planning as an integrative device. *Administrative Science Quarterly, 49*(3), 337–365.
[41] Mankins, M. C., & Steele, R. (2006). Stop making plans; start making decisions. *Harvard Business Review, 84*(1), 76.
[42] Poister & Streib, Elements of strategic planning and management.
[43] Levy, M., & Powell, P. (2000). Information systems strategy for small and medium sized enterprises: An organisational perspective. *The Journal of Strategic Information Systems, 9*(1), 63–84.
[44] Weick, K. E., & Quinn, R. E. (1999, February). Organizational change and development. *Annual Review of Psychology, 50*, 361–386.
[45] Drazin, R., Glynn, M. A., & Kazanjian, R. K. (1999). Multilevel theorizing about creativity in organizations: a sensemaking perspective. *Academy of Management Review, 24*(2), 286–307.
[46] Zahra, S. A., & George, G. (2002). The net-enabled business innovation cycle and the evolution of dynamic capabilities. Information Systems Research, 13(2), 147–150.
[47] Drazin, Glynn, & Kazanjian, Multilevel theorizing about creativity in organizations.

[48] Goudt, A. A. F. (2017, January 31). The perception of investor readiness: A study about the perception of investor readiness of VC professionals and tech venture teams in Twente [unpublished student thesis]. Retrieved from https://essay.utwente.nl/71793/
[49] Ibid.

Images:

Bulletin Board image by Gerd Altmann on Pixabay.
House image by ArtTower on Pixabay.
Blueprint image by Michael L. Hiraeth on Pixabay.

TEN

PRACTICAL TACTICS FOR COLLECTING BUSINESS DATA

by Alice Nkore, PsyD, MBA

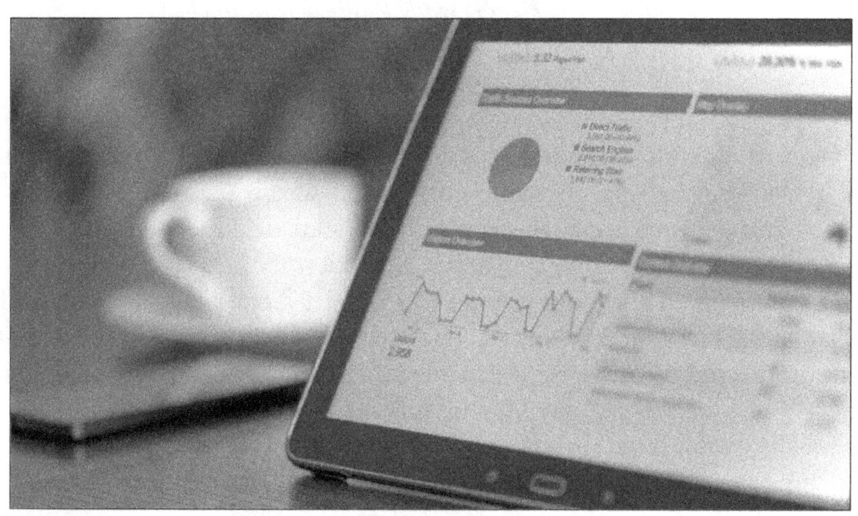

For start-ups seeking to write an effective business plan and for existing businesses that need to formulate a strategic plan or begin a process improvement initiative, the importance of data collection in key areas cannot be overemphasized.

Ray Smilor, who conducts entrepreneurial training for the Kauffman Foundation, says he looks for three pieces of information from a start-up's business plan: "Is there really an opportunity here? Can these people pull it off? Will the cash flow?" He acknowledges that such information comes from collecting data.[1]

Yet only *quality* data should be collected, because your organization will make strategic decisions based on that information, which makes data collection the most time intensive part of business planning. First, leaders should decide what data to collect and then create a plan for collecting it. The types and amount of data that can be collected depend on what your business can afford.

Data may include a scan of relevant literature, background research, focus groups, interviews, surveys, and electronic data from blogs, kiosks, website "cookies," and other more sophisticated electronic means.[2] Another way of collecting business data is by using the scientific method, as in creating a hypothesis about a business operation and testing it. Furthermore, business assessments can be placed into multiple categories: financial, market, customer, employee, operational, and "bare" analytics.[3]

What you really want to do is . . . get the data, but not just add up the columns of numbers. What you're really looking for is insight . . . this is why accountants don't run start-ups.
— Steve Blank, entrepreneur[4]

Once the data is collected, it then must be analyzed. Two ways of analyzing data are through thematic analysis, in which data are classified by subject, and quantitative analysis, which is a statistical method.

Yet the first step in your analysis is to identify how the data relate to your strategic plan and your company goals. In fact, data is only helpful if it is organized so that relationships between the data can be identified and then interpreted in order to attach meaning to it with the aim of drawing conclusions and making recommendations for action.

Ideally, your data should first be tested for validity, and once it is determined to be valid and reliable, then it should be communicated so that there will be constituent buy-in as the data is applied to strategic business planning in your organization.[5]

Key Areas for Research

Whether your business is a start-up, is already up and running, or is looking to expand nationally or internationally, some of the key areas for research include (but are not limited to): laws and regulations governing your business, customer analysis, competitive analysis and product positioning, pricing, selecting distribution channels, and globalization.

From the data you collect, you should be able to determine an effective response to the data, potential pitfalls in either the data collection process or in the data itself, and the pros and cons (advantages and disadvantages) in the collection process or in what the data reveals for your business plan.

Laws and Regulations

Any failure to know and abide by the laws and regulations instituted by city, state, and federal governments can result in severe violations of legal business practice and the resulting negative consequences to your business. Among others, these laws and regulations include: (a) a city business license, (b) business permits, (c) sales tax permits, (d) hazardous materials disposition, and (e) federal and state labor regulations.

An Effective Response to the Law. Policies and procedures predicated on data collection for business planning are established based on knowing applicable laws and regulations. Your organization must be effecttive in implementing the law in order to be in compliance—which is the only way to achieve both public, societal, and private business goals.

Furthermore, businesses can be more effective when they use these policies and procedures to strategically redefine their relationships with city, state, and federal governments to reduce uncertainty and promote goal-oriented collaboration.[6]

Potential Pitfalls. One of the potential pitfalls of collecting data about laws and regulations is that they can change at any time; business leaders must be constantly alert and ready to change policies and procedures to reflect current laws and regulations.

Specifically, some laws can change periodically. These are most likely to be those adopted by local governments in the United States that prohibit the acquisition of goods and services from parties that do not comply with certain minimum labor standards.[7]

Pros and Cons. One advantage in having laws and regulations for business is the notion that they are instituted primarily for the benefit of the public.

A disadvantage is that people with political power may seek to influence these laws and regulations to serve the private objectives of those being regulated rather than the public good.[8]

Customer Analysis

For an organization to be successful, business planning should include finding answers to the following questions:

- Who are our customers?
- Where are our customers?
- When do our customers buy?
- What do our customers want?
- How do our customers buy?

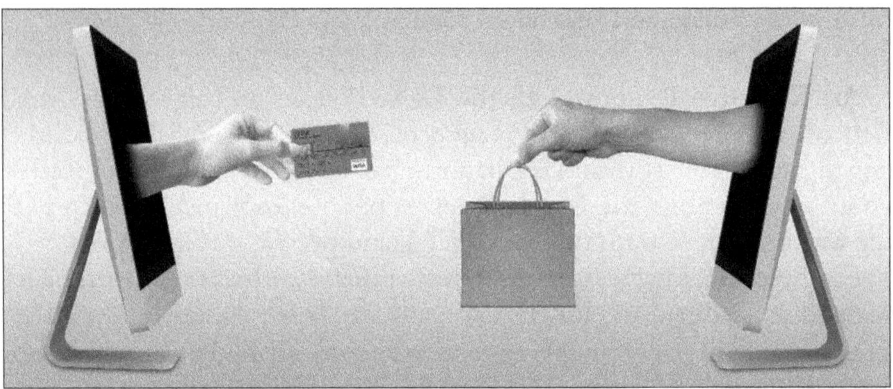

This data, if accurately gathered, can help businesses become customer oriented.[9] Also, identifying and concentrating on target markets can help an organization avoid falling into the trap of trying to be everything to everyone—which is almost impossible to do.[10]

An Effective Response to Your Customers. For it to be effective, data collection for business planning must target consumer preferences, such as durability, color, and price. Organizations should accurately measure these preferences in order to create products that will draw customers in so that, ultimately, they will purchase your business's products or services.[11]

Potential Pitfalls. According to data scientists Thomas Whelan and

Amy DuVernet, data collection for business planning is more than a passing trend in business analytics.[12] Although data collection is desirable for business planning, it is also critical that business leaders remain mindful of the pitfalls that could threaten the validity of conclusions made from these kinds of datasets.

Two categories of threats—namely to statistical conclusion and validity, are always potential pitfalls. Similarly, sample size can be significant. If the sample size is not correct, especially if it's too small, your business strategies might be jeopardized by inaccurate results.

Pros and Cons. One of the pros for data collection for customer analysis is discovering where customers are located. This information can be very useful in designing and implementing marketing strategies.[13]

One disadvantage is that data collection is often carried out on a target population that does not represent the general population. In fact, most assessment instruments used for data collection were designed and validated using a primarily white male population. Another problem is that many, if not most, of the measurement tools currently in existence were developed by European Americans, which means they could contain substantial measurement bias when applied to other ethnic groups.[14]

Competitive Analysis and Product Positioning

According to MBA professor Timothy Hatten, "Your competitive advantage is found by means of a competitive analysis. The heart of your company's strategy and reason for being in business is your competitive advantage. You must do something better than everyone else; otherwise your business isn't needed."[15]

During data collection for competitive analysis, the key questions to ask are:

- Who are our competitors?
- What are our relations with our competitors?
- How do we learn about our competitors?
- Where do we compete?
- How do we compete?
- How do we position our products?

Effective Competitive Analysis. Data collection for business planning ensures that an organization continually monitors customer information, competitor information, and marketplace information. This allows business leaders to design and provide superior value to their customers and earn their long-term loyalty. Research shows that higher levels of customer and market orientation among an organization's leaders results in a greater ability to reach objectives and achieve higher levels of performance.[16]

Potential Pitfalls. One of the pitfalls of data collection on competitors and product positioning is summarized by marketing expert Kenneth Simmonds: "When firms expand beyond single market boundaries, problems grow exponentially." He also stated, "Poor selection of markets, underestimation of competitors, misunderstanding customer differences, and entry at the wrong price are all common pitfalls."[17]

Pros and Cons. Having various competitive analytic tools can be helpful when making strategic decisions, because these tools increasingly require companies to expand their flexibility in their quest to achieve business objectives.[18] Data collection for competitive analysis and product positioning also enables businesses to focus on two main goals: First, to know competition borders, i.e., determining the scope of a business' potential competition, in order to define strategic areas and second, to examine your competitors' activities within the same industry.

At the same time, this type of data collection can be expensive. It may put small businesses, especially start-ups at a considerable disadvantage compared to large companies with almost unlimited funds who can conduct research across many sectors.[19]

Product Pricing

Product pricing is important, as it often affects the customer's decision to buy. Data collection to determine the right price for a product in relation to competitors' prices is a critical part of business planning. Factors to consider about pricing include:

- Determining the right price
- Choosing a pricing method
- Deciding when prices should be changed

Effectiveness in Pricing. Marketing management experts Douglas Dalrymple and Leonard Parsons argue that "pricing is a critical job in the successful operation of for-profit and not-for-profit organizations. Price is the primary element of the marketing mix that generates revenue."[20]

Other scholars have noted that an effective pricing framework helps companies ensure effective pricing strategy development and execution.[21] One example of a pricing system was introduced by marketing educators Michael Morris and Roger Calantone, who outlined their "strategic pricing program" (SPP). It consists of four components: price objectives, strategy, structure, and levels.[22]

Potential Pitfalls. Some challenges for collecting data to determine the right prices for your products or services include possible loss of revenue from charging fees and a degradation of client relationships.[23] If during data collection it is revealed that no competitor is charging fees, for example, a business may simply "go along to get along" even when its business model might be more successful when charging fees. Another example is when a business offers more products of superior quality than currently exist in the market; it may risk losing revenue to competitors who offer lower quality products at a low price.

Pros and Cons. One of the advantages to data collection on pricing is that leaders who create effective business models and allocate resources in ways that maximize pricing confidence can positively impact their bottom line. They can also enhance their competitive advantage and business performance compared to their competitors.[24] Another advantage is that effective data collection allows business leaders to look at pricing techniques and practices in other businesses and ask the important question: How can that concept be applied to our own business?[25]

There are two potential disadvantages to data collection on pricing. One, while most companies have become savvy about cutting costs, few have figured out how much money they are giving up by using pricing strategies. Two, there is the example of Ford (one of the world's largest companies), which tested new ground for pricing approaches. Ford stepped up its market research in order to find more accurate price structures and discovered that lack of detailed information on price changes routinely led to overpricing some products and underpricing others.[26]

Selecting Distribution Channels

Distribution has two meanings: the physical transportation of goods and services from one place to another and the relationships between intermediaries who move products, otherwise known as the channels of distribution.

Data collection on selecting distribution channels includes:

- Distribution alternatives
- Channel choices
- Managing the channels
- Organizing distribution

Effective Distribution. Hatten argues that collecting data on distribution channels "is especially significant for your small business because an effecttive distribution system can make or save a small business as much money as a hot advertising campaign can generate." This information can help businesses investigate what drives a firm's distribution strategies and the effects of distribution strategies on general business performance.[27]

Potential Pitfalls. Discovering how to select the most effective distribution channels for products and services can assist firms in exploiting market potential more efficiently while also avoiding overly intensive distribution, which can limit competition and cause channel "cannibalization," resulting in a reduction in sales volume, sales revenue, or market share.[28]

One pitfall to be mindful of is that losers and winners often emerge from changes made in distribution channel design and policy. What this means is that any changes made to the business plan as a result of data collection can lead to good decision making, but the contrary should also be expected. For example, Porsche and Nationwide Insurance both attempted to introduce changes in their distribution channels, and both ended up running into resistance that made them quickly abort their plans.[29]

Pros and Cons. One advantage that arises from data collection on distribution channels is that researchers have the opportunity to contribute to industry trends and best practices.[30] Another is that business leaders have the opportunity to "trim the fat" from their current distribution channels, reorganize their business scope, and provide better services or products to consumers.[31]

A disadvantage is that the data collected could generate information that might discourage business leaders from taking next steps. For instance, online trading is a new distribution channel, and yet these trading platforms are products of investment and financial service companies that have changed how organizations write and execute their business plans. In other words, product distribution, which traditionally was part of a business's portfolio, has changed the way business is handled for a lot of tech companies.[32]

Globalization

Globalization has forced businesses to implement decisions beyond borders, meaning that data collection must include scanning the external environment for international opportunities and potential threats.

For any business to be successful on the international scene, data collection must look into the following areas:

- International business environment
- Which markets to enter
- International market and business entry strategies
- Global versus local business

Global Effectiveness. Data collection focused on globalization enables business owners and leaders to find the right answers to the number one question about going global: What do you need in an international

business plan?

That information, at a minimum, is necessary to help owners analyze their ability to go international and chart the best course to follow once they're there.[33] Research has shown that one of the most popular ways businesses get involved in international operations is through international strategic alliances.[34]

One country that has successfully created business alliances throughout the world is Japan, with Toshiba in particular as an exemplar of negotiating successful strategic partnerships. Data collection is effective when it helps business leaders understand that they must form partnerships in order to effectively navigate chaotic global markets and share the increasing cost and complexity of product development.[35]

Potential Pitfalls. American leaders and the employees they send overseas are often notoriously unprepared for entering other cultures.[36] The term "Ugly American" was coined by Eugene Lederer and William Burdick in their 1958 novel and showed how other cultures often perceive Americans as overbearing, insensitive, and even reprehensible.

Is this information accurate, and should it be generalized to every American worker? And if the research is accurate, what should businesses be considering in terms of their workforce during the business planning process?[37]

Research suggests that even if this stereotype of Americans is not true, U.S. companies often stumble as they assess the culture of another country and whether their business venture is appropriate to a particular market.[38]

Pros and Cons. In his book *Team of Teams*, General Stanley McChrystal concluded that "the recently minted military acronym VUCA: volatility, uncertainty, complexity, and ambiguity" accurately describes the current international business environment.[39] Collecting data on globalization is therefore vital in a world in which business effectiveness is crucial to international economies that are often unstable.[40]

Through a systematic analysis of the issues that international ventures face, business leaders can integrate findings from research on globalization as they conduct their business planning and focus on the core business mission of small and midsize companies, which is to be competitive and sustainable in an active international market.[41] In addition, data collection focusing on globalization takes into account the cultural differences, tastes and preferences, and potential stereotypes that could jeopardize foreign business success.

One disadvantage, however, is that even among so-called global industries, companies are pressured to become more regionally focused or else face a competitive disadvantage. Similarly, companies that have attempted to pursue global opportunities have been pressured to scale back their efforts to meet regional competition.[42]

Research-Informed Decision Making

Data collection plays an important role in making research-informed business decisions during the process of business planning. Careful collection and analysis of data can ensure that business dealings are within the law, that information is gathered about how to favorably compete through focusing resources on the right target markets, and that the most cost-effective and efficient distribution strategies are used to serve customers in local, regional, and global markets.

Alice Nkore was born and raised in Uganda. She came to the United States as an international student. In addition to earning a Doctorate in Psychology with an emphasis in Organizational Management and Consulting, Dr. Nkore holds an MBA from the University of Dallas in Texas and a BA in Social Sciences from Makerere University, Uganda. She has worked with many organizations, including Walt Disney World Supply Chain Management and is currently a management and leadership consultant with the Institute of African Leadership based in Simi Valley, California.

Before enrolling in the doctoral program, Dr. Nkore was looking to acquire skills in the practice and profession of consulting, specifically in the areas of training and development, executive coaching, strategic planning, and change management so she could offer her clients tangible and relevant solutions to their personal, professional, and business problems. Her consulting focus is to develop individuals who in turn will be in a position to organize, manage, and transform organizations, whether that organization consists of their family, their community, a business, or a government.

Her goal is to make sense of complex issues and make them accessible and easily understood by common people so they are not left behind in the current wave of global transformation. She strongly believes that learning and knowledge acquisition can and should be a basic human right. Dr. Nkore has authored one book: Seeds of Ambition: Putting Together the Pieces of Your Life.

Dr. Deborah Jackson contributed to this chapter.

NOTES

[1] Smilor, R. (2000, December 25). The entrepreneur's Rosetta Stone: How to read a business plan. [Video log]. Retrieved from https://www.entrepreneurship.org/articles/2000/12/the-entrepreneurs-rosetta-stone-how-to-read-a-business-plan

[2] Barksdale, S., & Lund, T. (2006). *10 steps to successful strategic planning.* Alexandria, VA: American Society for Training and Development.

[3] Marr, B. (2016). *Key business analytics: The 60+ business analysis tools every manager needs to know.* Upper Saddle River, NJ: FT Press/Pearson.

[4] Blank, S. (2016, July 28). The lean approach: Customer development data [Video log]. Retrieved from https://www.entrepreneurship.org/videos/the-lean-approach/customer-development-data

[5] Barksdale, & Lund, *10 steps to successful strategic planning.*

[6] Fiorino D. J., & Bhan M. (2016). Supply chain management as private sector regulation: What does it mean for business strategy and public policy? *Business Strategy and the Environment, 25*, 310–322.

[7] Barnes, A. (2007). Do they have to buy from Burma? A preemption analysis of local antisweatshop procurement laws. *Columbia Law Review, 107*(2), 426–456.

[8] Stigler, G. F. (1971). The theory of economic regulation. *Bell Journal of Economics*, 3–21.

[9] Dalrymple, D. J., & Parsons, L. J. (2000). *Marketing management: Text and cases.* New York, NY: Wiley.

[10] Hatten, T. S. (2016). *Small business management: Entrepreneurship and beyond* (6th ed.). Boston, MA: Cengage.

[11] Dalrymple & Parsons, *Marketing management.*

[12] Whelan, T. J., & DuVernet, A. M. (2015). The big duplicity of big data. *Industrial and Organizational Psychology, 8*(4), 509–515.

[13] Dalrymple & Parsons, *Marketing management.*

[14] Royce, D., Thyer, B. A., & Padgett, D. K. (2016). *Program evaluation: An introduction to an evidence-based approach* (6th ed). Boston, MA: Cengage.

[15] Hatten, *Small business management.*

[16] Webster, R. L., Hammond, K. L., & Rothwell, J. C. (2010). Customer and market orientation within AACSB member business schools: Comparative views from three levels of administrators. *Journal of Business Education, 3*(7), 79–92.

[17] Simmonds, K. (1999). Executive insights: International marketing--avoiding the seven deadly traps. *Journal of International Marketing, 7*(2), 51–62.

[18] Kamalian, A. R., & Ghasemnezhad, M. (2015). Strategic analysis of business portfolios: Case study of Chabahar Fishery Cluster. *International Journal of Management, Accounting & Economics, 2* (6), 558–570.

[19] Suryadi, I. K., Ridwan , I. S., Dou, H., & Purnama, A. (1999). Technology forecasting in competitive intelligence: The use of patents analysis. *International Journal of Information Sciences for decision making*, 1–6.

[20] Dalrymple & Parsons, *Marketing management.*

[21] Bang-Ning, H., Tsai, J., Hsiao-Cheng, Y., & Shih-Chi, C. (2011). An effective pricing framework in a competitive industry: Management processes and implementation guidelines. *Journal of Revenue & Pricing Management*, 231–243.

[22] Morris, M. H., & Calantone, R. I. (1990). Four components of effective pricing. *Industrial Marketing Management, 19*(4), 321–329.

[23] Connell, R., & Zalan, T. (2012). Should management consultants charge clients on a contingency basis for merger and acquisition work? *Service Industries Journal, 32*(16), 2677–2689.
[24] Liozu, S. M. (2015). Pricing superheroes: How a confident sales team can influence firm performance. *Industrial Marketing Management, 47*, 26–38.
[25] Hatten, *Small business management.*
[26] Coy, P. (2000, April 10). *The power of smart pricing.* Retrieved from https://www.bloomberg.com/news/articles/2000-04-09/the-power-of-smart-pricing
[27] Hatten, *Small business management.*
[28] Käuferle, M., & Reinartz, W. (2015). Distributing through multiple channels in industrial wholesaling: How many and how much? *Journal of the Academy of Marketing Science*, 768–789.
[29] Magrath, A. J., & Hardy, K. G. (1987). Avoiding the pitfalls in managing distribution channels. *Business Horizons, 30*(5), 29.
[30] Käuferle, Reinartz, Distributing through multiple channels.
[31] Bassolino, F., & Leow, S. (2006, July 1). FICE and the Liberalization of distribution in China. *China Business Review, 33*(4), 16–30.
[32] Petric Iancu, I. A. (2015, July). Benefits and drawbacks of online trading versus traditional trading. Educational factors in online trading. *Cluj- Napoca: Annals of the University of Oradea, Economic Science Series, 1*(1), 1253–1259.
[33] Hatten, *Small business management.*
[34] Daft, R. L. (2013). *Organization theory & design* (11 ed.). Mason, OH: Cengage.
[35] Raffield, B. I. (1994). *How to make international strategic alliances work: One more business lesson from the Japanese.* Paper presented at the Thirteenth Annual EMU Conference on Language and Communications for World Business and the Professions, Ypsilanti, MI.
[36] Jin, B., Swinney, J., Cao, H., Muske, G., Nam, J., & Kang, J. H. (2011). Doing business with China: Curriculum internationalisation through an infusion method. *Innovations in Education and Teaching International, 48*(2), 171–181.
[37] Tomkiewicz, J., Bass, K., & Gibble, A. (2011). Potential pitfalls of ethnocentricism in a globalizing world. *College Student Journal, 45*(2), 369–375.
[38] Rhodes, J. (2016). *Accounting for culture.* New York, NY: NACD Directorship.
[39] McChrystal, S., Collins, T., Silverman, D., & Fussell, C. (2015). *Team of teams: New rules of engagement for a complex world.* New York, NY: Penguin.
[40] Fotiadis, A. K., Vassiliadis, C. A., & Piper, L. (2014). Measuring dimensions of business effectiveness in Greek rural tourism areas. *Journal of Hospitality Marketing & Management*, 21–48.
[41] Renko, M., Kundu, S. K., Shrader, R., & Carsrud, A. (2016). Liabilities, advantages, and buffers of newness: How young age makes internationalization possible. *Group & Organization Management*, 786–822.
[42] Morrison, A. J., Ricks, D. A., & Roth, K. (1991). Globalization versus regionalization: Which way for the multinational? *Organizational Dynamics*, 17–29.

Images:

Tablet Graph image by Photo Mix on Pixabay.
Computer image by Mediamodifier on Pixabay.
Calculator image by rawpixel on Pixabay.
Globe image by Gerd Altmann on Pixabay.

ELEVEN

PRACTICAL TACTICS FOR PLANNING BUSINESS STRUCTURE, POWER, AND COMMUNICATION

by Deborah A. Jackson, PsyD

Organizations are complex creatures. And once an entrepreneur has completed the footwork necessary to establish a business—with a certain vision in mind—it often takes on a life of its own.

This complex, systemic nature of organizations is why, after reading even part of this book, you may have noticed that there is some overlap in content. The chapter on change management, for example, also talks about the importance of communication, which is one of the subjects of this chapter. It's also the reason for including three complex and seemingly unrelated topics in one place. It turns out that how executives at the highest level of an organization choose to *structure* (a.k.a. design) it affects how *power* is distributed in that organization, which in turn affects the company's lines of *communication.* Furthermore, *strategy* affects the choice of organizational design, which is why this chapter is in the section on strategic planning.

In fact, ". . . the primary responsibility of top management is to determine an organization's goals, strategy, and *design*, thereby adapting the organization to a changing environment."[1]

Of course, most of us understand this innately. We know that this interconnectivity exists, because organizations are as complex as the people who work in them.

The Continuing Evolution of Organizational Structure

If you walk into a fast food restaurant today, you'll see one of the most prevalent of today's business structural designs, one that is hierarchical, mechanistic, and scientific. McDonald's especially has honed its processes so that its products are uniform and so that specific procedures are followed to the letter. That's why you know exactly what to expect no matter which McDonald's you visit anywhere in the country.

Classical/Scientific Organizations. The "classical" type of management and organizational design began with the genesis of the Industrial Revolution in the latter half of the nineteenth century and was in full force in the early twentieth century. At that time, it began to be common to view organizations as machines.[2]

In fact, it has been argued that the relatively unknown American engineer Frederick Taylor, through his now widespread ideas about scientific management, has had more influence on business and industry, and even on culture in America and worldwide, than anyone else in modern history.

Taylor purported that workers "could be retooled like machines, their physical and mental gears recalibrated for better productivity." He argued that decisions should no longer be based on tradition as they had been under the world's earlier, primarily agrarian, economies. Rather, he suggested that "precise, standard procedures" should be developed—after careful study—for doing each job, with the goal of increasing efficiency and productivity.[3]

Good Ol' Bureaucracy. The word "bureaucracy" currently has a negative connotation, conjuring images of red tape, slow decision-making, and power-tripping government employees. But it didn't start out that way.

When it was a new idea, it meant designing and managing organizations on a rational basis through deploying "clearly defined authority and responsibility, formal recordkeeping, and uniform application of standard rules," which worked well for the organizations prevalent in the Industrial Age. It still functions successfully for some companies today.[4]

Yet there was a major problem with mechanistic and some bureaucratic business structures: They didn't take into account the realities of the social needs of their very human workers.

The Hawthorne Studies. In the 1920s, Harvard Business School professors Elton Mayo and Fritz Roethlisberger conducted a series of experiments and observations at the Hawthorne plant of the Western Electric Company in Illinois. They concluded that treating employees positively (instead of like machines) "improved their motivation and productivity." Their research "led to a revolution in worker treatment and laid the groundwork for subsequent work examining treatment of workers, leadership, motivation, and human resource management."[5]

It took several decades for this paradigm shift[6] in thinking about employees and organizations to take hold, though the tide began to change as global enterprise began to grow:

> The 1980s produced new corporate cultures that valued lean staff, flexibility and learning, rapid response to the customer, engaged employees, and quality products. Organizations began experimenting with teams, flattened hierarchies, and participative management approaches.[7]

Flip a Coin and Choose a Structure?

Organizational theorist Richard Daft defines organizations as "social entities that are goal-directed, are designed as deliberately structured and coordinated activity systems, and are linked to the external environment."[8]

But what kind of structure should leaders choose as they are designing or restructuring their organizations in order to meet the needs of both their business and of the society in which it operates?

First, let's look at the key components of organizational structure. It:

1. Assigns formal reporting relationships among employees.

2. Specifies all levels in the organizational hierarchy.
3. Indicates the areas for which managers and supervisors are responsible.
4. Determines how departments should be organized and who works in which area.
5. Designates systems for coordination and integration of work efforts.
6. Determines the most effective means of communication between departments and divisions.[9]

Based on those criteria, some of the choices that can be made in terms of structure are whether it should be:

- Classical or contemporary
- Centralized or decentralized
- Vertical or horizontal
- Mechanistic or organic

These choices are not meant to be entirely either/or but rather a range on a spectrum of possible ways of designing your organization. The choice executives make about which structure to choose depends almost entirely on strategic intent, which in turn is based on a systematic analysis of organizational and environmental factors. That's why it's so important to go through a strategic business planning process prior to choosing an organizational design. The structure you choose becomes part of how you implement your business strategy.[10]

Here are some examples of how some organizations are designed:

Multifunctional Structure

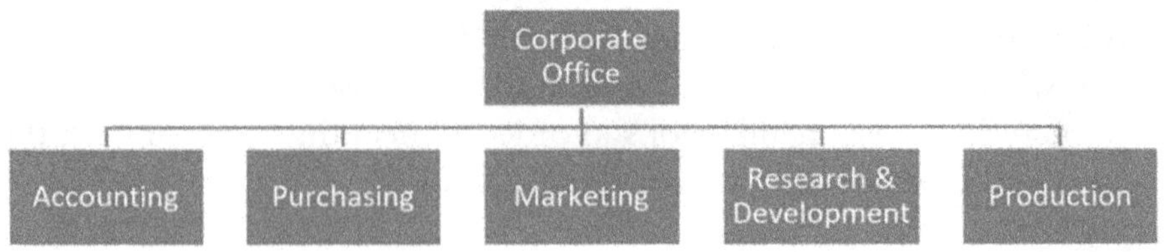

A **multifunctional structure** is organized according to a company's various inputs to its operations. This form works well when production methods and technologies for creating products can be shared. Employees often develop specializations within this design. Use this structure when you need to optimize your technology and when you need scale economies in production. This structure is not as effective when you need to be able to respond quickly to the changing needs of the market.[11]

Multidivisional Structure

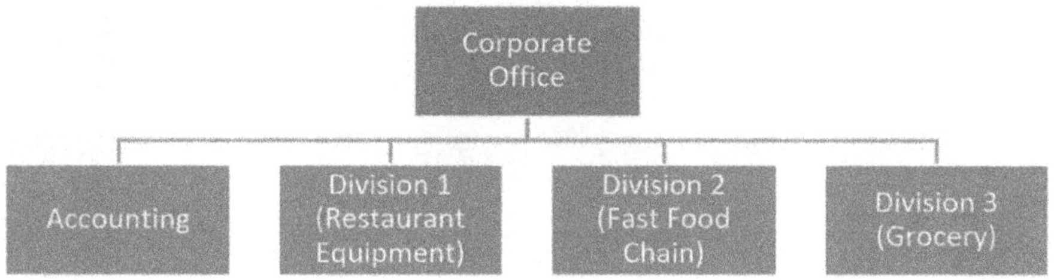

A **multidivisional structure** is just what it sounds like—multiple divisions based on creating individual product lines. Each division contains what is needed to make the end product—purchasing, manufacturing, and distribution. Use this structure only if you plan to manufacture more than one product or provide multiple services. It works well in terms of providing better focus in specific areas, such as marketing, and using this design makes it much easier to compare divisional performance. A challenge in using this design is that effort can sometimes be duplicated, as divisions often operate in silos. Duplicated effort means greater expenses.[12]

The main feature of a **matrix structure** is that employees often have multiple reporting relationships. Business consultant Ian Brooks describes this structure as having "One line of authority, often the function area," that "manages the formal side of the employment contract such as performance management and salary negotiations. The other lines of authority are used to involve employees in ongoing projects and initiatives that are part of their work."[13]

The matrix structure is often used "to coordinate projects and brands across countries." This structure is especially adept at responding to market needs and allows for better coordination across divisions. Managers need to understand the challenges of this structure in order to overcome possible confusion among employees about who has final authority over which areas.[14]

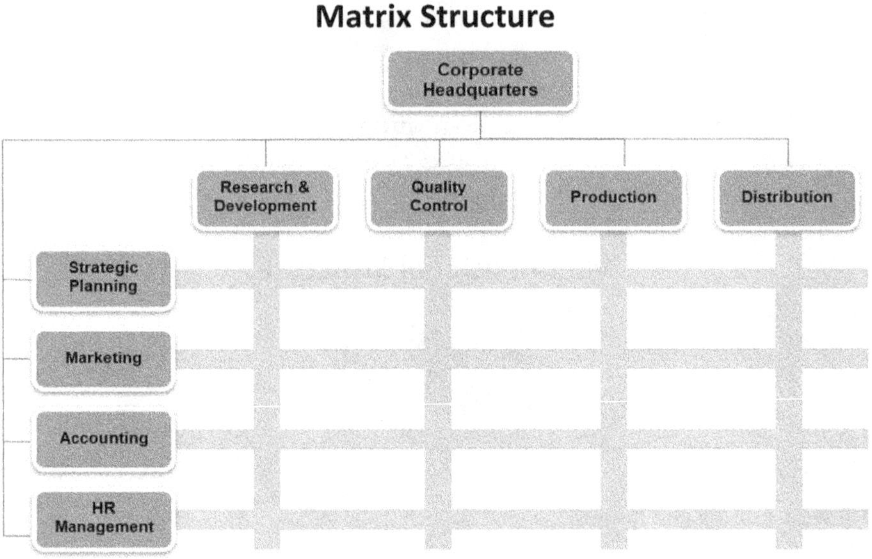

Matrix Structure

Corporate Headquarters

Research & Development

Quality Control

Production

Distribution

Strategic Planning

Marketing

Accounting

HR Management

Contemporary (and Futuristic) Business Structures. As was hinted at earlier, some business and nonprofit leaders are choosing a newer kind of structure for their organizations. These changes are a result of a greater emphasis on meeting human social needs in the workplace, including meeting the very human needs for meaning, purpose, and work-life balance.[15]

The idea is that employees who are happier at work are more invested in the company. Virgin Group founder Richard Branson ascribes much of his success to this principle. He said, "My philosophy has always been, if you can put staff first, your customer second, and shareholders third, effectively, in the end, the shareholders do well, the customers do better, and you, yourself, are happy."[16]

These newer structures are often less mechanistic, more organic, less formalized, more free-flowing, and, as a result, more adaptive to the business environment. They are also often less hierarchical (i.e., less vertical) and are therefore known as horizontal, flat (or flatt*er*) business structures. Let's look at a few examples.

- **Network Organizations.** A network organization consists of a small core organization coordinating various outsourced functions. It is sometimes likened to a "spider tugging on the strands of a web reaching out to the other organizations in the network."[17] I once consulted for an organization that only came together on a project-by-project basis. The CEO formed a new team for each new project, adding team members based on their specific skills and the needs of the job and the client. The CEO referred to it as "virtual," but since the work was primarily conducted in person, it was, in fact, a network with the CEO and a couple of assistants at its core.

- **Virtual Organizations.** Similarly, the virtual organization is a network enabled entirely by the innovations of technology. Work is conducted by various individuals at a distance using computers, the internet, telephones, virtual conferencing, and work-sharing software, such as Microsoft's SharePoint or other project management software options.

- **Hybrid Organizations.** This type has a functional structure with both permanent and temporary teams. Each team focuses on a core concern, such as research and development. There needs to be a high level of information sharing in this type of structure. In this type of organization, managers "have to negotiate and come to some agreement on which direction the company will take. Organizations with a social mission, for example, may have to hire business-minded people to sell the organization's services to provide additional income."[18]

- **Flat Organizations.** In flat organizations, there are typically no job titles, no executives, and no seniority. They are sometimes called self-managed organizations and are often radically decentralized.

  One example is the gaming company, Valve. "At Valve there are no job titles and nobody tells you what to work on. Instead all the employees . . . can see what projects are being worked on and can join whichever project they want. If an employee wants to start their own project then they are responsible for securing funding and building their team. For some this sounds like a dream. For others, their worst nightmare."[19]

  Another example is Morning Star, which processes tomato products for other companies, such as Heinz. In this company no one has a boss, employees negotiate their responsibilities among themselves, there are no promotions and no titles, your peers decide how much you get paid, and anyone can spend the company's money.[20]

- **Holacratic Organizations.** Holacracy is another type of flat organization that is so new the word isn't yet in Merriam-Webster's dictionary. It is based primarily around teams, or circles of teams, which can also be thought of as departments. This structure gained some notoriety when Zappos leaders announced that they intended to adopt it. Though it is widely thought of as another "boss-less" model, in a holacracy there is some structure and hierarchy. Yet decisions are typically made in ongoing meetings, and information is openly accessible to all employees.[21]

It is thought that flatter, less centralized organizational structures typically work better in small to medium-sized organizations or in the tech industry. Additionally, studies have indicated that organizations with less emphasis on hierarchy and formality are more effective in terms of having a competitive advantage, greater production and employee commitment, less internal conflict, and more effective leadership.[22] Yet, flatter structures are still emerging; it remains to be seen how effective these structures will be over time.[23]

Ultimately, choosing a structure for your business or nonprofit all depends on one thing: According to business consultant Ian Brooks, "What matters most in structuring organizations is not the type of structure used but how well it works."[24]

Lines of Power within Organizations

What is power? Traditionally, people have thought of power as the exertion of influence. Exerting power allows a leader to somehow persuade workers to do what is wanted or needed. German sociologist and political economist Max Weber defined power as "the probability that one actor within a social relationship will be in a position to carry out his own will despite resistance, regardless of the basis on which this probability rests."[25]

Yet where power rests within your organization, or in other words, who has the authority to make decisions, often depends on the structure you have chosen. If your organization is hierarchical and centralized, decision making typically rests with top management.

In flatter, decentralized organizations, employees have greater freedom to participate in and make decisions. This creates an environment where the workers who are most affected make decisions in the area where the work is conducted. These decisions often include spending (within a budget), determining how to organize tasks, and the ability to innovate procedures, products, and services, and to decide how to work with vendors and customers.[26]

Furthermore, as employees are empowered in these flatter organizations, studies have shown that morale and motivation are typically higher.[27]

Types of Power within Organizations

In 1959, American social psychologists John French and Bertram Raven identified five sources of power[28] that are still useful in helping leaders understand how power works and is distributed within organizations:

1. **Legitimate** or **position power** is what most people think of when determining who is in charge in a given organization. People with a formal title have authority because it has been given to them based on their position in the organizational hierarchy. The military is an example of an organization in which legitimate power is determined based on rank.

2. **Coercive power** is what we see in dictatorships. It depends on fear and sometimes on physical or psychological abuse or force. It is effective in that this power can get people to comply, and ineffective in that when applied in business situations, employees are likely to lack commitment to the organization or to its coercive leader, which can lead to high turnover rates.

3. **Reward power** uses incentives to tempt people to behave in a desired manner. The quasi-golden rule applies here: Whoever has the gold makes the rules. In other words, the person in the organization who has power over how resources are distributed has the power. Workers often comply if they consider the result of benefit to them. This doesn't always have to be negative—employers can use bonuses, perks, and raises as an incentive. But they can also threaten the loss of those same perks and incentives or even the loss of the job itself.

4. **Expert power** is based on having special knowledge or skills. Have you ever worked for a company where the IT director was let go and management later found out that she took vital knowledge with her about access to the company's information backup systems? I

have. I have also worked in a company where a lack of cross training meant that one employee had far more power than he ought to according to his level in the company hierarchy. This employee often slowed down his response to work requests as a way of exerting control. If your resident expert is a good character with a benevolent disposition, your company probably won't have difficulties. But watch out if he isn't. It's better to avoid this circumstance by ensuring that vital knowledge is not situated with just one employee.

5. **Referent power** is often based on personal charisma; it's derived from how much a person is respected and admired. And those who have it often have extraordinary persuasive power over their subordinates.

Interpersonal Power. Another kind of power to consider is the use of interpersonal power. This type of power is not so much wielded as it is employed as a leadership technique. Clinical professors Robert Hicks and John McCracken have argued that a "coaching mindset is one of the foundations of interpersonal power."[29] The idea is to recognize that colleagues and subordinates are capable of solving their own problems. To act as a coach is not so much to "diagnose and prescribe solutions" but to help employees instead "think through their problems" themselves.

This more positive type of power consists of "a collaborative process that helps an individual alter perceptions and behaviors in a way that increases personal effectiveness and fulfillment."[30] The idea is to point out possible solutions but to also let people discover and make their own conclusions. Hicks and McCracken further assert that this type of power builds confidence and trust and increases interpersonal influence. It works best in situations when you want to increase employee initiative and creativity.

The Links between Structure, Power, and Communication

Organizational structure, power, and communication are inextricably linked. One of the reasons for choosing a particular structure, for example, is to facilitate effective communication so that the people in your company can accomplish its overall mission.[31]

Vertical, formally structured companies typically use vertical information systems and formal means of communication, such as computer information and periodic reports that are distributed primarily to managers.

Flatter organizations encourage horizontal communication across departments, meetings, task forces, and project teams. You may not see horizontal communication mechanisms listed on an organizational chart, but that doesn't mean they don't exist.

Which type of structure, and therefore direction of communications, you choose depends on your goals for the company.[32] Vertical typically means you want stability and efficiency; horizontal communication is associated with flexibility, innovation, and learning.[33]

You can easily tell whether your communications systems are *not* working. If there is a lack of collaboration between departments, ineffective or delayed decision making, if your company can't respond quickly enough to changes in the business environment, or if employee performance is devolving, you may need to reconsider how to structure your business, and thereby your flow of communication.[34]

Establishing Effective Communication

Since most organizations still operate under a vertical structure, effective communication typically begins at the top. Additionally, the most successful communication is the kind that is planned and managed. In organizations, the goal of any communication is to help a company reach its strategic objectives.[35] (If that sounds familiar, it's because it is. That is also the goal of choosing the right structure and employing the right kinds of power within your organization.)

It's also important to the development of effective communication that the company's leaders clearly understand their organization's culture, especially in terms of what employees are concerned about. Leaders who don't may communicate one thing and their employees may hear another. For example, if employees trust management, they're more likely to take what is communicated at face value. If trust is lacking, your employees are likely to look for the hidden message within your messaging.

It's also true that what leaders communicate can actually shape corporate culture—if it's done effectively. In order to springboard a stronger, more open company culture, communication strategy should be focused mainly on creating awareness and understanding.[36]

Communicating Change. Employees are more committed and engaged when leaders communicate what direction they plan to take the company, especially when significant changes are planned.[37] This type of communication reduces conflict and enhances job satisfaction and performance. And it can actually improve an organization's reputation and credibility to outside stakeholders and the general public.[38]

It is even more important to communicate with stakeholders and employees when your company is experiencing a crisis. Often, the instinct among company leaders is to hide extreme difficulties. Yet in order to maintain or create greater trust, it is vital to communicate honestly and authentically when your company is experiencing a crisis.[39]

Diversity of Perspective. The effectiveness of your company's efforts at communication, and even its overall success will often be affected by its diversity. According to Larry Harrington, a vice president of internal audit at Raytheon, a global defense and security company:

> The real value of diversity in the global marketplace today is not just ethnicity, not just gender, but also the diversity of thought that allows a company to truly innovate. Traditionally, many professions . . . have tended to attract people of like minds, schooling, and backgrounds . . . but the danger of this trend is twofold. First, it creates monocultures that are insular and conservative in the way that they think. Second, people from minority cultures feel invisible in such organizations and often leave because their views are not heard or acted on.[40]

Perception Bias and the Johari Window. In working toward creating the most effective and successful lines of communication possible, it is important that company leaders be aware of perception bias. There are four well-known areas in which this bias occurs:

1. **Loss aversion.** This is when people make choices based on the fear of loss rather than the pursuit of gain.

2. **Anchoring.** This is when people rely on the first piece of information they hear about a person, product, or situation before making a decision.

3. **Choice-supportive bias.** This is a bias in favor of things that we like or of what is familiar.

4. **The framing effect.** This is when a choice is made based on how

> the choice is worded. For example, you see the glass as half full or half empty depending on how it is presented to you, when in reality, the amount in the glass is the same either way.[41]

It's also important to be aware of perception bias in teams and to understand that how you communicate can affect individual perceptions. As people work together, they are communicating information about themselves, and as others on a team observe each other, they develop opinions based on an individual's behavior.[42]

The Johari Window can be used as a group discussion tool to enhance individual awareness and perceptions of others within a team, including awareness of perception bias. That gives your team enough knowledge to call it out when they see it.

The top left section of the Johari Window represents the aspects that are known about the individual by others and those things the person knows about him or herself. The top right section refers to aspects of an individual's behavior which may be known to other people but of which the person is unaware—things that he is blind to about himself. A person might be unaware that she has a distracting habit of twisting her hair around her finger, for example. The bottom left section refers to things people know about themselves of which others are unaware. The bottom right area consists of those things that typically remain in the subconscious.[43]

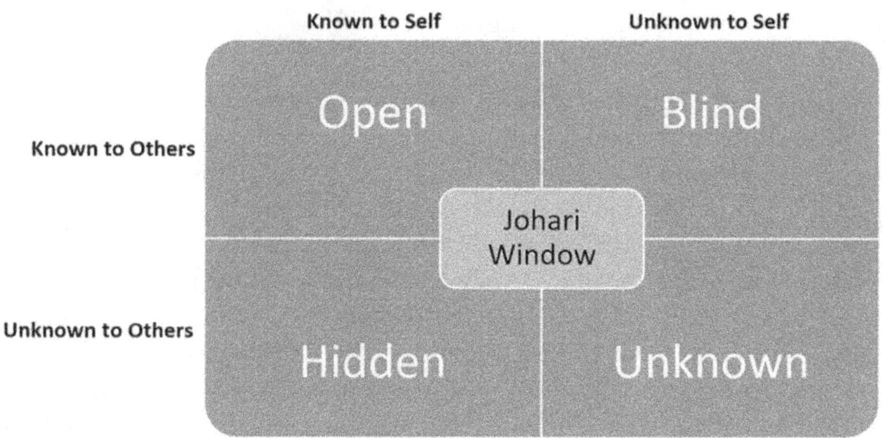

Improving Communication through Empathic Listening. In his book, *The 7 Habits of Highly Effective People*, Stephen Covey argues that people don't really know how to listen effectively. Instead, people often pretend to listen, listen selectively to only parts of what someone is saying, and only sometimes listen attentively. Yet, he remonstrates, people rarely listen with the intent to truly understand someone, which he terms *empathic listening*:

> The essence of empathic listening is not that you agree with someone; it's that you fully, deeply, understand that person, emotionally as well as intellectually. Empathic listening involves much more than registering, reflecting, or even understanding the words that are said. In empathic listening, you listen with your ears, but you also, and more importantly, listen with your eyes and with your heart. You listen for feeling, for meaning. You listen for behavior. You use your right brain as well as your left. You sense, you intuit, you feel. Empathic listening is so powerful because it gives you accurate data to work with.[44]

In today's jargon, this type of listening can be thought of as an aspect of *emotional intelligence*. The idea is, rather than rushing in to fix a business problem—or the person who is bringing it to you—to take the time to first deeply understand, and thereby come to an accurate diagnosis. Through empathic listening, in seeking to understand rather than to be understood, we are more likely to find alternative ways around obstacles and creative solutions to our business challenges.[45]

Discovering How DISC Can Improve Communication. The DISC profile is sometimes thought of as just another personality test, but DISC was actually designed to measure behavior.[46] One of the most important benefits of using this tool is in improving communication and in adapting to various working styles among team members.[47]

DISC categorizes behavior orientations along a continuum from Extrovert to Introvert and Controlling to Accepting. Those who are predominantly D-oriented tend to be extroverted and controlling. Those who are I-oriented tend to be extroverted and accepting. Those who are C-oriented tend to be introverted and controlling, and those who are S-oriented tend to be introverted and accepting. People typically have a dominant and a secondary orientation, such as someone who is a Ds or an Sc.

Extroversion and introversion have different meanings besides categorizing people as either outgoing or shy. Extroverts typically are more willing

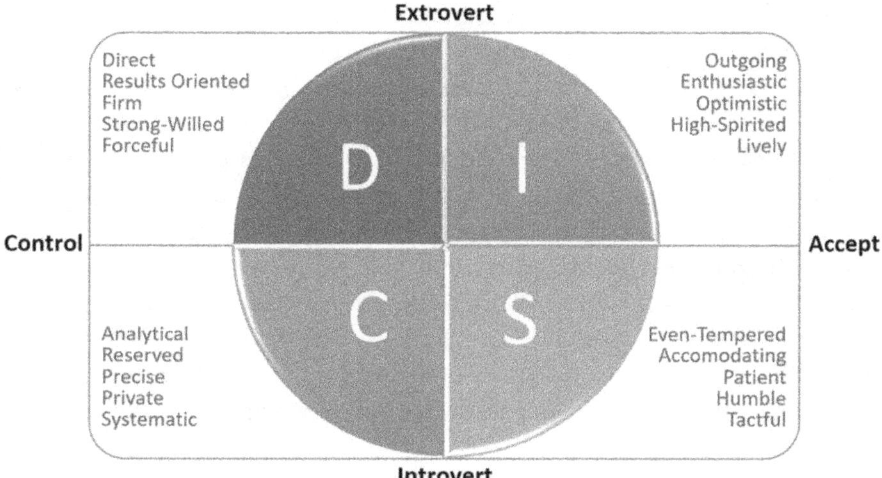

to express their thoughts and emotions, both verbally and nonverbally. They also tend to gain energy from being around people. Introverts are less likely to express their thoughts and emotions, either verbally or nonverbally. And they tend to gain energy from solitude.[48]

The Ken Blanchard version of the DISC describes the difference between control and accept orientations:

> When someone exhibits CONTROL-ORIENTED behavior, he or she tends to act on his or her environment in an effort to change it to meet his or her inner needs. Controlling your environment is not good or bad; it is merely a personal tendency to frequently want to change people or things in order to meet inner needs.
>
> When someone exhibits ACCEPT-ORIENTED behavior, he or she tends to accept what the environment gives him or her and uses it to meet his or her inner needs. Either tendency—to control and to accept—can be functional or dysfunctional depending on the frequency of use and the requirements of the situation.[49]

The DISC model can help people be more effective in their working relationships. It serves to increase self-knowledge about what inspires you, what gets you down, how you react when there's a conflict, and how you approach difficulties. It can also help you communicate more effectively with your colleagues.

For example, let's say an admin, an S, works for a D-type boss. The S-admin learns to approach his boss, a strong D, with bullet-point requests rather than a chatty, friendly email he might prefer himself, and as a result gets a more complete, faster response to those requests.

The DISC can also help people in sales positions communicate better by responding appropriately with a customer's DISC style. Managers can become more effective with their employees, since they know the various ways in which their subordinates prefer to be approached.[50]

NOTE: Because the founder of the DISC, William Marston, did not copyright it, there are many forms of this assessment available. If you decide to take the DISC or use it for your employees, make sure you research the options and choose one that has been determined to be both stable and valid.[51]

There's So Much More Info Out There

This chapter has barely scratched the surface of three topics of great importance to understanding and managing organizations. If you'd like to take a deeper dive into organizational structure, power, and communication, check out the references listed in the notes following this chapter and then check out the sources in *those* documents.

Dr. Deborah A. Jackson attained a PsyD with an emphasis in Organizational Management and Consulting at Phillips Graduate University (now the Phillips Education Center for Campbellsville University) in Chatsworth, California. She earned a BA in English from the University of Washington in Seattle, and after moving to Los Angeles, took a full array of journalism courses at Los Angeles Pierce College to further improve her editing and writing skills.

Dr. Jackson has worked as a freelance editor, writer, and ghostwriter, and over the years has created and edited marketing content for many business professionals, small businesses, and nonprofit organizations. She once again resides in the Pacific Northwest. Her next goal is to fulfill a lifelong ambition to write a novel.

NOTES

[1] Daft, R. (2016). *Organization theory and design* (12th ed.). Independence, KY: Cengage.
[2] Ibid.
[3] Ibid.
[4] Ibid.
[5] Ibid.
[6] April, K. A., & Hill, S. (2000). The uncertainty and ambiguity of leadership in the 21st century. *South African Journal of Business Management, 31*(2), 45–51; Wheeler, W. (2000). Emerging organizational theory and the youth development organization. *Applied Developmental Science, 4*(1), 46–54.
[7] Ibid.
[8] Ibid.
[9] Ibid.
[10] Ibid.
[11] Brooks, I. (2009). *Organisational behaviour* (4th ed.). London, UK: Pearson.
[12] Ibid.
[13] Ibid.
[14] Ibid.
[15] Conley, C. (2007). *Peak: How great companies get their mojo from Maslow*. San Francisco, CA: Jossey-Bass.
[16] Hasanaj, E. (2017, February 25). The Branson guide to customer service: Putting your employees first. Retrieved from http://customerthink.com/the-branson-guide-to-customer-service-putting-your-employees-first/
[17] Daft, *Organization theory and design.*
[18] Ibid.
[19] Morgan, J. (2015, July 13). The 5 types of organizational structures: Part 3, flat organizations. Retrieved from https://www.forbes.com/sites/jacobmorgan/2015/07/13/the-5-types-of-organizational-structures-part-3-flat-organizations/#cd6e66e6caa5
[20] Daft, *Organization theory and design.*
[21] Morgan, J. (2015, July 20). The 5 types of organizational structures: Part 5, holacratic organizations. Retrieved from https://www.forbes.com/sites/jacobmorgan/2015/07/20/the-5-types-of-organizational-structures-part-5-holacratic-organizations/#7f48933f48a2
[22] Bhargava, S., & Sinha, B. (2001). Prediction of Organizational effectiveness as a function of type of organizational structure. *The Journal of Social Psychology, 132*(2), 223–231; Lamoreaux, N. R., Raff, D. M. G., & Temin, P. (2003, April). Beyond markets and hierarchies. *American Historical Review*, 404–433; Tomer, J. F. (1995, Fall). Strategy and structure in the human firm: Beyond hierarchy. *Journal of Socio-Economics, 24*(3).
[23] Morgan, Holacratic organizations.
[24] Brooks, *Organisational behaviour.*
[25] Kippenbrock, T. A. (1992, July/August). Power at meetings: Strategies to move people. *Nursing Economics, 10*(4), 282–286.
[26] Brooks, *Organisational behaviour.*
[27] Daft, *Organization theory and design.*

[28] French, J., & Raven, B. (1959). The bases of social power. In D. Cartwright (Ed.), *Studies in Social Power*, (pp. 150–167), Ann Arbor, MI: Institute for Social Research.
[29] Hicks, R., & McCracken, J. (2013, September/October). Creating interpersonal power. *Physician Executive*, 82–84.
[30] Ibid.
[31] Daft, *Organization theory and design.*
[32] Miller, K. (2015). *Organizational communication: Approaches and processes* (7th ed.). Boston, MA: Cengage.
[33] Daft, *Organization theory and design.*
[34] Ibid.
[35] Wood, J. (1999). Establishing internal communication channels that work. *Journal of Higher Education Policy and Management, 21*(2), 135–149.
[36] Ibid.
[37] Kuchi, T. (2006). Constant change and the strategic role of communication: A selective annotated bibliography. *Library Management, 27*, 218–235.
[38] Suh, J., Harrington, J., & Goodman, D. (2018). Understanding the link between organizational communication and innovation: An examination of public, nonprofit, and for-profit organizations in South Korea. *Public Personnel Management, 47*(2), 217–244.
[39] Ziek, P. (2015, March). Crisis vs. controversy. *Journal of Contingencies and Crisis Management, 23*(1), 36–41.
[40] Piper, A. (2015, June). A focus on people. *Internal Auditor*, 47–51.
[41] Patel, N. (2015, November 26). 4 powerful cognitive biases that could transform your marketing. Retrieved from https://www.inc.com/neil-patel/4-powerful-cognitive-biases-that-could-transform-your-marketing.html
[42] Brooks, *Organisational behaviour.*
[43] Ibid.
[44] Covey, S. (2004). *The 7 habits of highly effective people* (25th anniversary ed.). New York, NY: Simon & Schuster.
[45] Ibid.
[46] Abelson, M. (2015, May 6). DISC: Myths and truths part 1. Retrieved from https://www.linkedin.com/pulse/disc-myths-truths-part-1-michael-abelson-ph-d-/
[47] Discprofile.com. (n.d.) DiSC overview. Retrieved from https://www.discprofile.com/what-is-disc/overview/
[48] Zigarmi, D., Fowler, S., & O'Conner, M. (2009). DISC profile. Escondido, CA: The Ken Blanchard Companies and Life Associates, Inc.
[49] Ibid.
[50] Discprofile.com. (n.d.) DiSC overview.
[51] Abelson, M. (2015, May 6). DISC: Myths and truths part 1.

Images:

Network image by Gordon Johnson on Pixabay.

TWELVE

PRACTICAL TACTICS FOR MARKETING IN A DIGITAL WORLD

by Deborah A. Jackson, PsyD

Marketing is the truth made fascinating.
— Jay Conrad Levinson in *Guerrilla Marketing*[1]

Marketing can be a dynamic and stimulating specialty, but it's also something all business professionals, consultants, entrepreneurs, and non-profit leaders should know something about. In fact, everyone needs to know some basics about marketing, because at some point—in order to make progress and earn a living—we all need to promote ourselves or hire someone to do it for us.

Yet we can't know or do it all, making it likely that at some point leaders of organizations will need to hire a professional to do some marketing. That's because the marketing umbrella encompasses not just traditional media advertising channels, but also branding services, community outreach, media training, public events, public relations (PR) services, search engine optimization, website design, and even word-of-mouth referrals.

And then there are the relatively new aspects of marketing: social media marketing (which has only been around since the mid-2000s), online reputation management (a focus that comes out of the social media revolution), content marketing (yes, that means knowing how to write), influencer marketing (it's not just about celebrities), and social enterprise (marketing with a conscience).

Although you aren't likely to use them all at once, at one time or another you are likely to use them all. That's because these various aspects of marketing are often interconnected, and typically several are used simultaneously during marketing campaigns.[2]

BUT—even though we can't do it all, that doesn't mean we can't do anything.

Fail to Plan = Plan to Fail?

Whether you hire an agency, an independent marketing consultant, or are a do-it-yourselfer, those who are considered "marketers" create plans that help organizations or individuals generate public or consumer interest in a specific person (such as a celebrity), in an organization, in an event, or in products or services typically with the aim of increasing income, job opportunities, participation, or sales.[3] We'll talk more later about marketing strategies for small business owners or nonprofits with a limited budget.

It's All About Connection

If you're like many, when you think of marketing and advertising you might feel the same thing you'd experience if you stepped on a piece of gum on a hot day: distaste for something that sticks with you when you'd really rather not have ever encountered the gooey mess. But, thankfully, marketing isn't always about aggressive telemarketers, salesmen who ring your doorbell and won't take no for an answer, or people persuading you to buy a product you don't want or need. Not even close.

Rather, according to marketing professional Karine Kim, marketing is "about knowing who you are as an organization, knowing your audience, and communicating how the organization can meet the needs of that audience."[4]

More than that, marketing has *significance* when it brings meaning into people's lives by *connecting* consumers with what they need. Think the top levels of Abraham Maslow's hierarchy of needs pyramid: love and belonging, esteem from others, and self-actualization.[5]

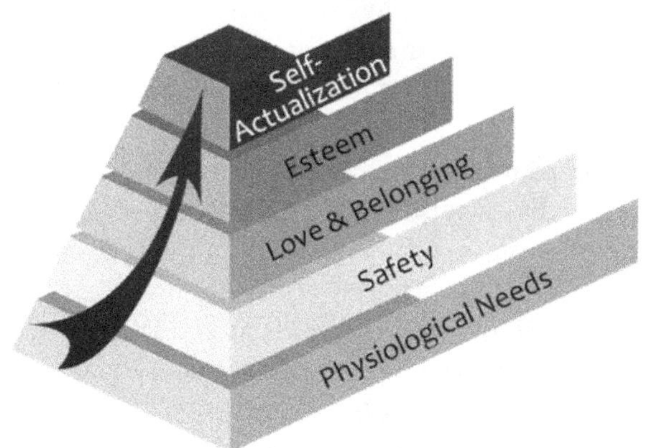

In his book *Peak: How Great Companies Get Their Mojo from Maslow*, Chip Conley[6] took Maslow's psychological theory and applied it to marketing by meeting customer's higher needs in his highly successful and unique boutique hotels. And according to Conley, it's just as important to market to your existing customers as it is to new ones. In that case, he advises, your customer service should almost be "telepathic."

> *Companies that lose their mojo forget about the emotional connection with the consumer . . . and concentrate on the process of business.*
> — Chip Conley in *Peak: How Great Companies Get Their Mojo from Maslow*

Other research also backs up the assertion that employing the right kind of marketing is important because it not only makes businesses more successful financially, but because it can also enhance customer and employee loyalty, pride, and satisfaction.[7]

Create a Marketing Plan

Because small businesses and nonprofits often work with limited resources, it is just as important that they create a strategic plan for their marketing efforts as it is for bigger businesses with a larger marketing budget—and perhaps even more so.[8]

What should be considered in a strategic marketing plan includes cost, what message should be delivered when and where, who will deliver it, and how the plan will be implemented. According to research, when and where to send your message is vital, since the average consumer receives more than two thousand commercial messages every day, meaning that organizations contend constantly for consumer attention.[9]

Free templates for marketing plans are easy enough to find on the internet.[10] A good template should include listing marketing objectives, conducting surveys, conducting a SWOT (Strengths, Weaknesses, Opportunities, Threats) analysis, creating a plan for implementation, defining a budget, and determining key performance indicators (KPIs) to determine whether your plan is working.[11]

Having a marketing plan also means your company's messages are more consistent, and consistency means that maybe the fourth or tenth or twelfth time a consumer sees or hears your message, it will finally register, and he or she will pay attention.[12]

One aspect of a marketing plan that is not often discussed is to ensure that organizational culture is communicated to and understood by all of a company's employees, not just business partners or consumers. Having a unified message will frame how staff represent your company in the marketplace.[13]

You'll know that your company's mission, vision, and values are being communicated effectively when you observe that your employees' job satisfaction is high, that they have a customer service focus, and that they feel committed, loyal, and empowered.[14] What that really means is that you need to think of everything in your business as marketing—from your business model to how you treat your employees to how you engage your investors.

Pay Attention to These Five Marketing Trends

Trend One: Social Media. The explosion of social media began sometime in the mid-2000s, and it didn't take long for marketing professionals to recognize its potential for promoting goods and services to consumers. Demonstrating the power of social media, in 2017 Facebook reached a new milestone at two billion users; if it were a country, it would be the most populous country on earth.[15]

According to social media expert Kathy Yanke, video is considered a top social media trend, with YouTube and Facebook Live taking the top spots for viewership.[16] This may be because "Videos enhance the public's impression of the organization's products or services, put a human face on the organization, and ultimately build the brand."[17] And the videos don't have to be serious. More than one mayor or city council has created a dance video and uploaded it to YouTube to highlight the best aspects of their city.[18]

Content is fire. Social media is gasoline.
— Tweet by Jay Baer, author of *Youtility*

Yanke also ranks the top five social media platforms that all businesses should participate in:[19]

Platform #5: Your Blog. Articles are big business now, and businesses are influencing people and selling products and services through them. You should aim to publish one blog post per week, but keep in mind that each blog post must be 250 words or more to be searchable according to current Google algorithms. Pull quotes, headlines, subheads, your bio, and your byline all count toward the total word count. Add a link to your blog on your website, which you can call "What's Happening" or "News."

Platform #4: Your Website. People don't think of a website necessarily as social, but it's an important part of your social media presence. It's the number one way people will use to find and research you or your company. Websites create a first impression about your company, so they should be clean, attractive, all links must work, and it must be ACTIVE. That means changing content or adding articles, photos, and videos regularly for prime search engine optimization (SEO).

Some tips to make your website better:

- Make sure you use large, in-focus, colorful photos. And they should not be boring.
- Use the right colors. Research indicates that rich, deep, dark colors stand out—you want people to be attracted to your website and stay for a while.
- Don't duplicate information—make it simple. People just don't have time to read a lot of complicated content.
- The "Contact Us" page must be very clear, and it must work.
- Go through your website page by page. Look at it on a desktop, laptop, iPad, other tablets, and most important, you must look at your website on two different brands of cell

phones. Note that links often will not work on mobile if you haven't updated your website in the last two years.

Platform #3: YouTube. This platform receives this rank simply because video is huge right now. For example, posting a helpful "how to" can drive people to your website.

Platform #2: LinkedIn. Businesses and business professionals should have a LinkedIn presence, because it's a business-focused network. If you haven't checked it out in a while, do—it has changed and grown quite a bit from its early days. It's a great place for content marketing and for reading a myriad of interesting business-focused information. Recruiters and other human resources professionals use it, so if you're looking for a job, make sure you have a complete and up-to-date profile.[20]

Platform #1: Facebook. Your business should be on Facebook because it's the number one platform in the world, meaning it is your largest potential audience.

Twitter, Instagram, and the baby of the social media world, Snapchat, can also be important, but if you must focus your efforts where they are needed most, focus first on these top five.

Businesses should also have an entry on Wikipedia with links to their website, but people who own or are employed by the business cannot add content.

Yelp can be scary for business owners, but your business should be on it. Someone in your business should monitor it and respond to the reviews. Yelp wants the company CEO or "someone important" in the business to provide the responses.

Some interesting facts about social media: [21]

- Ninety-three percent of buying decisions are now influenced by social media.
- Facebook is the most used platform with the largest demographic (70 percent of the U.S. public is on Facebook). They are loyal; half don't use other social media.
- The LinkedIn participation age was recently lowered to thirteen.
- Currently, the leading demographic on Twitter is grandparents.
- One in three marriages now begin online.
- The average *adult* attention span is seven seconds (think of the im-

pact that has on social media marketing).

Trend Two: Reputation Management. There's no question that word of mouth is an effective marketing tool. In fact, more than one study has demonstrated that word of mouth among consumers "is a more important source of information than print advertising, television advertising, marketing events, and media appearances." [22]

It works both ways, however—negative word-of-mouth messages are also quite powerful and can seriously affect an organization's reputation. Reputation management contributes to and helps to maintain an organization's *positive* reputation online and in other media, and it is a growing focus for marketing specialists.

For example, social media expert Kathy Yanke advises businesses to respond immediately to negative reviews. She suggests interacting positively with the person who listed the review and that you should fix whatever problem the person complained about as soon as possible. Then ask the person to change the number of stars he or she gave you or to delete the bad review.

Yanke says that you cannot delete reviews on Facebook unless you can prove that it's a disgruntled former employee or that the review comes from a fake profile. That's difficult, but not impossible. Who does fake business reviews? Typically, former employees and competitors. She further stresses the importance of being aware of and managing your company's social media reviews.[23]

Content is king.
— Bill Gates, 1996

Trend Three: Content Marketing. Bill Gates' 1996 definition of content as "king" is quite broad,[24] but the focus has narrowed somewhat since then. Today, what marketers mean when they talk about content is *storytelling.* Ann Handley, who wrote *Everybody Writes: Your Go-To Guide to Creating Ridiculously Good Content,* argues that "Our online words are our emissaries," making it important to "write with honest empathy for our customers . . . and tell a true story really, really well."[25]

You'll find examples of great content on LinkedIn in the form of user-posted articles and on Twitter, where magazines such as *Harvard Business Review*, *Inc.*, and *Forbes* post links to their articles (content) several times every day.

Handley's book is a how-to for business professionals who want to write better so they can create better online content. She asserts that everyone can learn to write and that everyone should, because it's *good* content that gets noticed, and because as businesspeople we have no choice but to promote the organizations through which we earn our living.[26]

Trend Four: Influencer Marketing. Influencer marketing is a relatively new phenomenon that is in reality an extension of word-of-mouth advertising; it's new enough that virtually no empirical research has been done on the topic.

However, research from marketing and business media leaders, including Forbes, Hootsuite, the Native Advertising Institute, Hubspot, Adweek, and Neilson indicates that influencer marketing is on the rise and that it works. Social media is the preferred channel, with Facebook and Instagram leading the way followed closely by Snapchat, Twitter, and YouTube. Marketers are also effectively employing influencer marketing in blog content.[27]

According to the marketing agency Mediakix, influencer marketing is "now one of the fastest growing categories in advertising and projected to be a $5–10 billion market by 2020." On Instagram alone, brands are now spending more than $1 billion per year on influencer marketing.[28] This rise in influencer marketing hit major cable and broadcast news channels in 2017 when singer/actress Selena Gomez posted a photo of herself on social media drinking a Coke with the name of her new song on the label.

But it's not just about celebrities. Markerly, a network that connects brands with influencers, recently found that partnering with micro-influencers can provide much better return on investment than working with big celebrities. They examined 800,000 Instagram users and discovered that influencers with 10,000 to 100,000 followers offer the best results in terms of reach and engagement.[29]

An Adweek survey showed that the top benefits of influencer marketing are "creating authentic content about brand (87%), driving engagement around brand (77%), and driving traffic to websites or landing pages (56%)."[30]

The marketing agency Tapinfluence says that influencer marketing can lead to increased sales. They provided an example of an influencer campaign in which thirty-nine bloggers created content "around a technology product . . . with a coupon. Within the first 24 hours, the first blog post generated 140,000 hits to the brand's URL, 5,000 shares on Facebook, and a 139% sales lift over the daily average."[31]

Of course, to use influencers, you have to pay them, so this option only works well for companies with a large enough marketing budget.

Trend Five: Social Enterprise. When you create a business on a philanthropic model or connect an existing business to a charity in order to promote both, you are using what is now known as "social enterprise."

California created a new business entity in 2012, which allows businesses "with a conscience" to have a dual purpose; some other states have done the same. Most corporations, by law, must create value for their shareholders; a benefit corporation, also known as a "B corp," allows these entities to also have another focus that benefits society.[32]

A prime example of this type of corporation is Ben & Jerry's, the ice cream company. According to the *Huffington Post*, "Ben & Jerry's has pursued the goal of linked prosperity in a number of ways. The company has been active in the fair-trade movement, worked with local dairy farms to find economically and environmentally sustainable practices, and even pioneered the use of new, energy-efficient freezer technology in the U.S."[33]

Although the social enterprise business model may not always be thought of as "marketing," per se, those companies who practice it certainly do not hide the fact that they are doing good; in fact, typically they highlight it on their websites, social media, and other marketing channels.

Two examples of this are TOMS Shoes and Subaru. TOMS Shoes was launched with its "One for One" business model (for each pair of shoes purchased TOMS gives a pair to a person in need); it has since expanded its giving to include "sight, water, safe birth and bullying prevention services."[34] Subaru also employs social enterprise by partnering with the American Society for the Prevention of Cruelty to Animals (ASPCA) to encourage pet adoption. Both companies showcase their social enterprise on their websites.[35]

The bottom line is that social enterprise benefits both the charitable organization and the businesses involved and appeals both to consumers' emotions and their need for meaningful, self-actualizing purchasing experiences.[36]

Ultimately, marketing is all about listening.
You want to be the equivalent of a good friend.
— Lynda Resnick (a.k.a. the POM Queen)
in *Rubies in the Orchard* [37]

Does Shoestring Marketing Work?

For leaders of businesses and nonprofits who need to do their marketing on a "shoestring budget," the short answer to the question of whether it can work is yes. It works, but the flip side is that you have to work hard at it. In other words, no matter who does your marketing, that person has to be willing to put in the time needed to develop a plan and then implement it.

The good news is that there are many ways of employing no-cost and low-cost marketing. Websites are inexpensive and relatively easy to set up with user-friendly tools (Google "free websites for business" and you'll see results like "twenty free website builders").

Social media is also free, but using the free tools means it takes more time to build an audience than if you have money to spend. In-person networking is another way to market your business at a lower cost.

Because marketing covers such a wide array of vehicles, marketing professionals must stay abreast of the latest marketing trends and channels. Owners of small businesses, independent business professionals, and nonprofit leaders can learn about marketing practices and trends by reading and researching on an ongoing basis.

Fortunately, because marketers are so good at self-promotion, there is no lack of content about what constitutes the latest best practices in marketing—a simple internet search will easily lead you to the information you need.

Dr. Deborah A. Jackson attained a PsyD with an emphasis in Organizational Management and Consulting at Phillips Graduate University (now the Phillips Education Center for Campbellsville University) in Chatsworth, California. She earned a BA in English from the University of Washington in Seattle, and after moving to Los Angeles, took a full array of journalism courses at Los Angeles Pierce College to further improve her editing and writing skills.

Dr. Jackson has worked as a freelance editor, writer, and ghostwriter, and over the years has created and edited marketing content for many business professionals, small businesses, and nonprofit organizations. She once again resides in the Pacific Northwest. Her next goal is to fulfill a lifelong ambition to write a novel.

NOTES

[1] Levinson, J. C. (2007). *Guerrilla marketing.* New York, NY: Houghton Mifflin.
[2] Influence & Co. (n.d.) *White paper: The 4-step guide to exceptional content marketing,* 1–9. Retrieved from https://www.influenceandco.com/services; Rokka, J., Karlsson, K., & Tienari, J. (2014). Balancing acts: Managing employees and reputation in social media. *Journal of Marketing Management, 30*(7–8), 802–827.
[3] Bureau of Labor Statistics, U.S. Department of Labor. (2015, December 17a). *Occupational outlook handbook, 2016–17 ed.: Advertising, promotions, and marketing managers.* Retrieved from http://www.bls.gov/ooh/management/advertising-promotions-and-marketing-managers.htm
[4] Kim, K. (2017, April 5). Personal communication with the author.
[5] Conley, C. (2007). *Peak: How great companies get their mojo from Maslow.* San Francisco, CA: Jossey-Bass.
[6] Ibid.
[7] Rokka et al., Balancing acts: Managing employees and reputation in social media; Helm, S. (2013). A matter of reputation and pride: Associations between perceived external reputation, pride in membership, job satisfaction and turnover intentions. *British Journal of Management, 24*, 542–556.
[8] Kline Henley, T. (2001). Integrated marketing communications for local nonprofit organizations: Developing an integrated marketing communications strategy. In Donald R. Self, Walter W. Wymer, Jr., & Teri Kline Henley (Eds.), *Integrated marketing communications for local nonprofit organizations* (pp. 141–155). Philadelphia, PA: Best Business Books.
[9] Ibid.
[10] Vital Design. (n.d.) Marketing template [Web log]. Retrieved from https://vtldesign.com/digital-marketing/digital-marketing-strategy/how-to-write-marketing-plan-template/
[11] Kline Henley, Integrated marketing communications for local nonprofit organizations.
[12] Ibid.
[13] Chapleo, C. (2015). Brand 'infrastructure' in nonprofit organizations: Challenges to successful brand building? *Journal of Marketing Communications, 21*(3).
[14] Ibid.
[15] Fleming, J. (2017, June 27). Facebook reaches 2 billion users. *Los Angeles Times.* Retrieved from http://www.latimes.com/business/la-fi-tn-facebook-hate-speech-20170627-story.html
[16] Yanke, K. (2017, January). *Social media marketing.* National Seminars Training/Skillpath Conference, Pasadena, CA.
[17] Waters, R. D., & Jones, P. J. (2011). Using video to build an organization's identity and brand: A content analysis of nonprofit organizations' YouTube videos. *Journal of Nonprofit & Public Sector Marketing, 23.*
[18] watchauburn. (2017, February 17). Auburn mayor Nancy Backus can't stop the feeling [Video file]. Retrieved from: https://www.youtube.com/watch?v=WgW4_RtwQc4
[19] Yanke, *Social media marketing.*
[20] Casey, A. (n.d.). Ten reasons why you should used Linkedin. [Web log]. Retrieved from http://maxmarketing.co.nz/10-reasons-why-you-should-use-linkedin/
[21] Ibid.

[22] Lang, B., & Lawson, R. (2013). Dissecting word-of-mouth's effectiveness and how to use it as a proconsumer tool. *Journal of Nonprofit & Public Sector Marketing, 25*, 374–399.
[23] Yanke, *Social media marketing.*
[24] Ria. (2017). Nearly two decades ago, Bill Gates declared "CONTENT IS KING"! [Web log]. Retrieved from https://www.silkstream.net/blog/2014/07/content-is-king-bill-gates-1996.html
[25] Handley, A. (2014). *Everybody writes: Your go-to guide to creating ridiculously good content.* Hoboken, NJ: Wiley.
[26] Ibid.
[27] Frost, A. (2017, June 14). Does influencer marketing actually work? A HubSpot blog experiment [Web log]. Retrieved from https://blog.hubspot.com/marketing/does-influencer-marketing-actually-work
[28] Mediakix. (2017, May 5). Instagram influencer marketing is a $1 billion dollar industry [Web log]. Retrieved from http://mediakix.com/2017/03/instagram-influencer-marketing-industry-size-how-big/#gs.QMXKMT4
[29] Medley, E. (2017, May 2). How to do influencer marketing campaigns that really work: Influencer marketing has taken on an entirely new meaning, and it promises to be the marketing buzzword in 2017 and beyond [Web log]. Retrieved from https://blog.hootsuite.com/influencer-marketing/
[30] Heine, C. (2016, December 1). 8 new stats about whether influencer marketing campaigns actually work: Brand practitioners weigh in [Web log]. Retrieved from http://www.adweek.com/digital/8-new-stats-about-whether-influencer-marketing-campaigns-actually-work-174868/
[31] Tapinfluence.com. (n.d.). Influencer marketing STATS [Web log]. Retrieved from https://www.tapinfluence.com/influencer-marketing-statistics/
[32] Baker, M. (2013, July 22). California benefit corporations [Web log]. Retrieved from http://www.nonprofitlawblog.com/california-benefit-corporations/
[33] Brussel, J. V. (2012, October 23). Ben & Jerry's Becomes B-Corp Certified, Adds Credibility To Impact Investing Movement. *HuffPost, U.S. Edition.* Retrieved from https://www.huffingtonpost.com/2012/10/23/ben-and-jerrys-b-corp-impact-investing_n_2005315.html
[34] TOMS. (2016). Improving lives [Web page]. Retrieved from: http://www.toms.com/improving-lives
[35] American Society for the Prevention of Cruelty to Animals (ASPCA). (2016). Subaru strategic cause partnerships [Web page]. Retrieved from http://www.aspca.org/about-us/strategic-cause-partnerships/subaru
[36] Claffey, E., & Brady, M. (2014). A model of consumer engagement in a virtual customer environment. *Journal of Customer Behaviour, 13*(4), 325–346.
[37] Resnick, L. (2009). *Rubies in the orchard.* New York, NY: Doubleday.

Images:

Pyramid image by jbmacros67 on Pixabay.

Social Media image by Gerd Altmann on Pixabay.

THIRTEEN

PRACTICAL TACTICS FOR THE FUTURE OF BUSINESS

by Margaret Easter, PsyD

Dr. Easter provides an overview of the future of technology in the workplace . . . with quite a few kernels of truth and wisdom—and a big dash of humor.

Robotics. Automation. Artificial intelligence (AI). These are just a few of the buzzwords you hear about the future of organizations and the future of work. Some believe that robots are already taking their jobs and that there will be no jobs in the future, at least not for humans.

Others believe that this new technology will create new jobs, jobs that have never existed before. Still others are harnessing this new technology and disrupting industries by creating new ways of doing business. Regardless of how you view the future, the truth is: *the future is already here.*

For years, scholars, thought leaders, and futurists have propagandized about the coming technological future and about how technology will improve our lives by making things go faster, doing things for us, and improving our lives.

Television shows like *Star Trek* and *The Jetsons* have shown us gadgets and devices that made life with technology look good, easy, and enhanced. Movies like *Transformers* and *Pacific Rim* have shown us super robots that could protect us and fight our enemies for us, while others like *Wall·E* and *Star Wars* have shown us what it would be like to live in space, should we humans destroy this planet and be forced to live elsewhere.

Video games are even preparing us for a technological future by allowing us to experience virtual reality and virtual worlds. In fact, some industries and the government are now using gaming for training simulations for their employees or for the armed forces.

Give Them What They Want; Let Them Enjoy It While They Can

Before we get into specifics about the future of technology, let's look at the future of the workforce. For years, employees have been the bane of an employer's existence. While companies need employees to do the work that needs to be done, managers often hate dealing with employee issues. Today's workers want more time off, more flexibility, and more pay. And because of a booming economy, it looks like employees are finally getting what they want: more time to goof off, more flexible work options, and high salaries.

The Employee Experience: The Demanding Girlfriend. Today, employees want a workplace where they can choose where they work, how they work, and when. They want open-concept offices, shared work spaces, espresso machines, full-course meals, ongoing training, longer vacations, maternity and paternity leave, movies at work, and the option to bring Fido or Fifi to the office.

They're overwhelmed and want more a relaxing, simplified work environment.[1] And whereas sleeping on the job at one time in workplace history was pooh-poohed, today employees have nap spaces and creative relaxation lounges to catch up on that much-needed rest they may not get enough of due to long hours at work.

Companies that fail to offer potential new hires these things and more are being ignored and overlooked in favor of employers who are willing to jump through hoops to get them.

Right now, organizations see this new "employee experience" expectation as a talent recruitment strategy to woo qualified people away from competitors. For now, it seems to be working. More and more potential new hires are asking for what they want, and they're getting it. They have employers jumping to the proverbial snap of their fingers.

However, this new talent should beware, as it won't be long before—just like the bloom of a new romance—the affection begins to wear off and employers begin to feel like the boyfriend being over-manipulated by the proverbial self-centered girlfriend. When that happens, it isn't long before the boyfriend begins to take interest in the new, easygoing girl.

The Flexible Employee: The Bored Wife. Some employees want even more flexibility in how they work, when they work, and where. In fact, flexibility is more important to this worker than pay. Flexibility trumps a high salary any day. They want to be employed, but with the option to go *where* they want, *when* they want, and do *what* they want when they do so.

They're like the stereotypical young wife married to an older husband. She'll do what he wants as long as he gives her money to spend as she pleases and with whom she pleases. She's bored but likes the money and security that being married to an older man provides.

The Gig Economy Worker: The Ex. These employees have divorced their employer and chucked the nine-to-five for self-employment as an independent contractor, because they see it as an opportunity to have more control over their work life and income. The potential to make more money and choose the type and duration of projects on which to work is what this type of worker desires most. This is your free agent, freelancer, your "can't-tie-me-down" type.

No longer are these workers willing to wait on someone to give them what they want; they have chosen to create what they want and go after it instead. Estimates are that the gig economy worker will represent more than

40 percent of the workforce in 2020.[2]

So Then, Replace Them

But just at the very point when employees are feeling like they're in control with their so-called "employee experience" and demands for flexible work options, employers are getting tired of the games and are busy coming up with creative ways to cut the biggest expense affecting their bottom line: their employees. And what better way to do that than with the new easygoing and submissive romantic attraction: automation?

Automation: The Dream Girl! Automation will do everything employers ask of it, when they want it done, and without all the hassle that employees have been giving them for eons. Automation doesn't require the things humans require. It doesn't need open concept offices, shared work spaces, espresso machines, full-course meals, ongoing training, longer vacations, maternity or paternity leave, movies at work, and the option to bring Fido or Fifi to the office just to feel good about working.

It doesn't even need you to pay it a salary or benefits. All it needs is some programming and occasional monitoring, and it's ready to go. It's like the Ronco rotisserie oven: You just set it and forget it![3]

Employers have grown tired of employee manipulation and have finally found what they believe they've been searching for all their lives. In fact, they're so excited, they've even asked for automation's hand in marriage. Automation has accepted their proposal and is already walking down the aisle. Is this true love at last?

Robotics: Automation's Child. If automation were a mother, then her child would be robotics. Robots don't get sick. Robots don't need vacations or family leave time. Robots don't need lunch or bathroom breaks. Robots don't need paychecks and benefits. Like the Energizer Bunny, they just keep going and going and going.

A few years ago, outsourcing (or offshoring) was the real threat to American jobs. Today, it's robotics.

Major corporations, looking for ways to cut labor costs or reduce their overhead, once sent many of their jobs overseas or contracted out whole departments that were not a core part of their businesses. Today, corporations view robotics as the answer to cutting real costs.

Proof of this shift can be seen in daily news reports about major corporations that are laying off thousands of employees because their jobs have been replaced by some form of technology.[4]

According to PricewaterhouseCoopers (PwC), in 1997 there were only 700,000 robots in the workplace; two years ago that number had exploded to 1.8 million. According to their estimates, the number of robots in use in the workplace currently is about 2.9 million.[5]

Unmanned Autonomous Vehicles. Employers are so excited by their new-found love with automation that they're practically throwing money at anything that automation can do.

For example, automation can drive vehicles, from drones to cargo trucks to self-driving cars.[6] Now, with the availability of drones, you don't need to hire more than one security guard to keep watch over your business.

Automation can take your food order at a restaurant, send it to the cook in the kitchen, take your electronic payment, and ensure your food is delivered to you promptly without using an employee. Just use an application on your mobile device or take your hot meal from a vending machine.

Automation can save you time by letting you shop online, guaranteeing two-day delivery, or allow you to self-checkout at the supermarket, thereby avoiding long lines in check stands that are supported by a cashier.[7]

Automation will even help you travel more safely and efficiently using sensors and communications systems that track the movement and speed of vehicles, ultimately connecting to intelligent self-driving vehicles in the very near future, likely in the next five to seven years.

Then, You'll Be Replaced

No Jobs or New Jobs. With the promise of everything that automa-

tion can do, who needs employees? Why invest in something that is never satisfied and is always finding something wrong with the workplace or the employer? Why invest in someone who will trade you in or swap you out for another place willing to jump through even more hoops when you can no longer (or simply refuse) to give it more?

Why, you could just take those extra dollars—the ones that were formerly being spent on employees and their needs and wants—and invest more of them into automation.

On the other hand, perhaps those dollars employers will invest in automation will yield new and different jobs, gigs perhaps, currently unknown to us this time, but that will enable employees to work easier and better. Even if more jobs aren't created, employers will certainly be happier.

Yet what some industry leaders see as an improvement, others see as their doom.[8]

Artificial Intelligence: Automation's Big Brother. You may be wondering, "How does it know what to do, what we want, and how we want it? How does it know how to please me?"

Where is automation getting all of its data? It's getting it from us! That's because automation has already given us something we can take wherever we go: a mobile device. We call it the smartphone. In fact, it's so smart it listens to everything we say, every text we send or receive, and responds to every request we make. And it's connected to the internet, a.k.a. the World Wide Web.

What we fail to realize is that every breath we take and every move we make is being watched by automation's Big Brother, artificial intelligence. Let's call him **Art** for short. Art wants to know and learn everything he can so that at the precise moment when your guard is down, he can just walk right in and take over your organization—and your leadership position.

The Internet of Things (IoT) in the Workplace. In fact, Art (a.k.a. Artificial Intelligence) is so smart that everything that automation shares with him just makes him smarter and stronger. Thanks to industry investment and innovation, Art is in almost every device that has a chip inside it and is connected to the internet. And he is well-connected.

Art knows so much he can now assist workers with all their work-related questions. He has reduced the amount of time it takes to find information that, in previous eras, would have taken days or months to figure out. Now, what used to take what seemed like forever only takes a few minutes at most, or a few seconds at least.

You, the employer, like Art a lot. Art is so sharp that your staff goes to him for advice before they come to you. In fact, he gives better answers and in a politer tone. He's happy to respond to their requests and then immediately gets out of their way, thereby eliminating the feeling that they're being micromanaged.

You, the employer, feel like since you brought Art into the office, your manager and staff appear a lot happier, are more productive, and you've even increased your revenue.[9] You can now take even more breaks, leave the office earlier, and maybe play a game of golf. You invest more money in Art, because you like how Art takes control.

You're Not the Boss of Me! I'm the Boss of You! Artificial Intelligence and the Alternative Organization of the Future

AI is in Control. You arrive at the office a little later than usual, now that Art is assisting you by giving directions to your staff on their projects. They don't really need you. When they're done working on a project, they just open their mobile app and ask Art, "What's next?"

In fact, when you arrive at the office, even you begin to ask, "What's next?" Then, when you attend a board meeting—which the board of directors demanded you attend—you're surprised at their announcement that Art is now a member of the board of directors. That's because the board now relies on Art to make critical business decisions, develop strategic plans, and direct your every move.

You suddenly realize that you let the enemy in when you were so busy falling in love with automation.

Alternative Organizational Structures. While there has been much discussion recently about new, sometimes experimental, organizational structures being implemented by various organizations, these alternative structures are actually very well aligned with Art (Artificial Intelligence).

The result is that because of Art, your organization doesn't need managers anymore. As a business leader, you're already aware that disintermediation occurred in the supply chain some time ago; because of Art it has now occurred in the workplace. No longer are managers needed to direct the activities of a department or team or to report on the status of an ongoing project or on your company's sales figures.

Art has already done that for you, and he's reported any discrepancies.

Because of Art, the structure of the organization has changed too. Employees feel like they can self-direct their work. There are fewer employees now as well, because Art has automated the processes of many jobs into one.

Holacratic and starfish organizational structures enable the employees—those few who remain—to work without managerial direction. In fact, there are no more managers in the new organization, because they are now obsolete.

The New Realities. There are other new realities on the horizon as well. Virtual reality enables the user to experience an environment that's not real, though it looks real. This is excellent for training and development in that it allows users to learn from experience, causing them to feel as if they really are in another environment.

Then there's augmented reality, which allows users to experience their current and real environment in a new way by overlaying it with artificial, yet realistic, images.

And *Star Wars* has come to life as holographic imagery enables individuals to send a 4-D image of themselves as if they were right in the space with you.

These new realities in the workplace will enable Art to train you better by virtually giving you a real-life experience and by providing elements in your workspace that alter your current environment.

Further, by projecting a humanlike image of himself, Art makes it easier for the human mind to accept him as an equal.

Artificial Intelligence: Your New CEO. If you can imagine all of this as a possibility, then you can see how easy it was for the employer to be seduced by automation, thereby clearing the way for Art to come into the organization to take it over. At the pace that we're going, sometime in the near future organizations will exist that are completely run by artificial intelligence—with Art fully in place at the helm.

Artificial Intelligence: Your Future Business Consultant. In fact, Art will gather so much more data from us, as we just keep freely giving it up, that he will become the organizational management consultant of the future.

Just as employees were the first to adopt this runaway technology, then whole boards of directors, it would not be surprising to see Art compile all the best business data in the world and take the premier business best practices and then provide answers to even the most difficult-to-solve business problems.

No longer will organizational management consultants, or any consultants for that matter, be needed to help organizational leaders or business teams solve their most pressing problems.

So Then, What Should You Do?

Run!

Dr. Margaret Easter holds a Doctorate in Psychology with an emphasis in Organizational Management and Consulting from Phillips Graduate University. She also graduated from California State University, Long Beach (CSULB) with a BA in Sociology. Her career experience includes sales, marketing, and business development. She has worked in biotechnology, commercial real estate, and in a business consulting firm as a marketing communications manager and business development administrator.

She is passionate about her family and improving the quality of life for others, not only at an individual level but also viewing the family as part of other systems within the community and the corporate world.

She specializes in business consulting in organizational change management and strategic planning and development.

Editor's Note: We acknowledge that it is possible that someone may be offended by the use of stereotypes in this chapter. It is our hope that readers will recognize the humorous intent of these words and see them exactly as that—exaggerations and stereotypes—and that they'll be able to laugh, or at least smile, at Dr. Easter's tongue-in-cheek descriptions of the "dangers" of automation and artificial intelligence.

NOTES

[1] Agarwal, D., van Berkel, A., & Rea, B. (2015, February 27). Simplification of work. Retrieved from https://dupress.deloitte.com/dup-us-en/focus/human-capital-trends/2015/work-simplification-human-capital-trends-2015.html

[2] Deloitte. (2016). Global human capital trends 2016. Deloitte University Press.

[3] Wikipedia. (2017, December 4). Automation: Recent and emerging applications. Retrieved from https://en.wikipedia.org/wiki/Automation#Recent_and_emerging_applications

[4] Daily Job Cuts. (2017). Daily job cuts. Retrieved from http://dailyjobcuts.com/

[5] PricewaterhouseCoopers. (2017, December 8). Managing man and machine. Retrieved from https://www.pwc.com/gx/en/ceo-agenda/ceosurvey/2017/gx/talent.html

[6] CARJAM TV. (2015, January 16). Mercedes self-driving truck driving itself: Mercedes future truck 2025 commercial. Retrieved from https://youtu.be/XZxZC0lgOlc

[7] Wikipedia. (2017, December 2). Ron Popeil. Retrieved from https://en.wikipedia.org/wiki/Ron_Popeil

[8] Kline, D. B. (2017, December 7). Here's how Americans feel about robots taking their jobs. Retrieved from https://www.fool.com/careers/2017/12/07/heres-how-americans-feel-about-robots-taking-their.aspx

[9] Johnson, K. (2017, November 30). Amazon launches Alexa for business platform, bringing voice services to the office. Retrieved from https://venturebeat.com/2017/11/30/amazon-launches-alexa-for-business-platform-bringing-voice-services-to-the-office/

Images:

Industry 4.0 image by Gerd Altmann on Pixabay.
Robot Calculator image by 849356 on Pixabay.
Drone image by Lars Nissen on Pixabay.
AI Globe image by Gerd Altmann on Pixabay.
Running Robot image by Janson_G on Pixabay.

In God We Trust. All others bring data.
— W. Edwards Deming, Engineer, Management Consultant

If a business is underperforming, then the assumptions are wrong.
— Fritz Shoemaker, Author of *ChEQmate*

When everything is a priority, nothing is a priority.
— Karen Martin, Business Consultant

The most dangerous kind of waste is the waste we do not recognize.
— Shigeo Shingo, Quality Control Specialist

If you define the problem correctly, you almost have the solution.
— Steve Jobs, Co-Founder of Apple, Inc.

PART FOUR

PEOPLE PRACTICS IN PROCESS IMPROVEMENT

FOURTEEN

PRACTICAL TACTICS FOR PROCESS IMPROVEMENT

by Greg Hilsenrath, PsyD

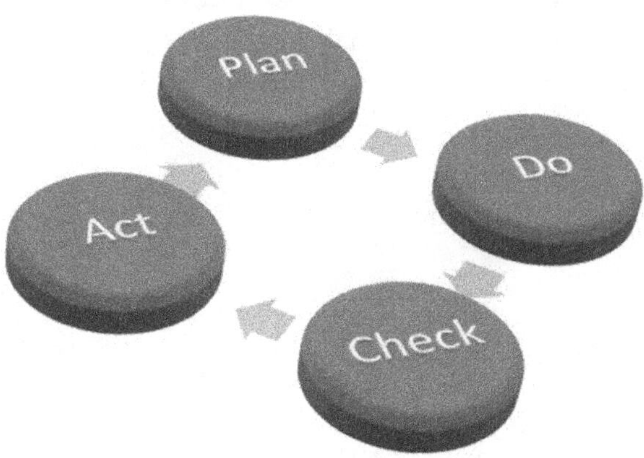

Process improvement concepts are now used in all types of organizations to improve all aspects of business operations, including productivity, quality, cycle time, and safety as well as optimizing financial and operational health.[1]

The roots of process improvement strategy can be traced back to the beginning of industrial engineering. Streamlining factory processes to increase productivity is one of the earliest efforts in organizational improvement.[2]

In 1911, Frederick Taylor wrote *The Principles of Scientific Management*,[3] and some of his ideas spurred modern-day business philosophies. Then, in 1950, W. Edwards Deming refined and publicized statistical process control, which became prominent in business concepts, such as the Plan-Do-Check-Act (PDCA) Cycle. Deming documented his theories in his book, *Out of the Crisis.*[4]

In 1989, Shigeo Shingo wrote *A Study of the Toyota Production System from an Industrial Engineering Viewpoint.*[5] Shingo, a renowned expert on improving the manufacturing process, was instrumental in designing the method the Toyota production system still uses today.[6]

The Organizational Process

A correctly implemented organizational process should result in a work environment in which all team members are aware of their responsibilities. Organizing the unified parts to get them to act in harmony—effectively and efficiently in order to achieve goals—is what author and business consultant Robert Hutcherson calls organizational optimization.[7]

But the organization of ideas and resources must be thoroughly vetted in order to be considered a functional process. This involves assigning tasks to individuals, determining what work is needed in order to accomplish a goal, and positioning those individuals in a high-functioning decision-making framework.

One way of structuring the organizational process is via the Five "Ds" shown below.

1. **Design: Review tactics and goals.** Leaders must first review the process and continue to evaluate as objectives change. Then, build the process to attain goals successfully and design specific activities to complete specific objectives.

2. **Departmentalize: Distribute job activities into manageable parts.** A manager can distribute specific job activities based on four models of departmentalization: functional, geographical, product, and customer.

3. **Delegate: Allocate activities.** Leaders should assign defined work activities to specific workers. Give each employee the authority to carry out their assigned tasks. In other words, delegate authority.

4. **Determine Purpose: Motivate.** Create a path for all employee expectations in order to achieve organizational objectives.

5. **Direction: Chain of Command.** Structure your organization's hierarchy in terms of horizontal (coordinating) and vertical (decision-making) relationships and diagram it.[8]

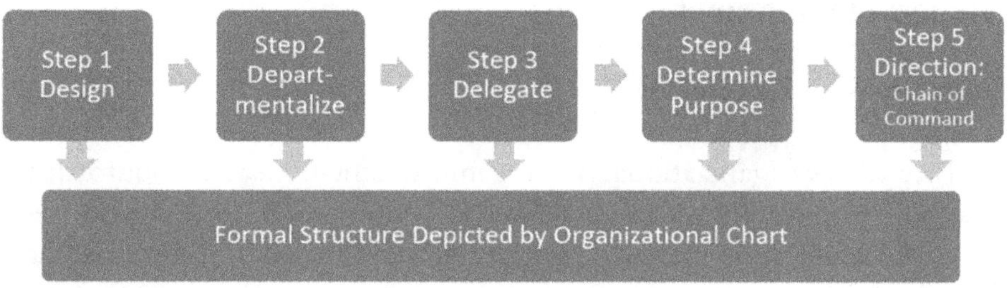

The Customer Is (Always?) Right

As you're considering process improvement, keep in mind that quality is challenging to achieve and that customers' expectations are always changing. To define what a quality product is, leaders must know what's most important to their customers and keep updating that knowledge over time. In other words, product excellence is what the customer says it is.

For example, automobile customers tend to vary on the features they want in a car. The vehicle and its features should feel unique to the customer, especially when the price is a significant factor in their decision to buy. Delivering what the target customer wants requires a concentrated effort among product design, marketing, operations, and production.

All Hands On Deck—Including the Leaders

It's also vital to remember that to improve organizational processes, participation by everyone across the organization is critical for success. That is, participation is essential for any quality improvement project.

One reason is that it's the everyday worker who is often the first to recognize regressions that contribute to poor quality. It is the frontline workers who are best resource for identifying and implementing improvements. Yet maximizing the potential of your line workers requires that they are educated and well-trained in the entire process, not just their specific job.

That means upper management support is critical, since implementing an improvement project will require substantial resources and support for those resources.

Here's another important thought: **Management must be willing to endure a probable short-term productivity decrease for the sake of long-term improvement**.

From Ideas to Execution

Today, new organizational process improvement ideas are put forth frequently. For example, through intelligent observation, leaders may see a more efficient way to maneuver paper through the office. They may have ideas about how to meet growing customer requirements or how to accomplish more within the same budget.

What to do with these observations and how to create ultimate efficiency and productivity becomes the challenge that separates true leaders and innovators from ordinary managers and owners.

Great ideas might come to leaders while in a meeting, during discussions at the water cooler, or in the middle of an assignment. Leaders will often jot down an idea to save it for a more appropriate time.

Leaders know that the best way to improve organizational processes is not to create difficulties, and this begins with leadership accountability and execution. A leader must first define the operational improvement challenge.[9] The challenge is likely something the business has dealt with for some time, so it's critical to gather and delineate every detail.

For example, when work is taking too long, it's important to discover which step in the process is slowing down the cycle or to figure out which piece is the cause of the problem. Yet that's only the beginning; leaders must also clearly define success. To do this, they must shift their focus away from who is accountable for deficiencies to how the *process* is creating inefficiency.

Quality guru W. Edwards Deming once stated, "Workers are responsible for 15 percent of the problems; the other 85 percent is the sys-tem, and the management is responsible for the system."[10] By "system," Deming meant the organizational *process*. Workers can only perform as well as the process allows them to.

In other words, process improvement starts with a change in focus:

EMPLOYEE FOCUS (Traditional Thinking)	PROCESS FOCUS (Innovative Thinking)
Who?	How?
Doing my job.	Getting things done.
Knowing my job.	Knowing the process.
Motivate.	Removing barriers.
Measure the workers.	Measure the process.

Improving the Value Stream

Next, leaders should consider the *value stream*, which is used to define, organize, and realize business objectives and to deliver product more rapidly. The value stream represents a series of steps that an organization uses to design solutions that provide a constant influx of value to the customer.[11]

Improve the value stream by creating a Value Stream Map (VSM), which is used to design processes and products before they are built. Furthermore, by using a value stream to create safety and order in the environment, leaders can recognize where waste happens.

The process for the value stream environment is to sort, straighten, scrub, standardize, and systematize while eliminating any unsafe conditions. This process is known specifically as "5S+."[12] After the VSM is operational, leaders will then identify areas for improvement. Below is an example of a VSM demonstrating the current state of a process and several potential areas for improvement:

Sample Value Stream Map

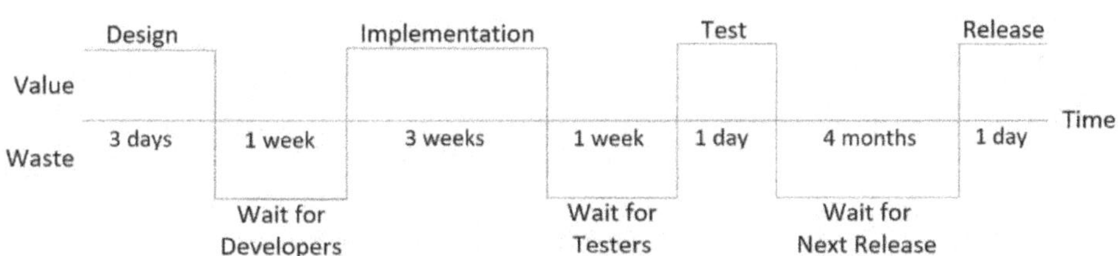

Lean

One of the most well-known process improvement models is Lean, which is designed to maximize customer value while minimizing waste. Lean is a customer-focused methodology that continuously improves any process by eliminating waste. Lean concepts consist of "continuous incremental improvement" and "respect for people." Simply stated, Lean methodologies create more value for customers with fewer resources.[13]

According to the Lean Enterprise Institute, "Lean applies to every business and every process. It is not a cost reduction or a specific program, but a way of thinking and acting for an entire organization. Minimizing waste throughout the value stream, instead of removing isolated points, creates a process that needs less capital, less space, less human effort, and less time to make products and services at much lower cost with far fewer defects than traditional business systems."[14] Using Lean, organizations can respond more efficiently to changing customer needs while maintaining high quality and low costs with faster production times.

Kaizen, a PDCA Cycle of Lean

Another way to improve processes is through *kaizen*, a Japanese philosophy that focuses on continuous improvement throughout all aspects of life. This belief system came from two Japanese characters: *kai*, meaning "change" and *zen*, meaning "continuous improvement."[15]

According to Lean experts Natalie Sayer and Bruce Williams, "The goal of *kaizen* is to eliminate waste in the value stream."[16] The working structure (or system) for executing kaizen is the Lean PDCA Cycle, which stands for:

Plan – Create a method for a change by first identifying what you want to change. Define the steps necessary to make the change and then predict the results of the change.

Do – Execute the plan in a beta or test environment on a small scale, under controlled conditions.

Check (or Study) – Scrutinize your trial run, verify the process improvement, then consider going live. No improvement? Repeat.

Act – Implement the changes you've verified on a broader scale and update your standard operating procedures.[17]

The Toyota Way

The Toyota process improvement methodology is also based on *kaizen*. Kaizen and its descendants, including Total Quality Management (also knowns as TQM, which focuses on employee commitment to high standards of quality) and Six Sigma (which is discussed below), are all systems for improving quality through a process-improvement approach.

Kaizen provides a new way to look at quality and focuses on the changing of organizational culture in order to achieve continuous improvement. Adding a focus on cultural change allows for maximum improvement.[18]

Gemba

For businesses to sustain a Lean organization, leaders must be different. One way this happens is that they lead from *Gemba* (also *Genba*), a Japanese word for "the real place." Japanese detectives call the crime scene *Gemba*, and Japanese reporters say they are reporting "from Gemba." In the business world, Gemba is where the value happens. In manufacturing specifically, Gemba is the factory floor where production materializes. The only way to accurately understand what is happening is to go to the place, the Gemba, where what's happening occurs.

Once there, leaders apply a process known as "3Gen" or the "Three Actuals":

- ***Genchi*** – (Like *Gemba*) Go to the actual place.
- ***Genbutsu*** – Observe the actual product, process or service.
- ***Genjitsu*** – Gather the facts.[19]

Six Sigma (6σ)

Another famous process improvement model is Six Sigma, which seeks to improve the quality of your company's product by identifying and getting rid of the source of any defects and by reducing variability in the process of manufacturing it.[20]

The principles of Six Sigma originated in 1986 with engineer Bill Smith, who incorporated its principles while working at Motorola.[21] In 1995, Jack Welch made it his business strategy at General Electric.[22] The term Six

Sigma (6σ) comes from a statistical model of the manufacturing process, which is given a *sigma* rating indicating the percentage of products it can create without defects.

A Six Sigma process is one that has a 99.99966% (3.4 per million) result based on all opportunities in the construction of a final product or part. The 99.99966% result is considered "statistically free" of defects. Motorola set the standard at "six sigma" for all its operations, and this goal then became a standard across many management and engineering practices.[23]

Each Six Sigma project follows a specific sequence of steps and has a particular end value in mind. For example, you may want to increase profits or customer satisfaction or reduce costs, cycle time, or even pollution.

In order to accomplish the Six Sigma type of process improvement, teams employ five steps, known as **DMAIC**: Define, Measure, Analyze, Improve, and Control:

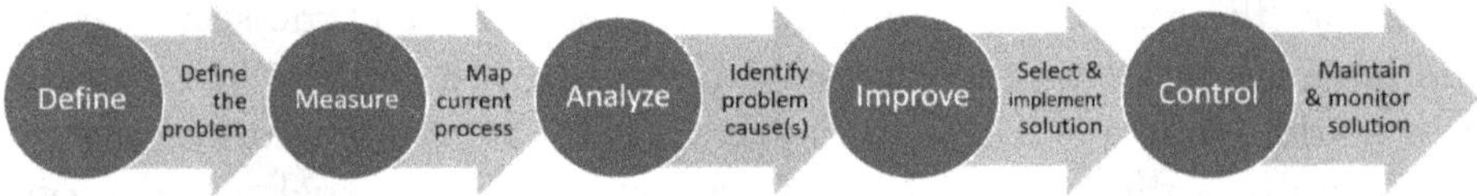

Lean Six Sigma

The business world has had an ongoing debate as to which is more effective when streamlining business processes and eliminating waste: Lean or Six Sigma. Both sides have advocates and critics who can cite situations in which one method yielded better results. Yet whoever is correct, experts agree that the best streamlining process, creating the most effective and efficient business structures, requires integrating Six Sigma and Lean principles.[24]

Most executives can quickly point out necessary improvements to their organization, yet they are often still unable to enhance productivity and profitability. This mishandling often occurs because they don't manage development systematically. Simply stated, without a system-wide strategy that includes planning, implementation, and support, continuous improvement initiatives are destined to plateau and eventually fail.

Continuous Process Improvement. Six Sigma improves the quality of operations and provides for efficient output by removing the causes of errors and inconsistency within a business process. Lean allows business procedures to be effective and efficient while decreasing cycle times and improving customer-minded production.

Using the Lean and Six Sigma approaches together will improve business process flow and increase speed via the precise and detailed gathering and analysis of data. Organizational innovators emphasize the idea that excellence links to the speed of the system and agree that even the most trivial opportunity for process improvement must be detected and acted upon. Doing so enables organizations to reach their maximum level of performance.

Any organization can achieve operational excellence under the following conditions:

- All business processes and workflow can be *defined*, are *measurable*, and can be *analyzed*, *improved*, and *controlled.*

- Competitive-advantage and process-improvement initiatives are *sustainable* and require company-wide *commitment* to the solution.[25]

Reducing Waste

A dictionary.com definition of "waste" is: "useless consumption or expenditure; use without adequate return." However, when referring to waste, Lean practitioners use the Japanese term *muda.*

Waste elimination is vital to effective business processes, though it's not always visible given the varying scope of logistics. Moreover, more than 80 percent of work takes place outside the view of supervision, further implying that precise, yet robust processes are important to all aspects of management.[26] (A useful tool that can help identify waste in a process is the value stream map.)

Taiichi Ohno, the author of *Toyota Production System*,[27] identified seven types of waste in manufacturing: Overproduction, Inventory, Over Processing, Correction, Waiting, Conveyance, and Motion.

These dimensions of waste can be more easily remembered by using the acronym **DOWNTIME** (which adds an eighth type to Ohno's seven):

1. **Defects** (Correction). One aspect of waste is doing things again that were not done right the first time. Quality can always be improved if the focus is on the source and when mistakes are not

passed down the supply chain.

2. **Overproduction.** Waste also happens when more is produced than the market demands. Lean focuses on building "*takt* time" (German for "the beat of the customer") in order to avoid overproduction.[28]

3. **Waiting.** Waste exists in lost time, in waiting for people, materials, customer orders, processes, and anything else that results in time wasted in delivering a product efficiently to customers.

4. **Not Utilizing Talent.** Waste happens when leaders fail to engage team members effectively or fail to share best practices and work collaboratively.

5. **Transportation** (Conveyance). Waste in transportation is defined in terms of conveying more than what is required, poor factory layout with underutilized equipment, or the movement of products from one location to another without good reason.

6. **Inventory.** This type of waste occurs when carrying more inventory than what is required to deliver such as through overproduction, forecasting errors, long lead times, and batch thinking.

7. **Movement** (Motion). Motion that does not add value to the process or to the desired result is considered waste, including employees walking around and searching for materials or tools.

8. **Excessive Processing** (Over Processing). Producing more than what is required to meet customer needs.

Operational Excellence

Author Andrew Miller states in his best seller, *Redefining Operational Excellence: New Strategies for Maximizing Performance and Profits Across the Organization* that "Operational excellence is the relentless pursuit of finding ways to improve performance and profitability."[29]

Operational excellence is the execution of business strategies that are more consistent and more reliable, with more output than the competition. Operational Excellence proves true through results. Examining two companies that have the same approach, the Operationally Excellent company will have lower operational risks, lower operating costs, and higher profit margins relative to its competitors, while creating value for customers and shareholders. Operational Excellence can also be thought of as "execution excellence."

Some interpretations of this leadership philosophy are based on earlier continuous improvement approaches, such as Lean or Six Sigma. Yet Operational Excellence goes beyond the traditional event-based model of improvement by seeking long-term changes in organizational culture.

Operational excellence innovators do two things significantly different than other companies.

1. They manage their business and operational processes systematically and invest in developing the right culture.

2. They focus on meeting customer expectations via the continuous improvement of operational processes and by improving organizational culture.[30]

Focus on the Fundamentals

"He began with the most elemental of statements: 'Gentlemen!' he said, holding a pigskin high in his right hand, 'this is a football.' "[31]

Legendary football coach Vince Lombardi started each season with the basics, believing that "fundamentals win championships."[32] This same philosophy applies to process improvement strategies in your organization: always review the fundamentals.

David Maraniss tells a story in his best-selling book, *When Pride Still Mattered: A Life of Vince Lombardi*, about when Lombardi entered training camp in 1961.[33] He was coaching professional football players who, just months prior, had come within minutes of winning the biggest prize their sport could offer. And yet he started the season from the very first page of the football playbook.

Lombardi's coverage of the fundamentals continued throughout camp. Each player revisited something they had been doing since they were kids, reviewing how to block and tackle. They opened the playbook and started from scratch. One player joked, "Uh, Coach, you're going too fast for us." Lombardi cracked a smile, and he merely continued with the basics. In 1962, the Green Bay Packers beat the New York Giants 37–0 to win the NFL Championship. The team became one of the best of all time—by starting with the basics.[34]

The Continuously Improving Organization

In this chapter, we have discovered that innovative leaders and ultra-efficient companies can be empowered by Lean Six Sigma as well as Kaizen, VSM, the 5Ds, PDCA, Gemba, Muda, and DOWNTIME as they reach for continuous process improvement and waste reduction. When these strategies are used in combination, the results are lean solutions that help the entire organization become more effective and efficient, leading ultimately to Operational Effectiveness.

But success also depends on authentic communication, an eye toward relationships, and a deep understanding of the power structure within your organization. Managerial processes involve tough choices about how to incorporate stakeholders—getting them to buy-in, commit, and have intrinsic motivation as the organization moves forward. Employees are essential to organizational success, and they must be valued before your company can thrive.

Improving your organizational processes while at the same time valuing your workers will have an invaluable positive effect on your organization. A precise, concise, Lean Six Sigma operation with buy-in will enhance just about any organization's ability to become as effective and as efficient as possible. The goal is Operational Excellence, which means getting the most from your organization and for all your valued employees and customers.

Dr. Greg Hilsenrath holds a Doctorate in Psychology with an emphasis in Organizational Management and Consulting from Phillips Graduate University in Chatsworth, California. He also earned an undergraduate degree in Economics from the University of Maryland. He has more than twenty years of sales and consulting experience in a career focused primarily on federal government contractors and their efficiency in selling to federal agencies. He has led unique, challenging, and exciting projects for hundreds of federal employees with the objective of implementing new technology.

Yet he moved to California to help young adults dealing with addiction, stuck in undesirable situations, and unsatisfied with their lives. He has worked with young adults and teens struggling with low self-esteem, poor physical condition, and lack of life education. He has also examined the relationships between insurance companies, government, and the trillion-dollar substance abuse industry with the hope of improving the rehabilitation process and lessening the epidemic of substance abuse.

Dr. Hilsenrath considers himself a "compassionate life strategist." He has spoken at seminars and conferences on behalf of the federal government about ways to improve efficiency and manage change. His passion is to find the most efficient, least expensive way to fix and solve problems and show growth in every person and project.

NOTES

[1] Seethamraju, R., & Marjanovic, O. (2009). Role of process knowledge in business process improvement methodology: A case study. *Business Process Management Journal, 15*(6), 920–936.
[2] Milakovich, M. E. (1991). Total quality management in the public sector. *National Productivity Review, 10*(2), 195–213.
[3] Taylor, F. W. (1911.) *The principles of scientific management.* New York, NY: Harper & Brothers.
[4] Deming, W. E. (2000). *Out of the crisis* (Reprint ed.). Cambridge, MA: The MIT Press.
[5] Shingo, S. (1989). *A study of the Toyota production system from an industrial engineering viewpoint.* New York, NY: Productivity Press.
[6] Monden, Y. (2011). *Toyota production system: an integrated approach to just-in-time.* Abingdon-on-Thames, UK: Productivity Press.
[7] Hutcherson, R. (2014). *Organizational optimization.* Bloomington, IN. Author House.
[8] Pride, W. M., Hughes, R. J., & Kapoor, J. R. (2012). *Introduction to business.* Boston, MA: Cengage.
[9] Basadur, M. (2004). Leading others to think innovatively together: Creative leadership. *The Leadership Quarterly, 15*(1), 103–121.
[10] Anderson, M. A., Anderson, E. J., & Parker, G. (n.d.) How to ensure quality in your operations management. Retrieved from https://www.dummies.com/business/operations-management/how-to-ensure-quality-in-your-operations-management/
[11] SAFe. (n.d.) Value streams. Retrieved from https://www.scaledagileframework.com/value-streams/
[12] Sayer, N. J., & Williams, B. (n.d.). Using Lean to define and improve the value stream. Retrieved from https://www.dummies.com/business/human-resources/workplace/using-lean-to-define-and-improve-the-value-stream/
[13] Sassanelli, C., Pezzotta, G., Rossi, M., Terzi, S., & Cavalieri, S. (2015). Towards a lean product service systems (PSS) design: State of the art, opportunities and challenges. *Procedia CIRP, 30,* 191–196.
[14] Lean Enterprise Institute. (n.d.) What is lean? Retrieved from https://www.lean.org/WhatsLean/
[15] Alukal, G. (2007). Lean kaizen in the 21st century. *Quality progress, 40*(8), 69.
[16] Sayer, N. J., & Williams, B. (2012). *Lean for dummies* (2nd ed.) Hoboken, NJ: For Dummies.
[17] Alukal, Lean kaizen in the 21st century.
[18] Ibid.
[19] Abed, A. M. (2015). Create Heijunka 5's matrix to control the dynamic gemba as lean tool. *Journal of Human Resource Management, 3*(2), 6–16.
[20] Ibid.
[21] iSixSigma Editorial. (n.d.) Remembering Bill Smith, father of Six Sigma. Retrieved from https://www.isixsigma.com/new-to-six-sigma/history/remembering-bill-smith-father-six-sigma/
[22] Watson, G. H. (n.d.) Cycles of learning: Observations of Jack Welch. Retrieved from http://asq.org/pub/sixsigma/past/vol1_issue1/cycles.html

[23] Koch, P. N., Yang, R. J., & Gu, L. (2004). Design for six sigma through robust optimization. *Structural and Multidisciplinary Optimization, 26*(3–4), 235–248.
[24] Crabtree, R. Shillingburg, C., Artzberger, B., Scheer, K., Goodman, D., Dubinsky, D., . . . Stewart, M. (2011). *Driving operational excellence: Successful lean six sigma secrets to improve the bottom line.* Pennsauken, NJ: BookBaby.
[25] Ibid.
[26] Abdi, F., Shavarini, S. K., Hoseini, S., & Mohammad, S. (2006). Glean lean: How to use lean approach in service industries? *Journal of Services Research, 6*, 191–206.
[27] Ohno, T. (1988). *Toyota production system: Beyond large-scale production.* New York, NY: Productivity Press.
[28] Aggarwal, P. (2010, August 31). What is Takt time? Retrieved from https://www.processexcellencenetwork.com/lean-six-sigma-business-performance/articles/what-is-takt-time
[29] Miller, A. (2014). *Redefining operational excellence: New strategies for maximizing performance and profits across the organization.* New York, NY: AMACOM.
[30] Jaeger, A., Matyas, K., & Sihn, W. (2014). Development of an assessment framework for operations excellence (OsE), based on the paradigm change in operational excellence (OE). *Procedia CIRP, 17*, 487–492.
[31] John, A. S. (2013). *Newton's football: The science behind America's game.* New York, NY: Ballantine Books.
[32] Ibid.
[33] Maraniss, D. (2000). *When pride still mattered: A life of Vince Lombardi.* New York, NY: Simon & Schuster.
[34] Williams, P. (2015). *Vince Lombardi on leadership: Life lessons from a five-time NFL championship coach.* Charleston, SC: Advantage Media Group.

Image:
Football image by Capri23auto on Pixabay.

FIFTEEN

PRACTICAL TACTICS FOR BUILDING SUCCESSFUL TEAMS

by Ramila Naziri, PsyD

Why include two chapters on teams in a section on process improvement? Because improving processes in your organization begins by first building a team that will successfully discover and carry out process tasks. Your team then needs to maintain its peak performance, which means being able to resolve team conflicts quickly and effectively.

The moment has come to build—and keep—your team and make it stronger than ever. Search "how to build a team" using Google, and you get about 55 million results. Perhaps that's because organizational leaders today face multiple difficulties in building effective teams.

The following is a list comprising the basic theoretical framework for building a winning team:[1]

- **Relevance of the work team.** What happens within a work team has great significance for feelings of satisfaction and competence.

- **Acceptance onto the team.** Most individuals wish to be accepted onto a team and to interact with great cooperation on all sides.

- **Need for delegation by the leader.** Delegation is a necessity, as leaders cannot perform all the functions of the team.

- **Need for openness in team operations**. Feelings and attitudes that are suppressed are likely to affect individual problem solving, personal growth, and job satisfaction.

- **Need for trust, support, and cooperation.** Research shows that levels of interpersonal trust, support, and cooperation are much lower than expected on most teams.

- **Solutions in work teams are transactional**. All members of the team must alter their work habits and relationships in order to create effective solutions within the team.

- **Team building is a continual process.** Team building is an on-going process, not a product.

Throughout this chapter, we will explore the foundations of building a cohesive team, from its psychological history to defining key steps. Keep in mind the common themes as you use these principles to build your own successful team: **LEADERSHIP**, **GOALS**, **DIVERSITY**, and **TRUST**.

Humans Are Hardwired to Be Social

Harvard scholar Robert D. Putnam's work *Bowling Alone: America's Declining Social Capital* ties into building successful teams. He defines two kinds of social capital: bonding capital and bridging capital:[2]

Bonding occurs in group formations of individuals who are alike in age, race, religion, and other similar characteristics. In organizations, it is those individuals who work in the same department, share the same lunch table, and so on.

Bridging occurs when individuals are not like each other, also known as "outsiders."

Putnam discovered that these two kinds of social capital strengthen each other. Similar research by U.S. Army Lt. Col. Chris Ellis also determined that new leaders benefit from the bridging kind of social capital, which they should use until there is acceptance and understanding within the bonds created.[3] In creating bridging between team members, leaders should also communicate and model policies for how team members should be treated. Furthermore, leaders who emphasize and protect the social bonds within their organizations earn the trust of their employees.

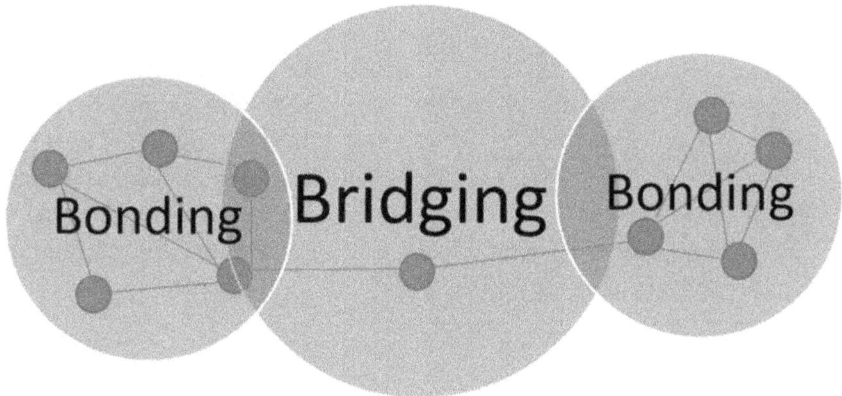

The Rewards of Conformity

Looking into the psychological history of team dynamics confirms that some types of team building can be negative or even dangerous. For example, in 1963 Stanley Milgram designed an experiment to explain the Nazi killings in World War II. The setup included a teacher (the participant), a student (the actor), and an experimenter (the authority figure).

The aim was to determine how far an individual would go in obeying an instruction even if it involved harming another person. The "teacher" asked the "student" a question, and if the student answered incorrectly, the teacher administered an electric shock. What Milgram's experiment proved is that individuals yield to perceived authority; 65 percent of participants administered deadly levels of shock upon the order of the "authority" in the setup.[4]

How does this tie into teams in organizations? Ellis concluded that Milgram's experiment spoke to the power of leadership, meaning that leaders should indicate what proper behavior is by setting standards. Milgram's experiment showed that standards set by leaders are often followed, even if they override the moral structures within the team.[5]

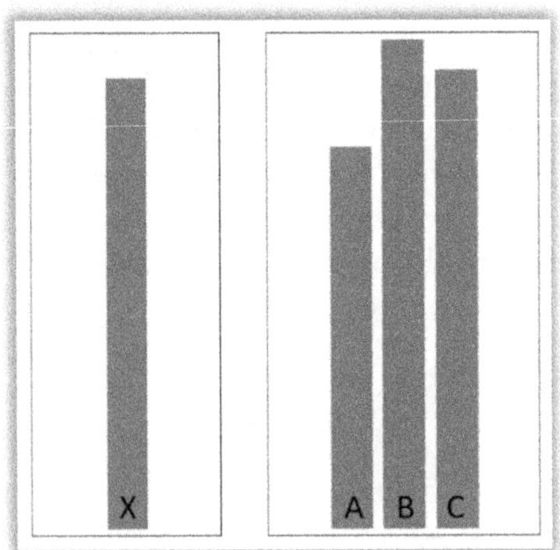

Another experiment tested conformity inside of a classroom. Solomon Asch presented images of vertical lines and asked the class which line was most like line X.

In the room, actors were mixed in with participants. When many of the actors gave the wrong answer (as they had been instructted), the participants began conforming to the group, even when they knew the answer was wrong.[6]

The reality is that team dynamics often reward conformity as a way of hindering feelings of retaliation, ostracism, and the fear of failing the leader or the rest of the team.

LEADERSHIP

Having a strong leader in a team is ideal for success.[7] As we saw in Milgram's 1963 experiment, leaders have direct effects on individuals within a team. According to Robert Katz's Skills-based Leadership Theory, there are three skills that anyone can learn to enhance their leadership abilities: technical, human, and conceptual.[8]

Technical Skills. Leaders who understand the methods, processes, procedures, and techniques of their industry or organization will excel at being a successful team leader. This increases trust among members of the team who feel they can look up to their leader, because they know that person understands their jobs and can provide adequate information in solving specific problems.

Human Skills. These skills are the most difficult to acquire. Essentially, having human skills means understanding and practicing emotional intelligence (EQ)—and EQ can enhance the human skills on your team.

Other aspects of human skills include the ability to empathize, listen to conflicting points of view, and create an atmosphere of approval in which the other team members can feel a sense of security. Human skills also pertain to the ability to motivate employees and keep them focused on the organization's mission and vision.

Conceptual Skills. These skills are the most difficult to learn and at the same time are the most essential to being an effective leader. Conceptual skills include the ability to strategize, plan, visualize, and set goals with your team. An effective way to obtain these skills is through attending goal-setting seminars and training.

Upon mastering each of these leadership skills, a leader must also learn to balance their use. Using one skill at the expense of another can lead a team into failure.

The Three Cs of Effective Leadership

Businessman Dennis Lejeck's three Cs of effective leadership is one method leaders can use to build cohesion within a company. His formula is: Communication + Collaboration = Cohesion.[9]

Communication. Communication skills are part of those human skills that are essential to being an effective leader, and effective communication is also key to team productivity.[10] According to Lejeck, electronic communication must be minimized, as it can impede full understanding of the message being sent.[11]

Forms of communication include verbal and nonverbal. For example, asking the right questions (verbal communication) can decrease misunderstandings between team members.

Examples of nonverbal cues include facial expressions, hand motions, body posture, and movements. Leaders should match their nonverbal cues to their words. When they do, they are more likely to be perceived as believable and trustworthy.[12]

Collaboration. The decision-making process is more worthwhile when leaders include other members of the team. According to business consultant Leo Denise, collaboration is about using information to create something new. It is with collaboration that communication thrives and therefore develops the team into a cohesive unit. With team collaboration, teams can solve problems, develop new understandings, and design new products.[13]

Cohesion. The final of the three Cs is cohesion. Cohesion is only possible if communication and collaboration are present. The foundation of a cohesive work team is trust, which will be discussed later in the chapter. Cohesiveness occurs when team members stick together and remain united throughout the pursuit of a common goal.[14]

GOALS

The most important of the steps to building a successful team is assuming that all members of the team share a common goal, or mission. The next step is to align your team to their mission and vision.

Author and consultant Lawler Kang's strategy for creating alignment with the team goal includes asking potential team members to look back at their life experiences and talk about which one they are most fond of.[15] The leader then asks them to connect those experiences with the core mission of the team. Through these open discussions, the leader is able to create alignment among the team members with the mission and vision of the team.

DIVERSITY

The best teams are composed of diverse individuals who bring a variety of perspectives and cognitive approaches to the task at hand.[16] Diversity, in this case, is defined as "individuals with differing genders, ages, cultures, capabilities, and experiences."[17]

As discussed earlier, bringing together a diverse group is a challenge; it means aligning the different perspectives and motivations of individual team members. Furthermore, diverse teams are composed of various personality types, which can be assessed with various instruments, such as Myers-Briggs and DISC. Yet strong leaders capitalize on these differences with a make-it-happen attitude that draws on the strengths of each individual's inputs.[18]

A study by NPR suggests that diversity in the workplace can ultimately lead to better organizational results.[19] Those positive results are, in fact, derived from the different perspectives, points of views, and backgrounds brought into the team and organization.

It's also important to increase cognitive diversity within a team because it helps teams avoid a singular groupthink approach, which often occurs when group members are similar.[20] One way to support team diversity is by training them in cross-cultural communication, conflict resolution, and multicultural team dynamics.[21]

TRUST

Strong leadership and common goals are two of the requisites for developing trust between individuals in a team, and motivation in teams increases when mutual trust and respect are established between team members and their leader.[22]

Trust is particularly difficult to obtain in diverse teams, especially when communication styles can vary across cultures.

Here are five tips leaders can follow to build trust between their team members:[23]

1. **Structure the team for success.** This includes having a clear and compelling direction and goals for the team. Members should also have access to the information and resources needed to accomplish team goals. And leaders should practice cultural and emotional intelligence in order to support the team.

2. **Understand the cross-cultural makeup of your team.** Leaders must be able to understand the different cultures, language differences, and issues within the team, including the potential for miscommunication.

3. **Set clear norms and stick to them.** Norms and expectations set a consistent structure and common ground in your team culture. These are best agreed to while in the process of setting common goals.

4. **Find ways to build personal bonds.** Depending on the culture, norms vary regarding relationship building in teams. Strong leaders must create an environment in which these connections can form. Leaders can create personal bonds through social events, pairing introverts with extroverts, or directly facilitating introductory activities, known as "icebreakers" that introduce team members to one another.

5. **When conflicts arise, address them immediately.** Conflict management is an important skill for strong leaders. The communication style employed when addressing these conflicts is just as important. This ability can turn a conflict into a group discussion or cause a leader to choose to address an individual confidentially instead of in front of the group.

Understanding Team Development

Once you have collected a group of people together in a room and have given them a task to accomplish, what happens to them as they move out of just-a-bunch-of-people status and into a team ready to work together?

Psychologist Bruce Tuckman's classic description of the four stages of teaming is one way of understanding how teams develop over time.[24] Tuckman's model is specifically helpful for leaders interested in process improvement in their organizations, since understanding effective team formation is essential prior to starting any process change initiative—but it also works for any type of team formation.

Stage One: Forming. At this point, your team is likely to be positive and polite—and either anxious or excited about their upcoming task. In

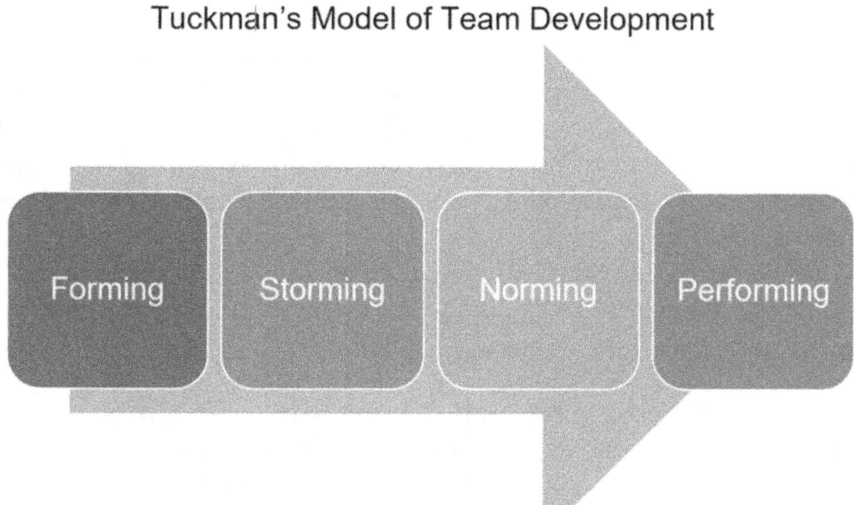

this stage the leader must be more involved. As discussed earlier, this is where it's important to get buy-in from your team members. You have a couple of jobs as a team leader in this stage: to get people to "enroll in the goal," i.e., understand and accept the team's mission, and to clearly define the team members' roles and responsibilities.

It's also important to build trust in this stage. That doesn't happen through team-building exercises—no icebreaker activity or "trust fall" will create lasting trust. It takes time. What builds trust is follow-through, which means your people know they can count on you.

Keep in mind that this stage can sometimes be lengthy. It takes time for people to get to know one another and to determine how they'll work together.[25]

Stage Two: Storming. If your team is going to fail, it will usually happen in this stage. This is the time when people are differentiating themselves from the other team members. Who's going to be the one who keeps everyone on task, the idea generator, the class clown?

Storming often happens as a result of differences in peoples' natural working styles. This is the time when people tend to bump heads, so leaders need to help the team members work through any conflict. That's why you set up the mission in stage one—leaders need to keep reminding the team what they're there to accomplish.[26]

Stage Three: Norming. In this stage, you as the manager need to let go and trust the team to get to know one another and do their work. In this stage, team members begin to resolve their differences, appreciate their coworkers' abilities, and respect you as a leader.

Because the team knows one another better, they feel comfortable enough to ask for help and give constructive feedback. They tend to develop a stronger commitment to the team goal, and the team makes good progress toward achieving it.

There is often an extended overlap between stages two and three, because as new tasks arise or if members come and go, the team may move from norming back into storming behavior.[27]

Stage Four: Performing. At this point the team has synergy; being on the team and doing the work is easier. If someone new joins or a team member leaves, performance isn't disrupted. Members often feel excited about participating on the team, there's little friction, and hard work leads to achievement of the team's goal. As the leader in this stage, you can concentrate less on managing and primarily on developing team members.[28]

Some teams—especially those that are project-related—experience a fifth stage: **Adjourning**. It's exactly what it sounds like—a time for saying goodbye.[29]

Team-Building Strategies

Now that you have read about the steps that can help you develop a successful team, it's time to discuss specific team-building strategies you can use to promote team effectiveness. Team building has significant benefits.[30] The following is a list of some of them:

- Improves morale and leadership skills
- Removes barriers to creative thinking
- Improves organizational productivity
- Identifies the team's strengths and weaknesses
- Improves the ability to problem-solve
- Promotes an active and healthy lifestyle

Here are some additional strategies leaders can use as they build a strong team:[31]

- ✓ **The power is in the planning.** Defining objectives and providing an atmosphere that invites open dialogue can encourage creative thinking, brain storming, and collaboration.
- ✓ **Education and skill development.** Considering the needs of the team is important in order to develop and maintain needed skills. About three-fourths of employees will at some time seek out opportunities for career growth, so strong leaders look out for signs of those needs.
- ✓ **Communication and problem solving**. Communication is key to solving problems within teams, enhancing teamwork, and improving emotional intelligence.
- ✓ **Self-reflection brings growth.** Facilitated group discussions can enhance emotional intelligence, intra-team relationships, skill development, productivity, and teamwork as well as reduce team conflict.
- ✓ **Gamification.** Simulations that create a fun and educational experiences can also drive engagement, reflection, understanding, and team cohesiveness.

Never forget that it is strong **LEADERSHIP**, common **GOALS**, **DIVERSITY** within the team, and mutual **TRUST** that are the key factors to building a cohesive team.

Remember also that team building is a continual process, not a product. Team building activities maintain the strengths and minimize the weaknesses of the team. Plus, as a leader, it's important to build up your leadership and team-building skills through adequate training.

Finally, it's important to recognize that leadership is about *who* you are being rather than *what* you are doing. Remember that, and you're more likely to develop successful teams.

Dr. Ramila Naziri earned a Doctorate in Psychology with an emphasis in Organizational Management and Consulting from Phillips Graduate University and a Bachelor of Arts in Psychology from the University of California, Riverside. She has worked as a behavioral therapist for children with behavioral and developmental disorders.

Dr. Naziri has always found the intermixing of psychology and business fascinating. Her business consulting focus is in personal and professional development coaching with emphasis in business start-ups, business planning, and bringing visions to life.

Dr. Deborah Jackson contributed to this chapter.

NOTES

[1] Sackton, F. (1993). How to build a winning team. *Armed Forces Comptroller, 38*(1), 26.
[2] Putnam, R. D. (2000). *Bowling alone: America's declining social capital.* New York, NY: Simon & Schuster.
[3] Ellis, C. (2017, December). Four insights to help build solid teams. *Army, 67*(12), 16–18.
[4] Ibid.
[5] Ibid.
[6] McLeod, S. (2018, December 28). Solomon Asch - Conformity Experiment. Retrieved from https://www.simplypsychology.org/asch-conformity.html
[7] Brox, J. (2015, Aug 31). *4 Essential characteristics of a successful team.* Retrieved from http://www.refreshleadership.com/index.php/2015/08/4-essential-characteristics-successful-team/
[8] Sackton, How to build a winning team.
[9] Lejeck, D. W. (2017, October). Team building: Without the three Cs you don't really have a team. *Smart Business Pittsburgh, 24*(5), 10.
[10] Ohler, L. (2004, March). Building effective teams in a high-tech world. *Progress in Transplantation, 14*(1), 7–8.
[11] Lejeck, Team building.
[12] Anthony, L. (2004). Effective communication & leadership. Retrieved from http://smallbusiness.chron.com/effective-communication-leadership-5090.html
[13] Denise, L. (2017). Collaboration vs. C-three (cooperation, coordination, and communication). *Innovating, 7*(3), 1–6.
[14] Molnau, D. (2013). *High-performance teams: Understanding team cohesiveness.* Retrieved from https://www.isixsigma.com/implementation/teams/high-performance-teams-understanding-team-cohesiveness/#comments
[15] Kang, L. (2012, May 11). How to bring passion and purpose to your executive job search. *Ivyexec.* Retrieved from https://www.slideshare.net/ivyexec/how-to-bring-passion-and-purpose-to-your-career-lawler-kang
[16] Santana, J. (2016, January/February). How to build a high-performing, diverse and inclusive super A-team. *Insight,* 54–55.
[17] Duggan, T. (2017). Examples of how diversity works within a group or a team. Retrieved from https://yourbusiness.azcentral.com/examples-diversity-works-within-group-team-21192.html
[18] Ohler, Building effective teams in a high-tech world.
[19] Vaccaro, A. (2014, March 25). Why diverse teams create better work. Retrieved from https://www.inc.com/adam-vaccaro/diversity-and-performance.html
[20] Santana, How to build a high-performing, diverse and inclusive super A-team.
[21] Lewis, B. J. (1999, September/October). How to build an effective management team. *Journal of Management in Engineering,* 5.
[22] Ohler, Building effective teams in a high-tech world.
[23] Molinsky, A., & Gundling, E. (2016, June 28). How to Build Trust on your Cross-Cultural Team. *Harvard Business Review,* 2–5.
[24] Tuckman, B. W. (1965). Developmental sequence in small groups. *Psychological Bulletin, 63*(6), 384–399.

[25] Mind Tools. (n.d.) Forming, storming, norming, and performing: Understanding the stages of team formation. Retrieved from https://www.mindtools.com/pages/article/newLDR_86.htm

[26] Ibid.

[27] Ibid.

[28] Tuckman, Developmental sequence in small groups.

[29] Mind Tools, Forming, storming, norming, and performing.

[30] d'ewes, D. (2016, June 9). Team-building for success. *Business Today*, 1–3.

[31] Keavney, A. (2016, April). Team building strategies. *Training & Development*, 26–28.

Images:

Team image by Gerd Altmann on Pixabay.
Puzzle image by Peggy and Marco Lachmann-Anke on Pixabay.
Team Cards image by Gerd Altmann on Pixabay.

SIXTEEN

PRACTICAL TACTICS FOR RESOLVING TEAM CONFLICT

by Raffi Islikaplan, PsyD

A few years ago, my mother and I went on a vacation to London to explore and sightsee. On our first night there, we ventured out to a pub for dinner and, deciding to "do what the Londoners do," we ordered fish-and-chips. About twenty minutes later, our waiter returned with a tray full of food and set down a plate of burgers and fries in front of each of us.

My mother and I looked at each other quizzically before turning to the waiter and mentioning that we had both ordered the fish-and-chips. Without missing a beat, the waiter replied, "No, you didn't."

This immediately sparked a conflict between my mother and our waiter. I, perhaps wisely, decided to excuse myself from the conversation. My mother argued that we would either be served our fish-and-chips, or we would leave the pub.

The waiter replied, "The food has already been made. I can't just take it back and throw it out. If we make you fish-and-chips, I'm going to charge you for both the burgers and the fish."

After a few more back-and-forth exchanges between my mother and our waiter, we left the pub without paying—and without dinner.

The reality is that conflict is inevitable. And it can pop up in the most unlikely of scenarios, just as it did in my fish-and-chips incident.

Can Conflict Ever Be Avoided?

My best friend's younger sister once asked me for advice about an issue she was having with her college dorm mate.

"How do I avoid having conflict with this person?"

My advice? "You could literally not say a single word and it could still be misconstrued into an argument. Conflict is inevitable; you just need to have the right tools and a cool head to manage yourself and assess the situation."

What Is Conflict and Why Does It Happen?

To properly assess conflict, lets first define it and ask ourselves, "Why does conflict exist?"

According to professors David H. Johnson and Frank P. Johnson in their book *Joining Together Group Therapy and Group Skills*, "Conflict is defined as a process that begins when an individual or a group perceives differences and oppositions between itself and another individual or group about interests, resources, beliefs, values, or practices that matter the most to them."[1]

In simpler terms, conflict is basically defined as ***having an opinion***.

There will always be someone somewhere that you interact with who has a different viewpoint. In an ideal world, human beings could have different opinions and respectfully acknowledge them. In reality, a difference of opinion typically means that *there will be conflict.*

This does not mean that the world has to end every time you run into someone who doesn't view things through the same lens as you do. This just means that understanding and operationalizing types of conflict, combined with the appropriate strategies to face them, can create a world of difference in your day-to-day life—in both your business and personal relationships.

Now that we have understood that conflict exists, what it is, and that it is always imminent, let's talk about the five types of conflict, which can also be thought of as five styles of managing (or reacting to) it. These styles are often used instinctively.

Styles of Dealing with Conflict

Compromising. Compromising could also be described as the "give-and-take" style of dealing with conflict. Both parties involved go back and forth between options in order to reach an agreement or a *compromise.*

In this situation, both parties ideally want to be "in the right," but either one or both can understand that neither will succeed unless there is give-and-take. Both parties end up giving up a piece of their initial argument in order to reach an agreement.

In the fish-and-chips scenario at the beginning of the chapter, my mother at one point tried to compromise with our waiter (albeit with a hell of an attitude). We were hungry and didn't want to go find another new restaurant on our first night in town. The waiter both didn't want to throw away the burgers that were already cooked and he did not want to have to get his manager involved. Therefore, we tried to compromise.

My mother said, "We'll eat the burgers, but we aren't going to pay for them."

Our waiter rebutted with, "My manager won't let me comp food, only drinks. I can comp your beers, but not your burgers."

At this point, those delicious burgers were taunting me, and I was so hungry I couldn't have cared less about the argument anymore. I would have happily eaten the burgers, but by that point my mother was out for blood. In the end, the compromise strategy did not pan out in our favor.[2]

Withdrawing. Withdrawing is also described as avoiding, as in "I just want to eat and not argue about fish anymore."

Withdrawing means removing yourself from a situation or conflict, or it could mean simply shutting down and letting the conflict pass. In this style of reacting to conflict, there really is no winner.

As I mentioned beforehand, being silent (withdrawing) will not make the problem disappear. Just as I told my best friend's sister regarding her conflict, you can literally not say anything and still come across as a conflict starter.

In the fish-and-chips debacle, I was so tired and hungry that I didn't have the energy or patience to fight with the waiter. I was willing and ready to accept defeat and eat the food given to me.

Needless to say, my mother had a different view.[3]

Problem-Solving. The problem-solving conflict style is basically a less threatening way of calling someone *confrontational.*

Ideally, this way of reacting to conflict creates a win-win situation, because the person who brings up the issue generally wants to clear the air and move forward.

Yet this means of handling conflict can easily be misconstrued as a threat because of the rather direct and forward approach many individuals take when employing it. In other words, some people have an issue with directness, which is a conflict within itself.

In the "Great Fish-and-Chips Debate of 2016," I was immediately caught off guard by our waiter's confrontational approach (which in turn caused me to withdraw from the conflict). He basically told my mother and me that we were lying when he asserted that we didn't order the fish-and-chips.

The waiter's next approach in this scenario (after my mother put her dukes up) was to problem-solve, but he went about it in the worst way possible.

I understood his intentions. He wasn't at liberty to make a decision without approval, was clearly afraid of the repercussions if he had to return our food to the kitchen, and he didn't want to involve additional staff or managers. In his head, he wanted all of us to win and be content, but what didn't work were his accusatory tone and sentiment—which turned a conflict into an argument.[4]

CONFLICT TIP #1: *NEVER accuse someone of something they may or may not have done. This triggers a fight-or-flight response and turns a conflict into an argument.*

Forcing. Forcing (as you may be able to tell from its name) is a conflict style that often does not go over well with people.

Forcing can also be referred to as competing, controlling, or dominating. This conflict style occurs when one person or group in a situation tries to win no matter what the circumstance, all while ignoring the other party's position or concerns.

Individuals who assume the forcing conflict style approach are likely inflexible and will not be satisfied unless all of their needs are met. Forcers often see situations as a "do or die" scenario and make snap judgments before considering all of their options (and consequences).

During "Fish-mageddon 2k16," our waiter immediately took a forceful stance in that the first thing that came out of his mouth when we told him we didn't order the burgers was, "No you didn't." He immediately prepared for a fight, and the only option was for him to win.[5]

Smoothing. Smoothing is also known as accommodating or obliging. In this approach, the smoother is willing to emphasize areas in which two parties agree and to downplay areas where they disagree. When applying smoothing, conflicts are not always solved; more often they're tabled for another time. Smoothers may sacrifice their own point of view for the betterment of the team or in order to move forward within the current situation, while creating as little tension as possible.[6]

Conflict within Teams

To help understand why conflict exists or what sparks it, let's view conflict from an organizational standpoint.[7] Whether inside or outside of the workplace, it has become human nature to compare ourselves to others. *Congrats! We have already created conflict!*

Working in an environment with other people can create a plethora of issues that affect us. I believe the following to be the top four reasons for why conflict is sparked in the workplace and what we can do to avoid and resolve it.

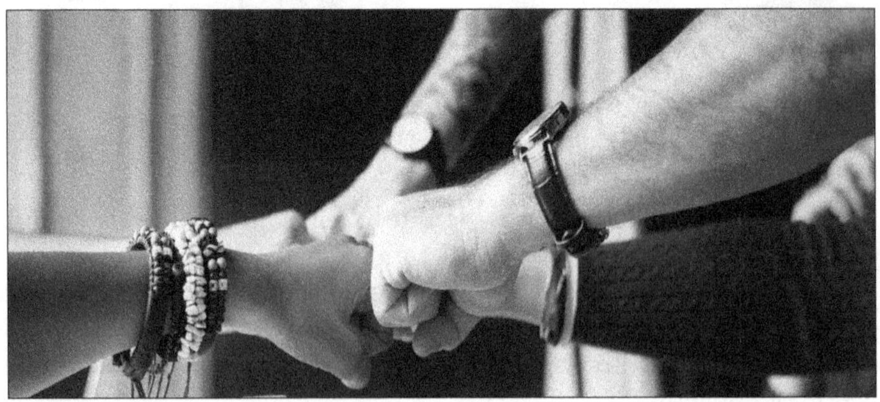

Conflict Over Position. Admit it; at one point in your life you've been envious of a person at work who just got promoted to the coveted corner office. You know in your heart that you're much more hardworking, dedicated, and have seniority, but apparently nobody else has noticed that. You're not alone here, but left to themselves, these emotions can begin to fester and hinder individual and team productivity. The best way to get out of this mindset is to be as upfront about the issue as possible.

CONFLICT TIP #2: *The only way to find an answer to a burning question is to ask it. Swallow your pride for a minute and be as genuine as possible with your supervisor. Maybe there is a valid reason why that other guy got the promotion and you didn't. Getting the answer you need could give you a new goal to work toward.*

Mistrust and Miscommunication. Uneven communication is a top concern in the workplace, yet it's important to keep in mind that *everybody communicates differently.* Some people instinctively dominate the conversation, while others fade into the background and listen. *It's natural.*

In organizations, communication can often be abused. For example, individuals often *don't even notice* that they're dominating the conversation. It's just in their nature to do so.

CONFLICT TIP #3: *If you feel like you're not being heard, a good strategy is to subtly point out that everyone else has had their chance to talk, and you'd like to get your two cents in. This way, colleagues who may have never valued your opinion can have another opportunity to notice your worth.*

Personality Clashes. I don't have to tell you that everybody is different. If personality styles and methods of operating in the workplace become a problem, take a leadership stance and assess how they work.

CONFLICT TIP #4: *If you're having a personality conflict with someone you're working with, have a conversation with him or her about the best way to be efficient. This way, if they tell you something like, "I just want to get from A to B without any interruptions," you can assess the answer and figure out how you can best fit that need into your work productivity. The same applies in reverse. You have the power to relay how you like to be efficient, which means you may be able to open the other person's eyes to a new perspective.*

Power Trips. What boss hasn't ever had a power trip? This is almost second nature when someone gets a promotion and is now the head honcho. Employees sometimes let their egos get the best of them, and all of a sudden they believe that they have the utmost power and control over you and the workplace. Unfortunately, there is not a great deal that can be done here, unless the situation gets out of hand.

CONFLICT TIP #5: *If you feel that your superior is truly stepping out of line, consider bringing the issue to the attention of his or her boss or your company's HR professional, though this must be done with careful consideration and tact. That person can then assess the best course of action to take. Never be afraid to speak your mind.*

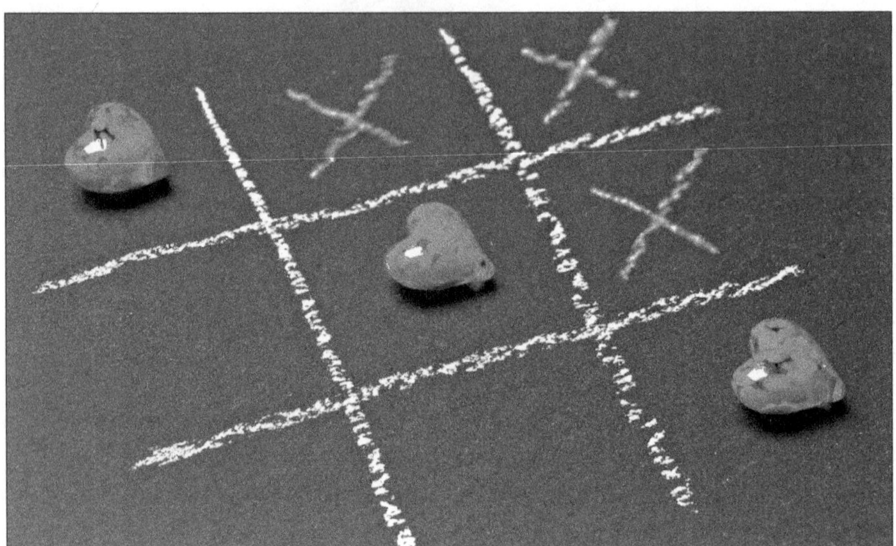

Conflict Strategies

By now you've become familiar with the different types of conflict, why conflict exists, and how it presents itself in an organization—and why I can never look at fish-and-chips the same way again.

What can you do with this information?

You can use it to your advantage. *Knowledge is power.* You now have the ability to accurately assess which conflict management strategy is best suited to your own scenario.

On the other hand, let's not underestimate the consequences if you choose to do nothing. Unmanaged conflict generally creates a lack of trust and loss of productivity in the workplace. The best course of action is to address it before it gets uncontrollable. Trust me—you'll thank yourself later.

Here are four conflict management strategies[8] that will help you get through most of the conflicts that inevitably will arise at work or at home:

Accommodating. Accommodating during a conflict essentially gives the opposing side what they want. This does not always have to mean accepting defeat. Instead, it signals that you value keeping the peace over driving your point home.

This style is best used when the issue is minor. In my mother's words, "Choose your battles." This particular issue may not be something you want to make a big deal about. A good tactic is to take note of minor conflicts to see if a pattern emerges in the future.

Avoiding. I know what you're thinking: *But you JUST told me that the best course of action is to address conflict before it gets uncontrollable!*

Hear me out. When I say avoid the conflict, I don't mean you should pretend it doesn't exist. In most cases, conflict arises because of tension or raised emotions. By delaying (or avoiding) the conflict for the time being, it gives both parties a chance to cool off and, later, to have a clearer understanding of the situation.

It's always a best practice to not try and resolve conflicts when emotions are high.

Collaborating. Collaborating with someone with whom you are having an issue can often be hard to wrap your head around, but doing so creates the ideal situation. With this strategy, both you and the other party can work together to find a solution that satisfies everyone's needs.

Collaborative decision-making requires a full understanding from both parties, so the best practice in this situation is to lay out all your cards and ask the other person to see things from your perspective. People who are willing to collaborate will relay the same information, and you can better understand where they're coming from as well.

Compromising. Earlier, we addressed compromising as a type of conflict, but now we're discussing compromising as a *strategy*. Typically, this strategy asks that both parties give up a piece of their argument for the sake of moving forward. The object of this game is to find a solution that is acceptable to everyone. It's the "meet me halfway" strategy.

This is the most prevalent of all the strategies, since the easiest course of action is to in a sense *haggle* with the other party until an agreement is reached. Consider it like a business contract. Addendums and amendments are always made before both parties sign off on a binding contract. The same goes (though it's unwritten) when compromising to resolve a conflict.

My hope is to have shed some light on what conflict is, where it stems from, and what you can do to resolve it. I have found these tips helpful in my everyday life.

Your biggest takeaway (and mine) should be to avoid starting an argument when your temper is high. As tempting as it may be, it seldom ever leads to a positive outcome. I try my best to remember that in my interactions with others.

Best of luck with your efforts at conflict resolution, my friend. Oh, and don't order the fish-and-chips!

Dr. Raffi Islikaplan earned a Doctorate in Psychology with an emphasis in Organizational Management and Consulting from Phillips Graduate University in Chatsworth, California. His undergraduate degree, also in Psychology, is from California State University, Northridge.

He has honed his leadership and organizational skills in a career focusing on market research development as well as customer-relationship management. As a business consultant he seeks to understand people's actions and behaviors on a professional level in to order to guide them to achieve the best version of themselves.

NOTES

---

[1] Johnson, D. W., & Johnson, F. P. (2013). *Joining together group theory and group skills*, 11th ed. Boston, MA: Pearson.
[2] Richards, F. (2011, July 10). *Recognizing common conflicts that can impede project progress.* Retrieved from http://www.brighthubpm.com/resource-management/95971-recognizing-common-conflicts-that-can-impede-project-progress/
[3] Ibid.
[4] Ibid.
[5] Ibid.
[6] Ibid.
[7] Witt, D. (2015, July 16). *4 Types of team conflict – and how to deal with each effectively.* Retrieved from https://leaderchat.org/2015/07/16/4-types-of-team-conflict-and-how-to-deal-with-each-effectively/
[8] Dontigney, E. (2019, March 6). *5 Conflict management strategies.* Retrieved from http://smallbusiness.chron.com/5-conflict-management-strategies-16131.html

Images:

Checkmate image by stevepb on Pixabay.
Fish-and-Chips image by ndemello on Pixabay.
Fist Bump image by rawpixel on Pixabay.
Hammer Egg image by stevepg on Pixabay.
Tic Tac Toe image by pixel2013 on Pixabay.
Tug-of-War image by mohamed_hassan on Pixabay.

SEVENTEEN

PRACTICAL TACTICS FOR RESEARCH IN ORGANIZATIONS

by Kristyl J. L. Smith, PsyD

People do not care how much you know
until they know how much you care.
— Teddy Roosevelt

One of the first aspects of a process improvement project is to discover what your stakeholders want and need. It's often referred to as determining "the voice of the customer."[1]

Whether you're a business owner or leader or a consultant who's been hired to come in and analyze a specific issue within a company, some of the most vital information you will gain is from the company's stakeholders, including its leaders, employees, vendors, and customers.[2]

Especially if you're an outsider, how you first enter the organization and how you conduct yourself while you're there will have great impact on the information you receive. Even if you're part of the organization and people already know you, it's still important to build and maintain trust so that you get the honest answers you need. After all, business leaders want to make decisions based on *correct* information.[3]

To that end, what follows is a list of steps you can take when you first seek to conduct research within any organization. Next, we'll explore the different ways of conducting that research. Finally, we'll dive deeper into methods that support employee and customer feedback.

SEVEN STEPS for Making a Great First Impression

STEP ONE: Understand Resistance and Build Trust. When walking into an organization, or into another department or division within your organization, it is important to remember that you are an outsider to them. As someone who is most likely external to where you're conducting research, your presence can either be a positive or it could be mean "trouble."

For example, have you ever had to call a specialist to inspect an issue in your home, such as a plumber or chimney expert? Do you remember the anxiety you felt knowing this person had the ability to deliver bad news during the inspection or the fear of the potential cost of the assessment? These experiences reflect a fear of the unknown.

With that in mind, it's important to consider that employees have similar anxieties. Their fears may be, "How much money is this consultant costing the company? Are they going to pay someone to tell them the same thing I've been saying all along? How is this going to affect my job? How much will I have to change? What if they decide my role is no longer an asset to the company? Can I trust that this person will keep my best interests in mind?"

All of these questions can breed animosity, resistance, avoidance, and tension in the work environment. Additionally, employees exhibiting these fears are likely the very people you will have to win over.[4] You can still present yourself as confident and as a subject-matter expert, but you should also remember to be cognizant of how others may perceive you. Be warm and patient while you build trust and remember not to take anyone's expression of fear personally.

STEP TWO: Learn to Blend In. As you work with people who don't know you well, be mindful of how you dress and present yourself. For example, if the employees at the company where you are conducting research generally wear jeans and T-shirts to work, you certainly don't want to show up on the first day in a three-piece suit. Try to ensure that your attire reflects the company's culture. You don't want to remind them by your heels or brown tips that you are really an outsider.[5] In addition, stay aware of cultural nuances and company norms.

Some organizations have an internal hierarchy of power that may not be reflected by title or on the organizational chart listed on the company website. For example, even if the regional director is on site, employees may have more regard for the area director. Working with and respecting the team's unofficial hierarchies can make it easier to build trust, absorb an authentic understanding of the company culture, and collect the information you need.

Our job as researchers is to find out how the hierarchy works, why it works, and to consider how a particular method of research will or will not align with your research goals. Sometimes the cultural norms and nuances we discover may seem out of order, but if they don't impact the end goal, it is best to adapt and stay on task.

STEP THREE: Maintain Confidentiality. Reassure staff that you are obligated to a code of confidentiality and that you will never reveal their identity under any circumstances, even if something unsavory is expressed in the process. In addition, never make subtle references to statements or comments made by staff. It is impossible to know what conversations staff members are having among themselves. Therefore, the best way to maintain confidentiality is to maintain the highest level of integrity.

Researchers cannot take shortcuts on Step Three if they want to build trust. Sign confidentially contracts in front of each employee, if you must.[6] And depending on the nature of your consulting/investigative work, you may also need to ask employees to sign nondisclosure agreements.

STEP FOUR: Don't Make Assumptions. If you don't ask, you don't know. Even more, you still don't really know without hearing from multiple sources at various levels in the organization. Sometimes what people think is happening is a reflection of their own bias and mental models.[7]

Let's say you are commissioned to investigate a troublesome accountant (we'll call her Melissa) to determine an effective intervention plan. The accountant's subordinates say that Melissa is overly critical, that she doesn't think any of their work is good enough. The accountant's coworkers say that Melissa is bitter because she was not given a promotion she worked hard for. Yet Melissa's managers express how she is simply trying to stay competitive in an ever-expanding market, which is why they take little notice of her behavior.

All of these perspectives are worth considering when building an employee intervention plan. This is an example of conducting diligent research before establishing a concrete "diagnosis" within any organization or of any individual employee.

STEP FIVE: Establish Boundaries. It's great to be down to earth and personable. However, remember that your professional boundaries and ethical obligations come first.[8]

If you're a consultant, and a client wants to have lunch and speak with you casually, that is certainly a great opportunity to learn about your client's values outside of work. However, this would not be an appropriate setting to discuss previously failed romantic relationships unless they involved someone on the client's team.

Perhaps the client (we'll call her Teresa) expresses that she has children, wants to share how much she misses being at home, and says she feels resentful that she often has to spend so much time redoing other people's work. You have now collected useful information that you can use as a motivator to move the change process along. However, what if Teresa starts venting about her marital life? Granted, this too may be impacting how she feels about work, but it's important to re-center the conversation toward topics that are less personal and more positive.

You don't want your clients to get the impression that they can vent to you like they would to a therapist. You may want to gently steer the conversation elsewhere. If it's warranted, you could ask Teresa if she would like to speak to a marriage and family specialist instead.[9]

Sometimes what people really need is help at home or help managing their emotions about what is happening at home. But unless you are a licensed mental health professional, it is important to remind the client that this area is not your professional expertise. In fact, you may also want to remind the client that it would be unethical for you to have discussions related to marital troubles (or sexual, or medical, or other personal information). You can and should show empathy, but you must also maintain your professional and ethical values.

STEP SIX: Use Simple Language. As you're introducing your research project, don't speak over people's heads to remind them how smart you are. Break down your concepts and theories in ways that are easy for people to understand. Your data displays should also be simple, unless otherwise requested.[10]

Remember that not everyone has studied industrial and organizational psychology or statistics. Using phrases like "founder's syndrome" or "systems theory" likely will not be understood in a roomful of accountants. If you happen to have clients who are already familiar with your formal terminology, then engage them at that level. But do your due diligence first in order to assess and respond to your clients' level of understanding.

You can always ask questions later through feedback loops to make sure your content is relatable and understandable.

STEP SEVEN: Practice Active Listening. Active listening increases your ability to connect with the employees during your interactions with them. It also increases memorization and cognition and reduces misinterpretation. Not only will the employees feel you really care about their perspective, but you also won't feel awkward asking a bunch of questions.[11]

Studies demonstrate that there is an increase of brain activity while a person is listening actively. By contrast, there is less cognitive activity when people listen passively.[12] Active listening increases our ability to remember what the speaker is saying, process what they said, and apply it effectively. Passive listening may allow us to take notes, but our ability to synthesize and process the information is limited.[13]

Seven active listening skills to practice include:

1. Be attentive.
2. Ask open-ended questions.
3. Ask probing questions.
4. Request clarification.
5. Paraphrase.
6. Be attuned to and reflect feelings.
7. Summarize.[14]

Types of Organizational Research

Observation. Observation is the act of watching the behaviors of employees within an organization, but from an external view. Observations can be participative or non-participative.[15]

According to studies of observational research, it is effective only when it incorporates semi-structured or unstructured research and interview designs.[16] These methods serve to collect qualitative data, which is not numerical, but instead approximates and characterizes the information.

Researchers who want to discover how employees at a company feel about their jobs could send out a company-wide survey. If none of the questions are open ended or allow for comments, that method is considered quantitative because thoughts, feelings, and opinions are converted into numerical systems.

However, if the same questions are formatted in an unstructured-interview style, the researcher would be able to observe the respondents' body language, posture, how frequently they smiled or made eye contact, their tonality, word choice, energy level, and much more. All of these variables are qualitative data that can give an organizational researcher an incredible amount of information that simply could not be captured in a survey.

So, let's say you ask a hundred employees to answer an employee satisfaction survey, because company leaders say that morale is low. After reviewing the results, it seems to you that employees are relatively satisfied. This is contrary to the overall feeling in the office. You then follow up with a series of unstructured interviews with a handful of the more expressive employees. As a result, you discover that employees generally enjoy their jobs and the company's culture, but they hate the office. Per your observations and interviews, you assess that the office has very few windows, little natural light or storage space, and is aesthetic displeasing overall.

You are now able to report to your client that employee morale is related to the office environment, not the company culture or leadership. Your recommendations would be very different if you had not performed both the survey and the unstructured interviews. It's important for researchers to capture both kinds of information to ensure the reliability and validity of the data.

Following are a few pointers that will help guide researchers as they conduct observations in an organization:[17]

1. ***Try to see things through other people's eyes.*** Rather than place judgment on employees, have an open mind and consider all possibilities, even in the midst of discomfort and conflict. It's also important to not take anything personally.

   If an employee yawns during an interview, you might conclude that the employee stayed up too late. But it's important to ask why before making such a conclusion. Let's say you are interviewing the receptionist at a start-up tech firm. Lin is twenty-four and identifies as gender neutral.

   You may be inexperienced with how to navigate a discussion in which you have to watch your pronoun use. Lin has picked up on this and has a watchful eye on your discomfort. There is clearly tension during the interview process. Nevertheless, Lin is responding to your questions regarding employee engagement.

   Then, in the middle of a response, Lin yawns exaggeratedly. Your initial reaction may be to feel upset. Perhaps Lin thinks your questions are boring. Perhaps Lin is intentionally being rude, because you've made a mistake on the preferred pronoun. Or, perhaps Lin is genuinely exhausted and wasn't able to catch the yawn in time to be more discreet. Perhaps Lin is still in school and just finished finals.

   There are many potential reasons for why Lin yawned, but it is important to ask discovery questions with genuine curiosity rather than assume the person is rude or irresponsible. This is also a great opportunity to change the temperature of your relationship. By showing genuine interest, you can simultaneous collect useful information and change the trajectory of the rest of the interview.

2. ***Pay attention to small details to reveal more layers.*** Subtle behaviors, such as two people speaking but not making direct eye contact with each other, could indicate an underlying issue that needs to be addressed, particularly if they do not belong to a culture that doesn't practice eye contact. Are they *both* not looking at each other directly in the eye? Is one making direct eye contact while the other is looking down or away? Are they both missing each other's eye contact as if they are both shy? Are their feet pointed toward each other? Did they roll their eyes after speaking or take a series of deep breaths?

   There could be a conflict that they are dealing with, or there could be a romantic attraction afoot.

3. ***Relate your observation to your wider social and historical knowledge about the organization.*** Ask yourself, how do these smaller pieces fit into the big picture?

   Let's say the organization routinely experiences conflict between the accounting and marketing departments as a result of a disagreement between the department directors. This conflict noticeably trickles down throughout the levels of the department but dilutes further down the hierarchy. Were the two directors ever employed in the other department? Are they decision makers, middle managers, or entry level employees?

   In this example, the circumstances of the organization may play a large impact on the way employees manage relationships with each other. It's important to ask all of these questions to determine if employee conflicts are a result of the culture or a result of independent circumstances.

4. ***Understand that all events are connected somehow.*** Rarely are social mishaps isolated events.

5. ***Avoid applying concepts and theories too early in the process.*** Making assumptions and decisions too quickly can lead to creating labels that do not accurately fit the circumstances.

Let's explore a fresh example; a forty-year-old nonprofit has a small number of employees and is primarily operated by the founding team consisting of the executive director and the associate director. They state that they experienced the most success in the late nineties, right before the internet boom, and they were able to advertise their services in local newspapers and magazines with much success.

Team members have since left, passed away, or retired; government grants have decreased; and the leaders don't trust online advertisements. Additionally, the leaders find it challenging to share their company strategy with other team members and find themselves working long hours. The staff often feels left in the dark, that assignments yield little to no return, and that the company operates like it is still 1997.

At first glance, it could be assumed that the company is experiencing founder's syndrome, a scenario in which the founding or long-time leaders do not want to release actual or perceived power and do not allow the organization to change and adapt to external changes in the industry or globally.

However, after building trust and interviewing both leaders separately, you discover that they actually have a hard time communicating with their young staff. They don't understand the way young people communicate and are used to professional communications being top-down. Both leaders are competent in their other leadership skills, but because they lack the confidence to communicate tasks to their staff, they find themselves spending three times as much time as they should performing administrative work, which their team should be doing.

What they actually need is help learning how to communicate cross-generationally, so they can explain to staff what they are trying to do without seeming authoritarian. They also may need help learning how to take feedback from their younger staff and how to harness their team's skills to make the organization flourish. It is organizational research, including observation, that will help company leaders understand what is really going on.

Interviews. The interview is an effective means of conducting vital research within an organization.

- **The Unstructured Interview.** This interview method is designed specifically for qualitative data collection and is utilized in all of the provided examples. This interview style may take a lot of practice before implementing. It is suggested that researchers learn skills that can make them more personable as well as willing to adjust to different personalities and communication styles. The following tips will help you conduct more effective unstructured interviews:

- This interview method is more informal and can incorporate multiple participants.
- Unstructured interviews are more like a guided conversation and are great for general discovery.
- Open-ended questions are used, it is flexible, and questions may be added or left out at the discretion of the researcher.
- Unstructured interviews provide qualitative data that can allow for more exploration and analysis.

- **The Structured Interview.** This interview method can be used for both qualitative and quantitative data collection, depending on how the questions are structured. Open-ended questions help to obtain qualitative data, and closed ended questions help to collect quantitative data. For example, asking, "Rate your satisfaction with your manager on a scale of 1–10" is quantitative. Asking, "How do you feel about your manager's leadership abilities?" is qualitative.

- This interview method will typically use the same questions for each participant.
- Questions must be asked exactly the way they are written and usually in the same order.
- This interview method does not allow for additional probing.
- Structured interviews are perfect for collecting quantitative data to determine satisfaction, behavioral trends, or engagement.

TIP: Consider using a semi-structured or unstructured research design to allow yourself the flexibility to adjust to each organization or department.[18] It may then be beneficial to follow up with a structured survey or questionnaire to collect more quantitative data, if needed.

Here's an example of why you should stay flexible and agile in your research methods: The research design used to question the Walmart Shipping Department may or may not be effective in assessing Walmart's Online Purchasing Department.

Questionnaires. Questionnaires, also known as surveys, are written versions of structured interviews.

- The benefit of using questionnaires during organizational research is that employees have an extra layer of anonymity. Questionnaires allow employees to express how they really feel while allowing researchers to collect quantitative data.
- Questionnaires are great for collecting massive amounts of data quickly from large organizations
- The downside of questionnaires, however, is that it is easier for participants to lie to protect their public image—even when the questionnaire is anonymous.
- The language of both a questionnaire and a structured interview

needs to be carefully curated to fit the overall demographics of the organization.

TIP: Questionnaires can include open- and closed-ended questions to collect both quantitative and qualitative data.[19]

Documentation Analysis. Documentation analysis consists of analyzing documents within an organization in order to discern what story they may tell. It is important to note that companies may not always abide by the structures outlined in their documents. As in the example mentioned earlier, when companies have unofficial hierarchies, they may also not abide by bylaws or company policy. Or they may have operational norms that are not specified in any operational documentation. Lastly, these documents may not always be accurate, so researchers should become familiar with standard versions of these type of documents.

- Records to review can include financial documents, debts, bills, bylaws, public records, meeting minutes, incident reports, marketing, and any other organizational documentation that seems relevant.

- Documentation analysis adds more credibility and complements other research methods performed. Documents also provide a base to develop goals and key performance indicators.

- Documentation analysis is a form of both qualitative and quantitative data.

- Collecting documents can be tedious, particularly in older organizations with decades worth of documents or in large corporations. Therefore, researchers should consider:

    - What documents are of the highest importance and relevance.

    - How to acquire documents. Can they be accessed in an online portal, through human resources, or does the executive team have sole access?

    - What expertise is needed to make sense of them. You may have to hire a legal or financial consultant to help dissect the material.

- What are your biases before assessing? Are you only looking for specific documents to prove a theory? You could end up overlooking other documents containing vital information.

- Consider any potential ethical issues that may arise. Be sure you are not viewing any documents with personal employee information without obtaining the appropriate legal approvals.

Conducting research in organizations can certainly be layered and sometimes strenuous. But the more you do it, the more skilled you will become. Be sure to utilize a variety of methods so you can have an array of reliable, valid, and relevant data from which to build your recommendations.[20]

Dr. Kristyl J. L. Smith earned a Doctorate in Psychology with an emphasis in Organizational Management and Consulting from Phillips Graduate University. Dr. Smith has more than five years of experience in both nonprofit management and marketing strategies. She is an author, public speaker, marketing consultant, professor, and account manager at an experiential marketing firm.

Dr. Smith also battles sickle cell anemia and has been an active advocate for disability rights, sickle cell awareness, and research-based pain management/prevention techniques. Her extensive professional career has been elevated by her love for research and for giving people more tools to empower their work and personal lives.

NOTES

[1] Tonkonogy, L. (2018). OC 922 Organizational Process Management lecture. Chatsworth, CA: Phillips Graduate University.
[2] Brooks, I. (2009). *Organisational behaviour: Individuals, groups and organisation* (4th ed.). Essex, England: Pearson.
[3] Barksdale, & Lund, *10 steps to successful strategic planning.* Alexandria, VA: American Society for Training and Development.
[4] Walsh, K., (2016). OC 805 Communications in Organizations lecture. Chatsworth, CA: Phillips Graduate University.
[5] Ibid.
[6] Gordon, S. (2017). OC 812 Legal and Ethical Decision Making in Organizations lecture. Chatsworth, CA: Phillips Graduate University.
[7] Walsh, OC 805 Communications in Organizations lecture.
[8] Trevino, L. K., & Nelson, K. A. (2013). *Managing business ethics: Straight talk about how to do it right* (6th ed.). Hoboken, NJ: Wiley.
[9] Walsh, OC 805 Communications in Organizations lecture.
[10] Ibid.
[11] Buttitta, D. (2016). OC 807 Survey of Psychological Theories lecture. Chatsworth, CA: Phillips Graduate University
[12] Dimitrijevic, A., Smith, M. L., Kadis, D. S., & Moore, D. R. (2017, February 24). Cortical alpha oscillations predict speech intelligibility. *Frontiers in Human Neuroscience, 11*(88). Retrieved from https://www.frontiersin.org/articles/10.3389/fnhum.2017.00088/full
[13] Brooks, B. (2006). The power of active listening. *American Salesman, 51*(6), 12–14.
[14] Allen, G. (2017, December 21). 7 key active listening skills [Web log post]. Retrieved from https://community.cengage.com/t5/Management-In-the-News-Blog/7-Key-Active-Listening-Skills/ba-p/5236
[15] Silverman, D., & Marvasti, A. (2008). *Doing qualitative research: A comprehensive guide.* Thousand Oaks, CA, US: Sage Publications, Inc.
[16] Ibid; Bryman, A., Bresnen, M. Beardsworth, A, & KeilFirst, T. (1988, January 1). Qualitative research and the study of leadership. *Human Relations, 41*(1), 13–30.
[17] Silverman, *Doing qualitative research: A comprehensive guide*; Bryman, Qualitative research and the study of leadership.
[18] McLeod S., (2014) The interview method [Web log post]. Retrieved from https://www.simplypsychology.org/interviews.html
[19] Ibid.
[20] Buchanan, A. D. & Bryman, A., (2007) Contextualizing methods choice in organizational research. *Organizational Research Methods, 10*, 483–501.

Images:

Interview image by Ibrahim Adabara on Pixabay.
Survey image by Andreas Breitling on Pixabay.

ÁCCENT ON WORDS PRESS

Thank you for reading this publication of Áccent on Words Press. To find out more about how you can also publish a book, contact the editor, Deborah Jackson, at djackson@accentonwords.com.

For more information, visit accentonwords.com.

www.ingramcontent.com/pod-product-compliance
Lightning Source LLC
Chambersburg PA
CBHW030240030426
42336CB00009B/182
* 9 7 8 1 7 3 4 2 6 0 5 0 2 *